# THE
# HENRY CLAY FRICK
# HOUSES

# THE HENRY CLAY FRICK HOUSES

## Architecture · Interiors · Landscapes
## in the Golden Era

MARTHA FRICK SYMINGTON SANGER

FOREWORD BY
WENDELL GARRETT

THE MONACELLI PRESS

First published in the United States of America in 2001 by
The Monacelli Press, Inc.
10 East 92nd Street, New York, New York 10128.

Library of Congress Cataloging-in-Publication Data

Sanger, Martha Frick Symington.
The Henry Clay Frick houses : architecture, interiors, landscapes in the golden era /
Martha Frick Symington Sanger ; foreword by Wendell Garrett.
p.  cm.
Includes bibliographical references and index.
ISBN 1-58093-104-9
1. Mansions—United States. 2. Frick, Henry Clay, 1849—1919—Homes and haunts.
3. Architecture—United States—19th century. 4. Interior decoration—United States—
History—19th century. 5. Frick family—History. I. Title.
NA7207.S26   2001
728.8'092—dc21                                              2001031201

Printed and bound in Italy

Project Consultant: Judith Joseph, Joseph Publishing Services
Designer: Alex Castro, Castro/Arts, Baltimore

Cover: Grand staircase, One East Seventieth Street, New York City, now the
Frick Collection, c. 1931

# CONTENTS

viii     Foreword   WENDELL GARRETT

  x     Preface

  2     INTRODUCTION
        Beginnings: Westmoreland County, Pennsylvania
        Influence on the Henry Clay Frick Houses

 14     CHAPTER I
        Clayton
        The Residence of Mr. and Mrs. Henry Clay Frick
        Pittsburgh, Pennsylvania

 84     CHAPTER II
        Eagle Rock
        A Summer Retreat, Boston's North Shore

136     CHAPTER III
        One East Seventieth Street
        The New York City Residence, The Frick Collection

218     CHAPTER IV
        The Clayton Estate
        The Home of Mr. and Mrs. Childs Frick
        Long Island, New York

278     EPILOGUE
        Endings: Westmoreland Farm
        The Country Home of Helen Clay Frick
        Westchester County, New York

282     Notes
285     Glossary
287     Bibliography
289     Archival Resources
290     Acknowledgments
292     Illustration Credits
293     Index

The captains and the kings depart, but the background[s] against which they moved are with us yet, to speak their names more loudly than their deeds.

— Sarah Lockwood

The story of houses is the story of life. Just as the history of a country is written down in architecture, so is the history of individuals to be traced by the houses in which they have lived. There it all is — their beginning, their growth, their development or deterioration, the realization or the destruction of their dreams, the very pattern of their destiny as it was etched line by line.

— Elsie de Wolfe

The ideals of the ruling class are in every epoch the ruling ideals.

— Karl Marx

To my great-aunt

HELEN CLAY FRICK (1888–1984)

Without her wisdom, courage, vision, and steadfast determination,
the spirit and integrity of the Henry Clay Frick houses might well have perished.

# FOREWORD

In the half century between the end of the Civil War and the outbreak of World War I, the United States underwent even greater changes than it had during the preceding hundred years. The Civil War radically altered the very character of the Union; with the conclusion of that conflict the territorial unity of the nation was established and seemed certain never again to be contested. As further assurance of unity, almost immediately following the peace, railroads reached across the continent to points west, and before the end of the century tracks had been laid over the entire country in a stout and binding web of steel. By then a gigantic industrial machine of rapidly and constantly increasing potential had been reared to appropriate and develop the resources that flowed into it from every quarter of the land. The American people prospered — most of them — as no people ever had prospered before. Aside from the natural increase in population, between the Civil War and World War I more than twenty million immigrants entered the country from all parts of the globe; that influx was in itself more than ten times the size of the entire American population at the close of the Revolutionary War.

Among the immigrants were craftsmen who brought with them the traditions of their different homelands and who adapted their skills to the demands of the American market. Increasingly this meant adapting to the mechanical processes that in the United States more generally than anywhere else were replacing age-old handicraft methods. Indeed, it began to seem that most Americans had little interest in anything that could not be mass produced. The Civil War had accelerated developments that were revolutionizing not only goods on the market but also the practical aspects of government, the nature of the American economy, and the very structure of American society. As Henry Adams, in retrospect, saw clearly, those years "had given to the great mechanical energies — coal, iron, steam — a distinct superiority in power over the old industrial elements — agriculture, handwork, and learning." In short, he concluded, the post–Civil War generation of Americans would have to create a new world of its own.

Whether the machine ever could be expected to serve the cause of good design and sound construction as well as the individual craftsman had done was a question hotly debated in the second half of the nineteenth century. Most early manufacturers went to great lengths and much expense to turn out machine-made goods that resembled in design and ornament traditional handmade products. Looking backward rather than forward for inspiration, they appropriated the style of the more or less distant past to lend prestige to their mechanically contrived articles. The spate of historical revivals that resulted presents a bewildering mixture of forms and motifs; the labels they were given — Gothic Revival, Renaissance Revival, French Revival — provided only a vague explanation.

During these postwar years a succession of critics and reformers, designers and decorators — from William Morris to Charles Eastlake, from John Ruskin to Edith Wharton and Elsie de Wolfe — produced a steady flow of advice on questions of good taste and sound practice in household and industrial arts. Although their individual pronouncements usually were issued with an air of finality and infallibility, their opinions varied widely. "No machine yet contrived, or hereafter contrivable," wrote the great English reformer Ruskin with almost biblical authority, "will ever equal the fine machinery of the human fingers" — a sentiment that Morris heavily endorsed. In general, however, what these critics and theorists had to say stemmed from one or the other of two major preoccupations of the age, industrialism and romanticism — two preoccupations that were giving shape to an evolving new culture. Industrialism faced the future, romanticism looked to the past; the one hoped to increase the material benefits of life with the aid of the machine, the other clung to, or sought to revive, what seemed to have been good in years gone by, with or without assistance from the machine. Those were not necessarily discordant attitudes; they were often more complementary than antagonistic — two sides of a single coin.

In the United States, as in England, the enthusiastic quest for "good taste" and "artistic" expression in domestic trappings became something of a craze after the Philadelphia Centennial in 1876. During the subsequent decade, the architectural style was characterized by light frame construction, irregular picturesque outlines, sharply peaked roofs, spindled verandas, upper-story balconies, and large, open interior spaces. Such designs, it was felt, were "sincere," "artistic," and "practical" and, at the same time, a fitting complement to the still-fashionable Eastlake-style furnishings. Here, in short, was a style for the times.

Nearing the turn of the century insurgent designers in various lands led a quest for styles that would be completely independent of the past, totally modern in character. Out of this search emerged the luxuriant, passing fashion of Art Nouveau, on the one hand, and, on the other, the more strictly functional designs that led into the mainstream of twentieth-century developments. In both cases the results differed greatly from the artifacts and fabrications of the post–Civil War period. No half century in history produced such a variety of styles and designs, or such a profusion of objects of every description, as appeared in America during those fifty years preceding World War I. After the war, however, with the rapid changes of outlook and lifestyle, the significance of much that previously had been built with great celebration was quickly forgotten — significance that we are only beginning to recall from what has survived from that period. The importance and beauty of these styles, trends, and structures are presented with rare insight and intellect by Martha Sanger in her carefully researched tribute to the Henry Clay Frick houses.

WENDELL GARRETT

# PREFACE

*Facing page:* THE SOUTH HALL, One East Seventieth Street, now the Frick Collection.

In this section of the hall, Frick placed the *Portrait of Lodovico Capponi* by Agnolo Bronzino. Of particular interest is the secrétaire à abattant by Jean-Henri Riesener, purchased by Frick in 1915 and made for Marie Antoinette, perhaps for her apartments in the Tuileries. The Living Hall can be seen beyond, with a photograph of Henry Clay Frick in the background. When this photograph of the South Hall was taken, c. 1931, Helen Frick had placed a picture of her father in each room, apparently to invoke his presence in the house he had so loved.

FOR AS LONG AS I CAN REMEMBER, I have been fascinated by houses. And no wonder. As a great-granddaughter of the steel baron and art collector Henry Clay Frick (1849–1919), I grew up in his residences, as well as his children's, and knew them as homes. Each is etched in my mind: Clayton, the châteauesque, high Victorian residence in Pittsburgh where generations of the Frick family lived from 1882 until 1984; Eagle Rock, my great-grandfather's Georgian Revival summer home in Prides Crossing, Massachusetts, built in 1904 and demolished in 1969; and One East Seventieth Street, his neoclassical Beaux Arts residence in New York City from 1914 until 1935 when it opened to the public as the Frick Collection. Then there was the Clayton Estate in Roslyn, Long Island, the English country house of my grandparents, Childs (1883–1965) and Frances Dixon Frick (1892–1953); and Westmoreland Farm in Bedford Village, New York, the rustic retreat of my great-aunt Helen Clay Frick (1888–1984). These were the houses that Henry Clay Frick, his wife, Adelaide (1859–1931), their son Childs Frick, and their daughter Helen Clay Frick lived in as a family. These were homes that I knew and loved. And these are houses whose stories have not been told until now.

During my childhood, when I visited my grandfather at his Long Island estate, or my great-aunt at her country place and at the houses she had inherited from her parents, little did I know as I dashed from one glorious room to another that these residences were examples of the evolving taste in the Golden Era of American domestic architecture. Each one was designed by a renowned architect of the period – such as Frederick J. Osterling, Daniel H. Burnham, Arthur Little and Herbert W. C. Browne, Ogden Codman Jr., Thomas Hastings, and John Russell Pope – and decorated to keep pace with the rapidly changing fashion in American interior design by such pioneers as Cottier & Company, who brought the English-inspired Aesthetic Movement with its emphasis on "art for art's sake" to America from London in the early 1880s; the American neoclassic tastemaker Ogden Codman Jr. and pioneer professional interior decorator Elsie de Wolfe; the internationally prominent dealer Joseph Duveen, who broadened many important art collections in America; and Britain's premier designer, Sir Charles Carrick Allom, knighted by King George V for his work on Buckingham Palace.

As a child — and well into adulthood — even the importance of the gardens belonging to these houses was lost on me. At ease as I was in the comfort and elegance of my surroundings, I largely was intent on catching an unsuspecting butterfly, squishing Japanese beetles, or savoring the smell of my grandmother's roses. An innocent child in a fairy-tale playground, I could not have understood that the grounds and gardens to these houses either had become parks, as in Pittsburgh, or were celebrated as historic masterpieces created by such prestigious pioneer landscape architects as Marian Cruger Coffin, Umberto Innocenti and Richard K. Webel, Guy Lowell, and the firm known as Olmsted Brothers.

For me, the houses were merely houses and the gardens simply places to frolic and dream. And as with any familiar place that one loves, I relished my time in all of them. I took everything for granted — their beauty, their fun, their place in history, and the treasures they contained. Living in a building designed by a famous architect, curling up on a lovely sofa, admiring a favorite painting, piece of porcelain, bronze, oriental rug, or wandering through manicured gardens never felt unusual or intimidating. My Maryland home was comfortable, filled with antiques and paintings, but certainly not on the scale of the Frick family houses. And yet, as a child visiting the homes of my relatives, I felt welcomed and loved, and not ever, not once, can I recall having heard the words "Do not touch." When I visited my great-aunt in Pittsburgh, Prides Crossing, Bedford Village, and New York, or stayed with my grandfather on Long Island, perhaps their love was the reason I had such an easy relationship with my surroundings.

Now, when I remember my times with great-aunt Helen at Clayton, Pittsburgh, I laugh at my innocence. As a child, I was preoccupied with using correct table manners, or searching for the family ghost behind the heavy velvet curtains (specifically Helen's ill-fated sister, Martha, for whom I am named, whose slow, harrowing death in 1891, one week before her sixth birthday, remains the family's great tragedy), or bouncing around in my great-grandfather's old-fashioned cars and carriages.

Of course, when summering at Eagle Rock, I was unaware that a team of architects and interior designers had labored there four decades earlier, determined to banish forever the once-fashionable, dark, cluttered Victorian ideal represented by Clayton. Such leaders in the stringent neoclassic movement of the Golden Era meant nothing to me. Eagle Rock meant swimming off the Atlantic beach, playing murder in the dark with the stream of third-floor closets for hiding places, dressing in costumes for celebrations such as the Fourth of July and our great-aunt Helen's birthday, gorging on cakes and cookies in the tea house, and playing capture the flag or leapfrog on the lush, green lawn.

I was, however, very much aware of the historical importance of One East Seventieth Street. It had opened to the public nine years before my birth, so I never knew this house as a home the way I did the other family houses. As a museum, it commanded respect and caution, and I understood that, as the Frick Collection, it contained one of the finest art collections in the world and was no longer "ours." Even so, despite the fact that I was told that important people came from around the world to see the collection — and once the art historian Sir Kenneth Clark held me firmly as I stood on a stool before Rembrandt's self-portrait and looked into the artist's penetrating eyes — in my mind the Frick Collection was still a family house, more of a home than a museum, as much a part of my everyday life as all the other Frick residences. This casual enjoyment and acceptance of the Frick Collection was made so because Helen Frick presented the museum to me and my family that way. Often, after lunch or tea in the Frick Art Reference Library next door — almost always on a Monday when the collection is closed to visitors — she would take me through the secret door connecting the library to the museum's East Gallery and give me the freedom of the house. I could walk round and round the gallery rooms, play hopscotch on the grand marble staircase, and if accompanied by Helen or a security guard, I could take a peek into the hotel-size kitchen, the laundry area, the paneled bowling alley, and the vast electrical panels in the basement. The best times in the house, however, were the family reunions. We played tag in the Garden Court, stuffed ourselves on pastries, and toured the galleries with our great-aunt. The finest treat was viewing Jan van Eyck's *Virgin and Child, with Saints and Donor* through the magnifying glass our great-aunt kept hidden in a secret panel in the Enamel Room. As we looked, minute swans, horsemen, and people not previously visible suddenly appeared in the painting's background.

Family gatherings always have been important to the Fricks, and none were more memorable than the Christmases with my grandfather, Childs Frick, at his Clayton Estate on Long Island. I awoke every morning at six to the sound of my grandfather driving his cotton golf balls into a sheet that had been strung across the hall. But on Christmas morning the sound of my grandfather's golf ball was not what interested me. I eagerly awaited the opening of the doors to the North Room. And as I dove into my stack of presents, I never suspected the importance of the room and its contents, much less the whole house and its Marian Cruger Coffin garden, to the history of American domestic architecture, interior design, and landscape architecture.

And certainly, until recently I had no idea that, with the exception of the Clayton Estate, I owed these childhood experiences to Helen Frick. Little did I know when I visited her at Westmoreland Farm that she had purchased the property with a multimillion-dollar inheritance from her father in 1919. Nor was I aware that she had chosen the place — a large tract of meadow and woodland — so she could be near her growing Frick Art Reference Library in New York, as well as One East Seventieth Street and her then widowed mother. There, on the farm, with a natural lake offering lazy days, good fishing, and a natural waterfall to lull family and friends to sleep, I also had no idea that my great-aunt had named the farm, with its nondescript, white clapboard farmhouse, for Westmoreland County, Pennsylvania, the area settled by her paternal Mennonite ancestors in 1800 and the place of her father's birth. And certainly while I dozed and dreamed, I had no idea that great-aunt Helen was musing about the historic preservation of the Frick family houses, including her father's West Overton birthplace. Here, in this idyllic setting, Helen Frick directed her art and historic preservation efforts — efforts that among other things safeguarded her father's homes and left them standing, or partially preserved in a museum as happened with Eagle Rock, as fine examples of the elegant architecture, opulent interiors, and luxurious lifestyle of the Golden Era.

But for Helen, Westmoreland Farm also represented a symbolic, full-circle return to the agrarian life of her forebears. And at Westmoreland Farm I enjoyed part of what was inherent in an agrarian lifestyle — home-cooked meals, the sweet smell of milking time and churning butter. But most of all I remember brisk walks through the woodland, and flowers — flowers and flowering trees everywhere. The dogwoods, daffodils, bluebells, and apple trees created a feeling of enchantment.

When my mother died in 1996 and I began rummaging through the more than twenty boxes filled with Frick family albums that came my way, I came to realize both the great gift I had been given in childhood and the gift I now had in my hands. Within the hundreds of archival photographs of the Frick family houses, I knew there lived the nucleus for this book. And now, after almost thirteen years of researching my Frick ancestors, and after the publication of *Henry Clay Frick: An Intimate Portrait* (New York: Abbeville Press, 1998), I understand the importance of these houses as examples of the Golden Era in domestic architecture in America, as well as that period's interior design and landscape architecture. Now I understand the great privilege of having grown up in these places of beauty and the extraordinary efforts taken by my great-aunt both to perpetuate them as family homes and to preserve them as symbols of the rise of wealth in America. Today, as fascinated as I am by my Frick heritage and as serious as I have become about this legacy as a Frick biographer, I feel the need to document these houses for others — to show how, although always just comfortable, livable homes to the Fricks, they represent some of the most extraordinary houses ever built in our country.

Apart from the fact that these houses were filled with the finest art, furniture, rugs, bronzes, and porcelain available in their day — and their architecture, interior design, and gardens represent the finest in the changing tastes of America — the decorative objects and stylistic trends stand today as symbols of the culture from which they were born. "The story of houses," as Elsie de Wolfe so aptly wrote, "is the story of life. Just as the history of a country is written down in architecture, so is the history of individuals to be traced by the houses in which they have lived. There it all is — their beginning, their growth, their development or deterioration, the realization or the destruction of their dreams, the very pattern of their destiny as it was etched line by line."

And here it all is, the story etched in historic photographs and architectural drawings — the very pattern of Henry Clay Frick's destiny explained and illustrated for us to consider and enjoy.

M.F.S.S.

# BEGINNINGS:
# WESTMORELAND COUNTY
# PENNSYLVANIA

## INFLUENCE ON THE HENRY CLAY FRICK HOUSES

*Facing page:* The springhouse where Henry Clay Frick was born on December 19, 1849.

THE STORY OF THE HENRY CLAY FRICK HOUSES is representative of developing taste, technology, and wealth in America during the Golden Era from 1880 through World War I. It begins with the life of Henry Overholt (1739–1831), Frick's maternal great-grandfather. At this time in rural America, home had not yet become a symbol of social status and cultural sophistication. Rather, home was synonymous with family farm; home meant survival and was therefore a center of economic production.

In 1762, a turn of fate occurred that had a direct impact on Henry Overholt. After the death of her first husband, Martin Overholt (1706–44), Henry's mother, Agnes, married William Nash (dates unknown), a prosperous Mennonite farmer and weaver from Deep Run, Pennsylvania. In 1762 he conveyed his homestead to Agnes — and died one month later. Good businesswoman that she was, Agnes expanded the Nash farm to include adjacent land, but ten years later — perhaps now an older woman (her dates and family name are unknown) and possibly uncomfortable with the burdens of owning such a large homestead — she conveyed this substantial property for the sum of 357 pounds, 17 shillings, and 2 pence to Henry, her son by Martin Overholt.

Whether or not the Nash family was upset that this valuable asset passed out of their hands is not recorded. Nor are the contents of the homestead known. What is known, however, is that the Nash farm came into capable hands. Thirty-three-year-old Henry Overholt was an expert weaver, as well as a successful farmer and distiller. An important member of the Mennonite community, he managed the thriving 175-acre farm for the next two decades. But when the new century dawned in 1800, sixty-one-year-old Henry had tired of life in Bucks County. His mother had been dead four years, and according to veterans of the American Revolution, cheap, fertile land lay to the west, across the Allegheny Mountains, on the Pennsylvania frontier of Westmoreland County. In fact, prior to 1800 a Mennonite community had settled on the banks of

*Left:* The Henry Overholt Homestead, Bedminster, Bucks County, Pennsylvania, c. 1903.

Jacobs Creek in what is now the Scottdale–Huntington Township area. Moreover, Henry's brother Martin lived there with his family of ten and long had been encouraging Henry to join him. So Henry Overholt followed the popular western migration, sold his homestead for 1,500 pounds of "gold and silver money," and packed his profits, his household goods, and his fifty-five-year-old wife, twelve children, and twenty or so other family members into covered wagons and headed for the wilderness.

After a six-month journey through the wilderness and over the mountains, Henry Overholt finally reached what only could have seemed to him like the proverbial Promised Land and purchased a tract of several hundred acres in coveted Westmoreland County. Playing on the Overholt name, he called it West Overton and there built a log cabin on the hill overlooking his property, as well as a smokehouse and a springhouse with walls eighteen inches thick. He also established himself in weaving and farming and constructed a small log distillery with a capacity of four bushels.

The few remaining records of this log cabin suggest that it resembled others of its day. Probably rectangular in shape with a dirt floor, a loft, and windows of waxed or "oiled" paper, it is known to have had a log chimney, a crude rock fireplace with no mantelpiece, and a roof made of cedar shingles, or shakes. Some Staffordshire china still survives to indicate the family's prosperity and interest in fine objects: a blue-transfer-print soup tureen of the Lady of the Lake pattern, c. 1810; a large Blue Willow platter, c. 1820; a rolled-glass mercury-backed mirror with a mahogany frame; and an eight-foot-high, twenty-eight-day walnut cabinet clock with burl veneer made in the German Palatinate in the 1770s and brought to America by Henry's grandfather, Marcus Overholt. Although Henry only would live another thirteen years in his wilderness outpost, by the time of his death in 1813, he had created another thriving center of economic production. And within his farming complex could be heard the first, muted strains of home becoming a way to claim status and display wealth.

*Right:* The Abraham Overholt Homestead (presently the Henry Clay Frick Birthplace, West Overton Museums), Westmoreland County, Pennsylvania, c. 1903.

Henry's sons, Abraham (1784–1870) and Christian (1786–1868), inherited the Overholt Homestead, but Abraham soon became the sole owner. A sixteen-year-old when the family crossed the Alleghenies, he had married Maria Stauffer (1791–1874) in 1809, and now at age twenty-nine, with his father's farming, weaving, and whiskey businesses to run and children of his own to raise, he was considered the head of the Overholt family. A five-foot-eight-inch-tall man with a forty-two inch chest — a solid, rugged individual — Abraham had his father's foresight, as well as his skills, and so he capitalized on, and expanded, the farm that Henry had created. In 1826, he built a three-story brick stock barn. A six-story brick barn followed in 1832, as well as a three-story hay barn in the German style with a high-pitched roof and x-shaped vents. Since whiskey was the staple of the day (every farm had a still and on average people drank twenty-four ounces of hard liquor a day), and demand for Overholt whiskey high, Abraham demolished his father's small log distillery and replaced it with a stone one boasting a fifty-bushel capacity. In 1834, thanks to the popularity of his Old Farm Straight Rye Whiskey, Abraham added a brick flour mill. Thus he could mill the grain himself, on site, rather than spend the time and money to haul it back and forth to someone else's mill.

In this way, Abraham — a Mennonite so unruly that had his wife's family not boasted a legacy of Mennonite bishops he probably would have been excommunicated — answered the call of his day: making money. In America, as the frontier opened with a rapid and efficient railway system, and steam engines and mechanized factories made goods available to a national market, houses began to assume a more definite character. The country had grown out of its survivalist mentality into one focused on material goods and acquisition. The pursuit of money had become equated with the pursuit of happiness. Everything was measured in money, for in America to acquire wealth was to gain social standing.

As Abraham prospered, the face of West Overton necessarily needed to change. So in 1838, fifty-four-year-old Abraham replaced his father's log home with a three-story house in the long-established vernacular Federal style with newer Greek Revival accents. Made of Overholt brick with foundations that Abraham dug by hand and twelve-inch-thick slate foundation stones laid by him as well the house represented more than Abraham's hard work. Its architectural style symbolized America in the 1830s — its freedom, the triumph of democracy, and a nation's pride.

The Federal style in American architecture and interior decoration was based on the light and delicate classical designs popularized by the eighteenth-century English architects Robert and James Adam. This Adamesque style, or Federal as it was called in America, flowered during the early decades of the new American republic. It represented the new nation's republican government, and it symbolized the ideals of America's founding fathers who had looked to Roman models for inspiration and guidance in everything from law to architecture. This slender, refined classicism long had dominated both the rural and urban architectural landscape, but by the 1830s, as Abraham was building his homestead, Greek Revival architecture was becoming fashionable. The Greeks were regarded as the creators of democracy and the rule of the common man. In the 1830s, therefore, when nationalism was growing in America, the wealth of the middle class was expanding, and democracy was widening with the westward migration, America was seen as Ancient Greece's spiritual successor. Greek Revival architecture thus became a symbol of both the new nation's form of government and its freedom from oppression.

The Overholt Homestead, in turn, is a charming representation of the transition between styles then under way. Porches grace the front and back. Elegantly trimmed in white, the homestead still displays graceful wrought-iron work on its exterior stairway made on site by the West Overton blacksmith. Bridged chimneys define the roof, and the cornice boasts a double-dentil brick Greek motif — a design that is repeated in the new kitchen, wash house, and carriage house built for Abraham's wagon and buggy, the only "fancy one" in the area.

An efficient house, the rooms on each of the three stories duplicate the ones below in size and shape, and the front door opens onto a hall that leads straight to the back door. The few remaining records in its archive, established by Helen Frick when she created a historic site of the Overholt Homestead in the 1920s, show that it originally had windows of rolled glass protected by exterior shutters and interior green wooden Venetian blinds; that the fireplaces burned coal, not wood; and that each bedroom had a fireplace closet where clothes could be warmed or dried. With the exception of the floral wallpaper in Abraham's bedroom, all the solid brick interior walls were plastered white.

*Above*: Lithograph of West Overton Village, 1864.

Maria Overholt maintained a kitchen garden full of medicinal and culinary herbs, as well as flowers and vegetables. She also seems to have added Wedgwood china from England's Staffordshire region to the family's collection. Today the dining-room cabinet contains a Flow Blue china teapot, c. 1840; an English ceramic vegetable dish, c. 1845; an Etruria soap dish and cup; an ironstone vase in a Geneva pattern; and Abraham's favorite Staffordshire cup dating from 1860. A piano and other objects typically purchased by the rising middle class in the mid-nineteenth century could be found in the rooms, most notably four cast-iron firebacks of elaborate design and construction. The one in Abraham's bedroom, for instance, depicts Leonardo da Vinci's *Last Supper*. Abraham's writing desk also is of interest. Made so Abraham could stand when working, it is of inlaid walnut. This desk, and his maple and birch ladder-back rocking chair, would have been cherished by the family as examples of their growing prosperity.

Although the contents, construction, and design of the homestead give full indication that Abraham already was the most prosperous farmer in the area, like his father he was never content to rest on his accomplishments. In 1859 he built a new brick distillery, six stories high, with a capacity of two hundred bushels. Located just outside Abraham's back door, it was taller than the local churches. And by now, an entire village of Overholt brick houses with their kitchens, barns, and gardens clustered around it.

So in 1762, when Agnes Nash suddenly inherited her second husband's prosperous homestead, and later transferred it to her son, the story of the Henry Clay Frick houses as showcases of wealth and social standing within the community was set in motion. In that single stroke of fortune, home came to symbolize for Henry Clay Frick's maternal ancestors what domestic architecture symbolized for the evolution of America — a fervent longing to own the new and fashionable, a desire to be recognized as genteel. Humble Mennonites though the Overholts were, and deeply religious as they were known to be, by the mid-nineteenth century their houses were among the finest in the West Overton farming community of Westmoreland County, Pennsylvania. And for Henry Clay Frick, the sickly Mennonite farm boy turned millionaire, the aesthete who would be forced into the harsh business world to win his fortune, home would become the place, if not the *only* place, where the self-made millionaire could give full expression both to the rewards of his hard-won fortune and to his aesthetic taste.

On December 19, 1849, Henry Clay Frick was born into this prosperous, democracy-loving, agrarian environment. The second child of Abraham Overholt's daughter Elizabeth (1819–1905) and her husband, John Wilson Frick (1822–89) — whose grandfather, Johann Nicholas Frick (c. 1735–96), had come to Westmoreland County in 1786 — was named for Henry Clay of Kentucky, the Whig speaker of the U.S. House of Representatives and secretary of state, known as "the great pacificator." His first home was his great-grandfather's two-room, stone springhouse that lay just beyond the eastern corner of his grandfather's fine Federal house. A sunny little dwelling, the springhouse still is fed by three springs in the hillside to the west. When Frick was born, it contained a small, three-day clock with etched-glass doors and portraits of Whig presidents such as Washington, Adams, and Monroe, as well as one of Senator Henry Clay. A red rag rug lay in front of the fireplace and a Pennsylvania long rifle was fastened to the wooden mantelpiece. For all its modest furnishings, however, the springhouse provided essential warmth and cheer for the young Henry Clay Frick, a sickly, stay-at-home child who became unable to work in the fields or walk the mile to school with the other children.

As a youth, Frick often helped the women with their baskets and babies and, as his health improved, clerked for his Overholt uncle, did bookkeeping for his grandfather, and worked in a Pittsburgh linens, lace, and notions store. When Abraham Overholt died in 1870 and his property was sold for $395,000, Frick received no inheritance, although he had been Abraham's favorite grandchild. Yet Frick had claimed throughout his childhood that he would make more money than his grandfather — and could do more with his grandfather's money than his grandfather was doing. So at age twenty-one, Frick made a decision. Knowing he was not strong enough to be a farmer and sensing that his fortune, if he were to make one, lay not in Pittsburgh's linens and lace or in Westmoreland County's farming or distilling businesses, Frick searched for his opportunity and found it. Just as his great-grandfather's imagination had been caught by the Pennsylvania farming frontier, Frick's was captured by the coming industrial revolution — particularly the nascent industry of manufacturing coke, a necessary ingredient for making steel. Abraham had experimented with the process of baking bituminous coal in beehive-shaped ovens until the impurities burned off and the purified coal, or pure carbon coal cake, remained. Certain this industry was both his and America's future, Frick went into the business.

With loans from Judge Thomas Mellon — a family friend who just had founded the Mellon Bank and was looking for profitable investments — and loans from his mother's and grandmother's inheritance from Abraham, Frick moved from West Overton to nearby Broad Ford, where he was bookkeeper for the second Overholt distillery. He built his first coke ovens there and alternately lived in a boardinghouse and a miner's shack. Although his business was threatened by the financial panic of 1873, and twice during these years he almost died from immune system attacks then known as inflammatory rheumatism, determination and good luck saw him through. When the panic broke in 1879, both he and his Frick Coke Company had managed not only to survive but to flourish. Since Frick had acquired in only nine short years the majority of the coking-coal fields in the region at depression prices, he was well-positioned to take advantage of new opportunities. The economic recovery required steel for the rebuilding of railroads, and demand for coke was high. In fact, with the dramatic rise in the price of coke, Henry Clay Frick became a millionaire. Frick coke had become so famous that the once frail Mennonite farm boy now was referred to as the Coke King.

At this same moment, Andrew Carnegie was expanding his steel empire and searching for a guaranteed supply of coke for his mills. In 1881 he approached Frick with a proposition: Carnegie would purchase the majority of the recently restructured H. C. Frick Coke Company stock so Frick could convert his paper fortune to cash. Frick would remain the chairman of the company, but in return Carnegie's mills would receive a guaranteed supply of coke at a favorable rate.

With the partnership struck, thirty-two-year-old Henry Clay Frick was out of debt for the first time, and like Henry Overholt, he was ready for new surroundings. His youth had been spent within the confines of West Overton, and his early adulthood had passed while living in an immaculately maintained miner's shack. Already, Frick had displayed an artistic temperament and interest in collecting paintings, having filled his tidy abode with so many pictures that in 1871 a Mellon Bank loan officer had made note of the young industrialist's near-obsession but nevertheless advised Judge Mellon that the passion was "not enough to hurt."

Now, with his fortune made, Henry Clay Frick desired a change in residence. He packed up his collection of prints and drawings and moved to the more cosmopolitan setting of

*Left:* The Monongahela House, Pittsburgh, 1898.

Pittsburgh's luxurious residential hotel known as the Monongahela House — the finest hotel between the Atlantic seaboard and New Orleans. Five stories high and of the late Victorian period, it featured a lobby trimmed in gilt and an impressive walnut staircase. The Monongahela House was where Pittsburgh society danced and mingled, and where politicians and businessmen from the South, New York, Chicago, and Philadelphia converged. Frick knew it well. He often had stayed there when in Pittsburgh selling his coke and conducting business on the Mon Wharf — the sandbank on the Monongahela River, at the confluence of the Monongahela, Allegheny, and Ohio Rivers, where the hotel was located.

Frick took a three-bedroom suite and agreed to pay a rent of $150 a month, an amount high even then despite the attraction that meals were included. Unconcerned, Frick embarked on a spending campaign that would be repeated — exponentially — for the rest of his life. According to family records, within three months he spent $5,000 on furnishings, largely from Pittsburgh dealers. Of high quality and in current East Coast styles, his furnishings, interior decoration, and art purchases included an $850 onyx and gilt-bronze clock and candelabra in the Louis XVI style from Tiffany & Company. Two workmen spent two days hanging the art collection — an indication that Henry Clay Frick from this point forward intended to have only the finest and most fashionable in his home.

Then, to celebrate his millionaireship and his debut into both high society and the upper echelons of the business world, Henry Clay Frick took a four-month tour of Europe. Accompanying him was his good friend and banker, Andrew Mellon, son of Judge Mellon and now the head of the family bank. On the trip, Frick's horizons were greatly expanded. He saw the important monuments, museums, and art galleries of Ireland, England, France, and Germany. But on his return, he seemed to want more in his life than just business, art, and sight-seeing. A wife would complete the home, and as luck would have it, in the summer of 1881 he met — and within three months married — Adelaide Howard Childs (1859–1931) of the Pittsburgh shoe and bootmaking family. And then, on August 15, 1882, with his wife pregnant and the two looking forward to more children, he paid the then high price of $25,000 for Homewood, a small Italianate house in the Point Breeze section of Pittsburgh's fashionable East End.

Unlike the Overholt tradition, home no longer represented the family's economic center. With the post–Civil War large-scale production of manufactured goods — and the vast selection available to consumers — home had become a showcase for wealth, not its source. Wealthy individuals could select and combine the exotic Oriental and Turkish styles with French and Renaissance Revivals, or with the rectilinear, medieval-inspired, modern Gothic furniture made fashionable in the 1870s by Charles L. Eastlake — a nationalist who was England's fore-most authority on interior decoration and author of *Hints on Household Taste.* At a time when more truly was not enough, home had become a place to show wealth and status through the best material goods that could be purchased — whether made by machine or by hand. Pluralism was in vogue and fashion demanded finely crafted objects such as "art furniture" with its abun-dant ebonizing and decorative painting; marquetry in contrasting materials; artistic metalwork; exotic ceramics, wall coverings, and textiles; tripartite wall treatments with horizontal, mixed imagery on a high dado, filling, and deep frieze.

From the moment Frick returned from Europe in 1880 his taste and direction were defined. He had seen some of the world's finest architecture, interiors, art, furniture, decorative objects, and landscapes. And now he would demand only the best and the most fashionable for his res-idence. Oddly, however, although the grandeur of his houses to come — Clayton, Eagle Rock, One East Seventieth Street, and the Clayton Estate — echoed Europe's finest traditions and par-alleled the evolution of decorative styles in America's Golden Era, Henry Clay Frick always insisted that home, however grand and fashionable, nevertheless must feel "homelike" — be a place of comfort and solace as it had been in the Mennonite village of West Overton, the village where he had spent the first thirty years of his life.

*Following pages:* CLAYTON, NOW THE FRICK ART AND HISTORICAL CENTER, PITTSBURGH

# CLAYTON

THE RESIDENCE OF MR. AND MRS. HENRY CLAY FRICK

PITTSBURGH, PENNSYLVANIA

*Right:* Adelaide and Henry Clay Frick on their honeymoon in 1881.

*Facing page:* THE RECEPTION ROOM, c. 1900
The first room visitors entered when the Fricks entertained in a formal manner was the reception room. It underwent three distinct phases of decoration as Henry Clay Frick's fortune grew and styles changed. The 1882 decor is unknown, but during the Osterling renovation of 1892, seen here, the Fricks chose reproduction Louis XV furniture and heavily fringed lambrequins with Aubusson panels directly from the A. Kimbel & Sons catalogue. A painted frieze of roses on a trellis, ornately carved overmantel, door frames, and gold-plated metalwork added to the splendor.

In front of the window is Orazio Andreoni's 1893 posthumous portrait bust of the Fricks' daughter, Martha. Four paintings that recall Frick's agrarian origins can be seen on either side of the portrait bust: *The Knitting Lesson* by Jean-François Millet (above left), *Road Near Woods* by Constant Troyon (below left), *The Sower* by Millet (above right), and another landscape painting (below right).

WHEN THIRTY-ONE-YEAR-OLD HENRY CLAY FRICK MOVED into the fashionable Monongahela House hotel in 1880, Pittsburgh was just as dark and dirty as the Coke Region he had left behind. "Forge of the Universe," "Hell with the lid taken off," cried the Boston journalist James Parton. "A smoky dismal city at her best," wrote Willard Glazier. "At her worst, nothing darker, dingier or more dispiriting can be imagined . . . the smoke from her dwellings, stores, factories, foundries, steamboats, uniting, settles in a cloud over the narrow valley in which she is built, until the very sun looks coppery through the sooty haze."

The Point Breeze area of the East End, on the other hand, with its burgeoning social, political, and cultural environment, promised escape. A remote area in the 1830s when Abraham Overholt was improving his father's homestead, by the 1860s it was served by two railroads and boasted as its most prominent residents Andrew Carnegie and his partner, William Coleman, the father-in-law of Carnegie's younger brother Thomas. By 1880, although Andrew Carnegie long since had made New York his permanent home, many of his Carnegie Steel partners lived in the area, as did such other prominent Pittsburghers as Henry John Heinz, the bottling, canning, and food-processing tycoon; Philander K. Knox, attorney for the Carnegie enterprises; Robert Pitcairn, head of the Western Division of the Pennsylvania Railroad; and Richard Beatty Mellon, son of Judge Thomas Mellon, founder of the Mellon Bank. Here, the many conflicting styles inherent in the late Victorian period flourished in gracious houses surrounded by ancient trees and vast lawns. And with the means to select beautiful objects and the freedom to employ a variety of styles within the home, the city's elite looked to artistry, craftsmanship, and ornament to separate itself from the industrialization and factory-dependent enterprises upon which their new wealth and status depended. In their own homes — containing custom-designed objects whose beauty was arbitrated either by their own evolving tastes or by that of the legions of architects who also served as decorators and designers — aesthetics reigned.

After a trip to Europe in 1880, where Henry Clay Frick undoubtedly noted and absorbed the many historic architectural and interior styles inherent in its cultural development, he met Adelaide Howard Childs of the distinguished Pittsburgh bootmaking family. They married in December 1881, just when Henry Clay Frick entered into a coke partnership with Andrew Carnegie. The Fricks, therefore, almost immediately became one of America's wealthiest young couples. They continued to live in the stylish Monongahela House, but when Adelaide became pregnant in June 1882, the couple began looking for a permanent home. That summer, Thomas Carnegie told the Fricks about Homewood, a two-story, eleven-room, Italianate house located on an acre and a half of land, one block east of his own home in the Point Breeze neighborhood. Built in the 1860s when Andrew Carnegie and his partners were taking up residence there, Homewood was owned by the widow of the plant manager for Carnegie Steel Brothers, Benjamin Vandervort. Although small and in poor condition — and located on a narrow dirt lane with planks serving as footpaths across the deep drainage ditches on each side — it was adjacent to a large wooded wilderness to the south and within easy commuting distance of Carnegie's mills on the banks of the Monongahela River, as well as downtown Pittsburgh. Just as important, it was in an area that boasted a total of three dozen millionaires — a place that was socially appealing and far enough away from Pittsburgh, and the mills, to ensure safety. So Frick purchased Homewood from Vandervort's widow for the then astonishing sum of $25,000 and gave it to Adelaide as a delayed wedding present. Anticipating a bright future and a house to show off their cultural refinement and status, Frick followed the Overholt family tradition of naming homes after themselves and called the house Clayton.

Frick then engaged a Scottish immigrant and prominent local architect, Andrew W. Peebles, to supervise a renovation of the almost twenty-year-old house. Perhaps conscious of the fact that he was trying to fit in with an already established elite in Point Breeze — a group who had achieved positions of wealth and social status far earlier than he — Frick decided to spend $50,000 on the project, twice the purchase price. During this time, however, the new industrial aristocracy, with its unprecedented consumption on a grand and conspicuous scale, had taken full advantage of what wealth offered. And a fashion-conscious Henry Clay Frick would not be left behind. Although now and throughout his life Frick would show more

*Right:* Adelaide Frick with her children in 1888. From left to right are Childs, Helen, and ill-fated Martha, seen here three years before her death.

restraint than most millionaires of the period, he wanted to update Clayton in the characteristic high Victorian manner with its prescribed proliferation of ornament, dense arrangements of objects, use of complex patterns, and abundance of drapery. He engaged a little-known New York firm, D. S. Hess & Company, to provide furniture and advise on everything from the installation of light fixtures to curtains, carpets, and wall coverings. In turning to New York, rather than to Pittsburgh as he had when he refurbished his Monongahela House apartment, Frick signaled that he had current fashion and social aspirations on his mind. Correspondence in the Frick Family Archives shows how high his expectations and anxieties were. He wrote the company on January 20, 1883: "I would like your Mr. Hess to make a run out. I am very much

disappointed in some of the furniture and mantels. [It is] really embarrassing to me to show it to my friends and say that it was purchased in New York."

The only documented example remaining of D. S. Hess's work in America (through invoices in the Frick Family Archives, not photographs), Clayton provides evidence of the company's taste, skill, and workmanship. In this initial renovation, the decor seems to have been in the then stylish Victorian Orientalist style: the overstuffed "Turkish" parlor furniture had long fringes and short, turned legs; the newlyweds' Anglo-Oriental bedroom furniture was carved in deep relief with flowers, vines, and urns; European decorative accessories were patterned after Japanese and Chinese models; other decorative objects came from the Orient; and the dining-room furniture was custom-made and monogrammed in the then fashionable rectilinear, Charles Eastlake style. New mantels were ordered for most of the rooms and decorative carving was placed on the stairs. At the time of this renovation, Eastlake's groundbreaking book, *Hints on Household Taste* (published in London in 1868 and Boston in 1872), was in its sixth American edition.

When the Fricks moved into Clayton, although the interior decor was entirely updated, it could not compare with the sixty-room mansions belonging to their peers. Nevertheless, the couple loved their new home. Frick took a few days off work to help unpack, and a man from D. S. Hess & Company came from New York to hang the curtains and place the furniture.

By 1890, however, the Fricks wanted to redo the house. Less than ten years had passed, but in 1889 Frick had become chairman of a division of the Carnegie empire, Carnegie

*Above left:* Homewood, later known as Clayton, when purchased by the Fricks on August 15, 1882.

*Above right:* Proposed design for the renovation of Clayton, c. 1890, by Frederick J. Osterling.

*Above:* Clayton, c. 1898, showing the porte cochère dating from the 1860s; the c. 1882 stained-glass bay window by A. Godwin & Company of Philadelphia, entitled *Love in the Tower*; the 1892 porch before it was enclosed; and Henry Clay Frick's new bathroom (to the above right of the porch), added in 1897.

Brothers & Company, and in 1892 would become chairman of the consolidated Carnegie steel works, the Carnegie Steel Company, the largest steel concern in the world and the employer of over thirty thousand workers. As Ellen M. Rosenthal notes in "Clayton: Portrait of the House," "At no other time in American history has the home been considered so important, both as a formative environment for the family and as an emblem defining its owners' social standing." Thus, to accommodate their heightened business and social position, as well as their growing family (the Fricks now had three children: seven-year-old Childs, five-year-old Martha, and two-year-old Helen), Frick and his wife embarked on a second renovation. They rented a house nearby and hired Frederick J. Osterling, a twenty-five-year-old Pittsburgh architect, known to be prolific, though quarrelsome, brilliantly adept at a range of styles including Richardsonian Romanesque, Classical Revival, and Gothic Revival. Significantly, Osterling was then

Pittsburgh's favorite architect. He had completed many homes in the East End, as well as an ornate residence in the Queen Anne manner for Charles M. Schwab, superintendent of Carnegie's Braddock steel mill. In addition, he had designed a Romanesque Revival switching hall for the Bell Telephone Company of Pennsylvania; handsome brick foundries for the Westinghouse Air-Brake Works in Wilmerding, Pennsylvania; the Bellefield Presbyterian Church in Pittsburgh; a renovation of the Bridge of Sighs connecting the Allegheny Courthouse to the jail; and the *Pittsburgh Times*'s Magee Building with its grotesque carvings.

But Osterling's first architectural rendering for Clayton's remodeling failed. Although he had turned the small Italianate house into a massive Loire Valley château as popularized for America's newly rich by the Vanderbilt family's famed New York architect, Richard Morris Hunt, Frick thought the overall design too elaborate — too many Romanesque arches, too many porches, bays, windows, and turrets. But the reworked plan, although for a smaller and greatly simplified house, was nevertheless imposing. Italianate Clayton still would resemble a Loire Valley château, but a lighter, more graceful one. And achieving this style — French for the preexisting Italian — still would represent an astonishing architectural feat by young Osterling. To accomplish the transformation, he removed Clayton's roof and added two floors, in addition to enveloping the original house with a greatly enlarged floor plan. On the north facade, where the bays on the front rooms had been, he placed a wide, arcaded stone porch with an intricate mosaic floor. The former dining room (the breakfast room today) and those above it on the west side received a bay, and the entire southeast corner of the original building was demolished and replaced with a grander dining room, butler's pantry with a metal-lined warming cabinet, scullery, cold room, and bedrooms above. Although still smaller than most millionaires' houses in the East End, Clayton now consisted of four stories and twenty-three rooms, including a children's entrance decorated with then fashionable stenciled walls, a small basin, towel racks, and a bench with hat-and-coat racks made of oak. Storm windows, three central furnaces, and $4,000 worth of plumbing completed the renovation. A house that virtually had doubled in size now required a staff of fourteen including chambermaids, cook, gardeners, stablemen, and coachman.

No doubt Frick was happy with all the remodeling, and no doubt he recognized that the job was a complex and difficult one. But Frick often was displeased with his architect's performance. On June 25, 1891, he wrote Osterling in the curt tones representative of the way he typically complained to those in his employ: "I think it simply outrageous the way you are looking after my house. If I had any idea that your business methods were as bad as they appear to be I would not have had anything to do with you . . . If you cannot give my matters better attention, I will expect you to turn over your work to some other man, whom I shall select. I am not accustomed to having business done in the manner in which you do it, and am out of all patience with you." Nevertheless, when the $300,000 renovation was finished Frick was satisfied. He had an impressive, fully updated, entirely modernized house.

By the time the Frick family moved back into Clayton in the spring of 1892, a stunning interior greeted them. Fully fashionable with textiles, painted designs, or stenciling on the walls, fine parquet floors, and lush curtains, Clayton had been entirely refurbished by another New

*Right:* Chairs by D. S. Hess & Company, c. 1882.

During the 1892 Osterling renovation, the mahogany furniture dating from the 1882 Peebles renovation and manufactured by D. S. Hess & Company in New York (and probably original to the room the Fricks now called the breakfast room) remained in place. Eastlake-inspired, the set includes a table, monogrammed chairs, and two monogrammed high chairs.

York firm, A. Kimbel & Sons, operating under Osterling's direction. Though not as prestigious as New York's Herter Brothers or Philadelphia's Daniel Pabst, this family firm of German cabinetmakers had introduced Gothic Revival to the American public at the 1876 Philadelphia Centennial Exposition, and in 1892 it had kept current with changing taste and was the leading purveyor of furniture in the style of Charles Eastlake, as well as in architectural woodwork and decoration.

For the Clayton dining room and library, Kimbel manufactured the Louis XIV–style furniture *en suite* to design specifications by Osterling and helped coordinate all the other decorative details. Others contributed as well. For the door between the entrance hall and kitchen quarters, A. Godwin & Company of Philadelphia, known for using semiprecious stones in stained-glass windows, provided a small, golden-hued panel framed in moonstones that depicts a woman dressed in blue, holding an overflowing cornucopia. In addition this firm provided a series of large romantic panels entitled *Love in the Tower* for the bay windows on the stair landing. The first-floor woodwork was made by P. Hansen Hiss of Baltimore, New York, and Washington; $5,000 worth of bold parquet floors were created by G. W. Koch & Sons of New York; and second-floor woodwork and the Blue Guest Room's French Renaissance Revival furniture were ordered from a prominent Wisconsin firm, Mathews Brothers of Milwaukee. Machine-made carpets, then a new technology and deemed highly fashionable; luxurious, handmade, heavy velvet curtains and portieres (new and fashionable at the time because they provided a way to display needlework skills); patterned brocades; damasks with tassels and trim; and furniture either ordered from the Kimbel catalogue or custom-made by them from Osterling's designs — all were entirely new and in the latest taste. Although still subscribing to the eclecticism of the high Victorian period and selecting a variety of mass-marketed styles for Clayton's furnishings, the tenets of the then popular Aesthetic Movement had not been forgotten by the Fricks and their designers. Tripartite wall treatment could be found in the entrance hall, breakfast room, second-floor hall, library, and sitting room, and everywhere — in fabrics, furniture, and decorative objects — the artist reigned supreme. Even the art Frick collected was by contemporary masters, albeit primarily European, not American.

But achieving the interior design had been just as trying for the Fricks as the architectural renovation. Their secretary, George Megrew, wrote to Kimbel on March 11, 1892, expressing his concern. Using softer language than Frick had with Osterling, Megrew, however, warned: "You could to very good advantage employ more men here, and it is Mrs. Frick's earnest desire that you facilitate matters for her . . . She knows that if your work is allowed to drift along, as it has been doing for the last few weeks, that Mr. Frick will be disappointed and indignant at the slow progress that has been made."

Through Clayton, the Fricks were solidifying their place in Pittsburgh society, and like other individuals of means in late nineteenth-century America, they had developed an unprecedented interest in, and concern for, interior decoration. The Fricks owned such books as *Modern Dwellings in Town and Country* (1878) by the prominent architect and writer H. Hudson Holly, who influenced the Aesthetic Movement in America and advocated the ideas

*Above:* Helen Clay Frick as a young girl, showing her spunk, independent nature, and feisty personality.

of Charles Eastlake, and the prestigious 1883 folio edition of East Coast millionaires' residences, *Artistic Houses: Being a Series of Interior Views of a Number of the Most Beautiful and Celebrated Homes in the United States.* As exacting as Frick was in business detail, and as oriented toward perfection as he was in every aspect of his work and person, so he was in his home. With fine books to educate his eye and his innate sense of beauty to guide him, he and Adelaide personally monitored every aspect of this Clayton renovation, sending measurements to suppliers, explaining the finish they wanted on certain items, and complaining about the quality of delivered objects not made to their satisfaction. Another letter from George Megrew to Kimbel shows their demand for perfection: "The decorated [window] shades you put in Mr. Frick's sitting room are not at all satisfactory and Mrs. Frick wishes you to send others. They are not wide enough to go over the rollers. It is almost impossible to make them go up straight. They are so thin and filmy that they are broken and curled up at the edges. They look very badly."

Once back in Clayton in the spring of 1892, the Fricks continued the process of using their home to reveal their wealth and emerging taste. In keeping with the late Victorian ideal mandating that every surface display something, and that motifs from conflicting styles could be combined in one object, Clayton contained a dizzying array of decorative objects and ornaments. Porcelain, sculpture, silver, glass ornaments, souvenirs from trips, and family photographs covered every inch of space on the tables, mantels, and tops of bookshelves. And as Helen recalled in her Clayton memoir, the walls were "rapidly being hung" with paintings. In fact, the house was so crammed with objects that paintings also were hung on shuttered windows and various doors.

But the splendor of Clayton was darkened by a series of family tragedies: the death of the Fricks' daughter Martha in 1891 after a four-year illness from ingesting a pin; a near-successful attempt on Frick's life by an anarchist, Alexander Berkman, during the 1892 Homestead Steel Strike; the death of his twenty-eight-day-old son, Henry Clay Frick Jr., while Frick was recovering from the assassin's attack; and Adelaide's near-death from complications in childbirth. Yet Frick's business life thrived, and in 1897, although the house now was filled with pictures of their deceased children and their mourning still remained profound, the Fricks made more improvements to Clayton. A Pittsburgh firm, Alden & Harlow, was asked to build a greenhouse and playhouse for the children, as well as add three bathrooms to the house: one for Henry Clay Frick; one for his fourteen-year-old son, Childs; and another for the Blue Guest Room. The well-regarded firm had completed several important projects no doubt known to Frick, among them Pittsburgh's prestigious Duquesne Club; the first Carnegie Library branch, located in Lawrenceville; the Carnegie Institute; and Sunnyledge, the home of the Fricks' family doctor, James McClelland. Nevertheless, and true to form, Frick was displeased with Alden & Harlow's initial efforts and again showed his wrath. Of the new, $2,300 bathrooms, an aesthetic-minded Frick, who obviously understood that in the new vogue a bathroom was meant to be pleasurable as well as functional, fumed: "[The work] is rough, you seem to have given construction of these bathrooms very little thought. There is nothing artistic about them. If you were attaching a bathroom to a stable, the one for my room might do."

The following year, Frick ordered a new walnut mantel for Adelaide's room (as newlyweds the couple may have shared the same bedroom but now had separate ones, as was the custom), as well as an oak and walnut parquet floor. He enclosed the arcaded porch, removed a large musical instrument called an orchestrion from the parlor, and installed it on the porch. A Freemason who had risen to the top of the York and Scottish Rites in the late 1870s, Frick seemed almost obsessed with building. Freemasons subscribed to the belief that God was the "architect" of the universe, and so for Frick erecting a building was a near sacred act. Restless, critical, and exacting in his quest, he now commissioned Alden & Harlow to design an art gallery wing off Clayton's parlor and dining room. Larger than Clayton itself, the wing would be in the English Tudor style and would provide, in addition, a ballroom, new kitchen, and more servants' rooms. But after nearly a year's deliberation, Frick changed his mind about the wing. He wrote his art-dealer friend Roland Knoedler: "Have asked Mr. Hiss to show you the plans of the proposed art gallery . . . am afraid he is inclined to make it more of a living room than an art gallery, and I hope you will give him your views frankly. Of course we have not decided positively to build it, but expect to make up our minds after the 1st of January."

In 1900 Frick hired an important Chicago architect, Daniel Hudson Burnham, to design the Frick Building in downtown Pittsburgh — intended to outshine the adjacent Carnegie Building by being the most modern office building to date in Pittsburgh. Although it represented his first Pittsburgh commission, Burnham's reputation had preceded him. In 1893 this renowned Beaux Arts architect headed the architectural arm of the World's Columbian Exposition held in Chicago — an important event in the development of classical architecture in America. But Frick, knowing that Burnham represented the height of cachet as an architect, also knew from personal experience that he needed his own man on-site, available to him at all

*Left:* THE PARLOR, c. 1903

In 1899 Henry Clay Frick acquired one of his first Old Master paintings — *Portrait of a Young Artist,* then believed to be a work by Rembrandt. Previously, Frick had collected paintings by contemporary French Academic and Barbizon artists. The year he purchased the Rembrandt, however, he prevailed in a lawsuit against Andrew Carnegie, withdrew his $15 million fortune from Carnegie Steel, and became an extremely wealthy man. Moreover, with the formation of U.S. Steel, his wealth would further increase. In this photograph, Frick clearly is showing his heightened status: *Portrait of a Young Artist* is placed above the sofa, on the east wall, directly opposite the doorway visitors used when entering the parlor.

times. Frick, therefore, asked the architect responsible for Clayton's 1882 renovation, Andrew W. Peebles, to be Burnham's local assistant, supervising construction, work progress, and interior arrangements.

While Frick persevered with Burnham, Peebles, and the Frick Building, he also asked Burnham to design a new residence on nearby Gunn's Hill, a high ridge overlooking the

Monongahela River and the Carnegie mills to the south. Two years earlier, Frick, who may have suffered both a delayed reaction to his children's deaths and a nervous collapse, also suffered the first permanent setback of his business career. He had been demoted in Carnegie Steel. And by 1899 he and Carnegie had quarreled so bitterly over the price of coke and other issues that Frick — after almost twenty years managing the H. C. Frick Coke Company and ten years as chairman of the Carnegie Steel Company — had resigned. But he did not go quietly. He sued Carnegie for the full market share of his Carnegie Steel stock and successfully extricated his $15 million fortune. The money, however, was not enough to compensate for his lost position in Pittsburgh's business and social arenas. Although a millionaire many times over, in 1900 Frick was only fifty-one years old and seemingly at the end of his active business career. Clayton, therefore, for all its improvements and status statements, now represented the home of Pittsburgh's odd-man-out. A new house on Gunn's Hill overlooking Carnegie's mills, on the other hand, would give Frick what he needed — a renewed sense of power and control.

After seeing the plans for the new house, however, Frick changed his mind. Apart from the fact that Adelaide wanted to remain at Clayton, where her children were born — and Frick sarcastically claimed that the smoke from the nearby steel mills might harm his growing art collection (the paintings were protected by glass) — Frick must have guessed that neither a new house nor an exquisite downtown office building would give him a power base or renew his position in Pittsburgh's business and social circles. He wrote Burnham on January 11, 1900: "Mrs. Frick and I are going over the plans left with us. Just when we will be able to return them, I am unable to say, but I have about reached the conclusion that it would be a mistake to build anything like so large a house, and we may decide to have you take the matter up in a different shape, looking towards making a more moderate house, and relying on the art gallery for giving us such room as we might need when giving a large reception."

But hosting large receptions was not going to become a regular social event for Henry Clay Frick and his wife. Frick had soured on Pittsburgh. He now began spending an increased amount of time in New York helping John D. Rockefeller Sr. and J. P. Morgan iron out the details of the merger between the restructured Carnegie Company and U. S. Steel. Indeed, the pied-à-terre he rented in New York's Sherry's Hotel may be seen as his first step toward making a final break with Pittsburgh. But in making his exodus, Frick did not leave silently. Apart from the fact that a forty-seven-ton granite cenotaph bearing Frick's name, designed by Daniel Burnham, remained in the Frick plot at the Homewood Cemetery; at the groundbreaking ceremony for the Frick Building, he laid the granite cornerstone with a silver trowel. When the Frick Building was completed in 1901, it was declared the finest office building erected in Pittsburgh to date, and no doubt its delighted owner reveled in the fact that the structure left its immediate neighbor to the west, the smaller Carnegie Building, in shadow.

The coup must have so pleased Frick that on August 2, 1901, he purchased from Patek Philippe a one-of-a-kind, 1892 gold pocket watch and had it engraved with a front view of the Frick Building. Frick gave it to Peebles for completing the building six months ahead of schedule. In time Burnham too would be rewarded: five years later Frick asked him to design yet another edifice in downtown Pittsburgh — the Allegheny Building. It would block the Carnegie Building's light from the south, just as the Frick Building did from the east.

Despite Carnegie's attempt to crush him financially and sideline him, Frick began to show that he was not yet finished in business circles. His fortune had tripled with the formation of U.S. Steel, and as a director of the giant steel trust (Carnegie did not become a director), he was in New York monitoring the company's progress and watching his fortune grow. Clayton, however, remained the family's primary residence and as such it now demanded another update to reflect both the dramatic shift taking place in interior design and Frick's reclaimed position in the financial and steel world.

The new principles governing interior design resulted largely from the publication in 1897 of the groundbreaking book on interior design *The Decoration of Houses*, by Edith Wharton and Ogden Codman Jr. They called for an end to the dense, dark, hodgepodge of the Victorian era and advocated either a neutral color for walls such as ivory or gray, or a single wallpaper from ceiling to baseboard; painted woodwork; fewer colors in a room; an end to portieres and the return of light and air; and the use of historically accurate classical designs. Having abandoned his plans for a new wing or even an entirely new house — possibly because his Mennonite farming heritage drew him to the ideals of simplicity and restraint, even as he was trying to make a statement about power — in 1903 Frick settled for a $100,000 interior renovation of Clayton consistent with the new ideal. He hired Cottier & Company, a prominent New York and London firm founded in the 1870s by a Scotsman, Daniel Cottier, a talented and charismatic designer, interior decorator, and art and antique dealer responsible for having brought the Aesthetic Movement to America from England in the 1870s. His firm intuitively understood the relationship between success and reinvention and now was creating interiors inspired by Wharton and Codman. Although Clayton always would remain a fine example of the late Victorian period, Cottier & Company reduced its ornamental detail and covered the walls in plainer, striped fabrics, consistent with the changing taste in America. In addition, the firm spruced up the places most often seen by guests: the stair landing, reception room, parlor, and third-floor guest rooms. Lighter colors, less drapery, less complicated treatment, and a non-layered look reigned. As this new look ruled, the decidedly romantic stained-glass bay window on Clayton's stair landing, entitled *Love in the Tower*, was replaced with panels entitled *The Four Virgins*, depictions of four adolescent girls from antiquity. In their conspicuous placement, the windows might well have been a message to Frick's fifteen-year-old daughter, Helen.

As was their custom, the Fricks kept a discerning eye on every aspect of the Cottier redecoration. On October 17, 1903, Henry Clay Frick wrote Mr. Inglis of Cottier & Company: "Mrs. Frick is inclined to think the rugs in the library are a little dark, and it may be we will wish to return them. There are several things in the rooms you have fitted up that we will probably want to return, and some I have already told you we did not care for." And ten days later he expressed concern for the way his newly acquired *Portrait of a Young Artist* by Rembrandt looked. He insisted: "[Mrs. Frick] also objects to the background of the Rembrandt; thinks you should supply something with more red in it, and not so expensive." The desired effect must have been achieved because the January 24, 1903, edition of the Pittsburgh *Bulletin* praised "the superb art of Clayton [that] in itself rendered this beautiful home famous in the art and social world"; and in 1904, Frederick Taylor Gates, a trusted advisor to John D. Rockefeller Sr., wrote: "The few hours spent in your home, with its wonderful treasures, will always be among the most memorable of my life. Long may it be yours to adorn this precious home and to share its treasures with your loving and admiring friends."

At this time, however, Henry Clay Frick no longer felt Clayton so precious. His power base in Pittsburgh was gone. Although Clayton long had symbolized his prominent business and social rank in Pittsburgh, even with the Cottier & Company redecoration, the house no longer felt fashionable to him. Perhaps for Frick, Clayton forever would represent Pittsburgh's odd-man-out, a man no longer engaged in active business management, a man whose partners had turned against him and sided with Carnegie.

Thus, when he rented the New York apartment at Sherry's in 1900, he also had begun searching for a summer home in Prides Crossing, a small town on Boston's North Shore then being invaded by the new industrialists and their families. In 1902 the Fricks had purchased a site there overlooking the Atlantic Ocean and had started renting a house on the nearby Robert S. Bradley estate. The location allowed the couple the dual pleasure of being with their artist friends in nearby Magnolia, as well as socializing with their powerful railroad and political associates. By 1904, construction of the Frick family summer residence began, and the next year, Frick made his Pittsburgh exodus final. He rented William H. Vanderbilt's New York house, 640 Fifth Avenue.

Apart from sporadic business trips by Frick, the family returned to Clayton only for Christmas, their daughter Helen's 1908 debutante party, and Henry Clay Frick's funeral in 1919. After her husband's death, Adelaide never again stayed there. Helen, on the other hand, adored the house. As the place where she most deeply had felt her parents' love and protection, it was her favorite home. In 1911 twenty-three-year-old Helen supervised the recovering of furniture in the library and breakfast room and visited often, even as her parents remained in New York. When her mother died in 1931, Helen inherited the house. Although she then owned Westmoreland Farm in Bedford Village, New York, and also inherited Eagle Rock, as the family summer home would be called, Helen kept a full staff at Clayton and forever maintained it as her legal residence. She culled many of the lesser paintings from her father's collection and also removed two small stained-glass windows at the back stairs in the second-floor hall, installed a bookcase, and reused the windows as doors for a medicine cabinet in the Blue Guest Room's bathroom. She also renovated the third-floor rooms for more guest rooms and a servant's suite, had the large double bed in the Blue Guest Room made into twin beds, and installed the furniture from her former bedroom at One East Seventieth Street in her Clayton bedroom, while her former childhood suite was placed in a new guest room on the third floor.

Helen's devotion to Clayton never waned. More than any other place, this was where she felt safe and secure, where she could escape New York society and enjoy the comfort of her childhood friends, where she could remember and feel her parents. And she was proud of its casual opulence. When living in New York, she reminded her father in a 1914 Friendship Calendar, "East to West Clayton's Best." Those who knew Helen heard her refer to Clayton as her "dear old home" and saw her dog play dead if she said New York yet jump for joy if she said Pittsburgh. In the 1950s she expressed her feelings more clearly. She wrote in her Clayton memoir: "Very often in the summer, we went abroad for a couple of months. I was always happy to return to 'Clayton' as no other place could compare with it in my opinion."

In 1951, Helen found a way to keep Clayton forever. For the previous six years, she had battled the Frick Collection trustees to prevent hundreds of articles belonging to John D. Rockefeller Jr. from entering her father's collection. When a 1948 court order permitted the Frick Collection to accept gifts from the public — and the trustees agreed to take Rockefeller's art objects on his death — Helen was livid. With her efforts to maintain the integrity of her father's one-man collection defeated, Helen, who had warned Rockefeller in a letter on July 24, 1947, that she, as Henry Clay Frick's daughter, could "neither condone nor forget" his actions, decided to take revenge. She left her entire fortune to the Helen Clay Frick Foundation, instructed its future trustees to create a house-museum of Clayton, and in a pointed allusion to the Rockefeller fiasco stipulated that no gifts or loans were to be accepted unless given by blood descendants of her parents. Helen's plan was criticized then and now as a sentimental effort to preserve her childhood home and keep it purely Frick. This action also was perceived, as she intended it to be, as a rebuff to the Frick Collection trustees for accepting the Rockefeller bequest. Indeed, although she bequested $400,000 for annual operating expenses, in this same will Helen also canceled a $33 million trust fund for the Frick Art Reference Library in New York. Instead she bequeathed the money to the Helen Clay Frick Foundation for the eventual restoration of Clayton. As a woman never permitted by her father to marry, one who had lived solely at his behest, and his defender and immortalizer to a fault — for Frick was a harsh strikebreaker and, as a man of his day, had little interest in the fate of the working men off whose backs his wealth, art collection, and residences were, in part, made — Helen certainly was trying both to get even with the Frick Collection trustees and hoping to insulate her father. But time has shown that her preservation effort also was visionary and Clayton has become a gift — in the true sense of the word — to the people of Pittsburgh and a monument to its past.

This was no accident. When Helen made the decision to preserve Clayton as a museum, she did so as a highly cultured woman with a genuine sense of history and understanding of the fine arts. Helen Frick already had founded two art reference libraries, had acquired art for her collection, the Frick Collection, and the Henry Clay Frick Fine Arts Building in Pittsburgh, and had published articles on her favorite sculptor, Jean-Antoine Houdon. Moreover, by the 1950s in New York, the Gilded Age mansions were disappearing and Pittsburgh was undergoing a postwar renaissance regarded by Franklin Toker, professor of art history and architecture at the University of Pittsburgh, "as the most intensive peacetime reconstruction of any city center in history." But for Helen, the loss of grand houses in New York, as well as in Pittsburgh, represented the destruction of an extraordinary period in American cultural history. In down-town Pittsburgh, for instance, new glass and steel skyscrapers were replacing the older, historic stone buildings she had known as a child. And in the suburbs many of the millionaires' houses Helen had frequented were being bulldozed to make way for what has replaced them — large commercial and residential developments. Today, Clayton is the only house that remains on Millionaires' Row, an estate now flanked by mid- to low-income housing to the north, mid-income housing to the west, upper- to mid-income housing to the east, and Frick Park and the Homewood and Smithfield Cemeteries to the south. A piece of turn-of-the-century Pittsburgh, and America, it also is the only millionaire's house that remains from the emerging steel indus-try, untouched since 1905.

In this way, Helen Frick was a pioneer in what we regard today as historic preservation. In explaining her motives, she wrote that the house was "to be preserved [so] future generations may better understand the kind of life that was lived within its walls." And she stipulated that the trustees of her foundation were to perpetuate Clayton and its contents not only "as a land-mark of the end of the Victorian era, but also as a place where students [can] study the decora-tive arts and do creative work." To this end she instructed that "a scrapbook in my possession at [Westmoreland Farm] containing photographs of Clayton by Lewis Stephany, will serve as guide to those whose responsibility it will be to hang the paintings or to place the furniture. Everything should be as nearly as possible like it was in the days when the family lived there." Additional archival material — invoices, inventories, letters, and memorabilia stashed away in drawers, closets, attic, and basement, as well as stored in the Frick Art Reference Library, Westmoreland Farm, and downtown Pittsburgh — was to be gathered and similarly utilized. Immediately, Helen began putting Clayton in order. She restored the water-damaged walls and ceiling of her bedroom, painted with lilacs, roses, chrysanthemums, morning glories, birds, and butterflies in the 1892 Osterling renovation. In 1953 she asked a prominent Long Island landscape design firm, Innocenti & Webel, to draw a site plan identifying every tree on the grounds. She also initiated a program of cleaning and protecting the Clayton furniture, as well as duplicating worn upholstery and curtains.

Like her father, Helen had a gift for knowing exactly how she wanted things. She left explicit directions for the way visitors should view the rooms. As far as possible, paintings that had been moved from Clayton to Eagle Rock were to be returned. And as Helen noted, "I have indicated on slips glued to the back of canvases which pictures I intend to leave to the Helen Clay Frick Foundation and these will be hung at Clayton. There were some paintings that were never [at Clayton], but these will add to the beauty and interest and value of the Collection, and they need not be hung at one time." In fact, at the Clayton property today, all the paintings from Eagle Rock can be seen: *Portrait of Margaret Beaumont* and *Portrait of Sir George Howland Beaumont* by Sir Joshua Reynolds; *Portrait of Richard Brinsley Sheriden* by Thomas Gainsborough; *Portrait of the Honorable John Hamilton* by William Hogarth; *Portrait of the Marquise du Blaizel* by Thomas Lawrence, now considered the School of David; and *Portrait of Julio Ascencio* by Francisco de Goya y Lucientes.

*Right:* The Henry Clay Frick Fine Arts Building at the University of Pittsburgh.

In the early 1960s Helen, now in her seventies, expanded her Pittsburgh philanthropy to include a fine arts building for the University of Pittsburgh donated in memory of her father. Designed by the firm of B. Kenneth Johnstone, the two-story, light gray limestone building has a roof of red tiles, a relief sculpture by Malvina Hoffman of Henry Clay Frick over the entrance, and an inner cloister patterned after Santa Maria Novella in Florence. It has classrooms and studios, as well as art galleries, period rooms, and a two-story art reference library with a wrought-iron balcony, natural cherry paneling, custom-made study tables, and open stacks filled with the books and catalogues that Helen began purchasing for the fine arts department she had founded in 1927.

Everything for the public galleries was carefully chosen — wall coverings, woods, curtain material, rugs, and furniture. The lecture hall curtains were woven in a blue-figured brocade Helen selected in Italy. One period room with *boiserie* (French carved panels) was designated to house fine pieces of Eagle Rock's Louis XVI furniture, and another was meant to reuse the Jacobean paneling from Eagle Rock's billiard room. The Eagle Rock organ was installed in the rotunda in memory of Helen's mother and was to play as visitors toured the galleries. In addition, Helen gave the building the Nicholas Lochoff frescoes she had acquired from Bernard Berenson — reconstructions of such works as *Expulsion from Paradise* by Masaccio, *The Birth of Venus* by Botticelli, and *The Arrival of the Ambassadors* by Carpaccio. While Helen planned to install the frescoes in the building, she also intended to exhibit her own collection of Italian, French, and Flemish paintings — including rare fourteenth- and fifteenth-century works from Florence and Siena by such masters as Duccio, Sassetta, and Giovanni di Paolo. In addition, she planned to buy more art works for the university's permanent collection. As if this were not

enough, on November 1, 1963, Helen increased the size and quality of her bequest, adding twelve barrels of Chinese porcelains, a drawing-room suite of French design upholstered in Aubusson tapestry, and Italian Renaissance bronzes bought by her father from the Morgan Collection, then housed in the Frick Collection vault.

*Above:* The Frick Art Museum.

But none of these gifts would be freely given. From 1963, when ground was broken, to 1967, when the building was up and running, Helen tried to attach a retroactive qualification to the bequest that placed restrictions on the curriculum and the hiring of professors and directors that the university found unreasonable and unacceptable. As a result, the university terminated its relationship with Helen and assumed all financial responsibility for the Henry Clay Frick Fine Arts Building. Although the Eagle Rock organ, Lochoff frescoes, and library books stayed, Helen was permitted to reclaim all the art objects she had donated.

The failure of her plans for the Henry Clay Frick Fine Arts Building only fueled Helen's desire to build an art museum on the Clayton site. She immediately engaged the Pittsburgh architects Pratt, Schafer, and Slowik and began designing what would become the Frick Art Museum — a Renaissance-style building constructed of Alabama limestone. In 1969 — one year before the new museum opened to the public — overly burdened by Eagle Rock, she took measures to incorporate its treasures in her new dream. Over that next year, she had a demolition company carefully raze Eagle Rock, room by room, so she could donate as much of the architectural ornamentation as possible to her new museum and distribute the balance to members of the Frick family. The Jacobean paneling from the billiard room — originally intended for the Henry Clay Frick Fine Arts Building — was to be installed in the new museum's trustees' room. In addition, Helen transferred her father's One East Seventieth Street bedroom furniture, then housed at Eagle Rock, to the Frick Art Museum and also gave the museum most of the remaining Eagle Rock porcelains and Renaissance bronzes.

As the Frick Art Museum took shape, the Clayton house was not left behind. Helen turned the reception room into a small gallery with walls covered in pink silk damask from Scalamandré. Here she installed more of the Eagle Rock collection: two ormolu mounted vitrines filled with approximately 125 miniature porcelains from the George B. Warren Collection; a mahogany, marble, and ormolu commode by Jean-Henri Riesener, c. 1780; an eighteenth-century, mahogany, Louis XVI–style bureau-plat inset with a Sèvres porcelain plaque, attributed to Martin Carlin; and other pieces of authentic and reproduction eighteenth-century furniture. Together with the many paintings in the Eagle Rock collection she gave to the Helen Clay Frick Foundation, she also returned eight pastels and two drawings by Jean-François Millet that were original to Clayton but then housed in the Frick Art Reference Library in New York.

*Below:* Clayton first-floor plan as conceived by Frederick J. Osterling in 1892, as it remains today.

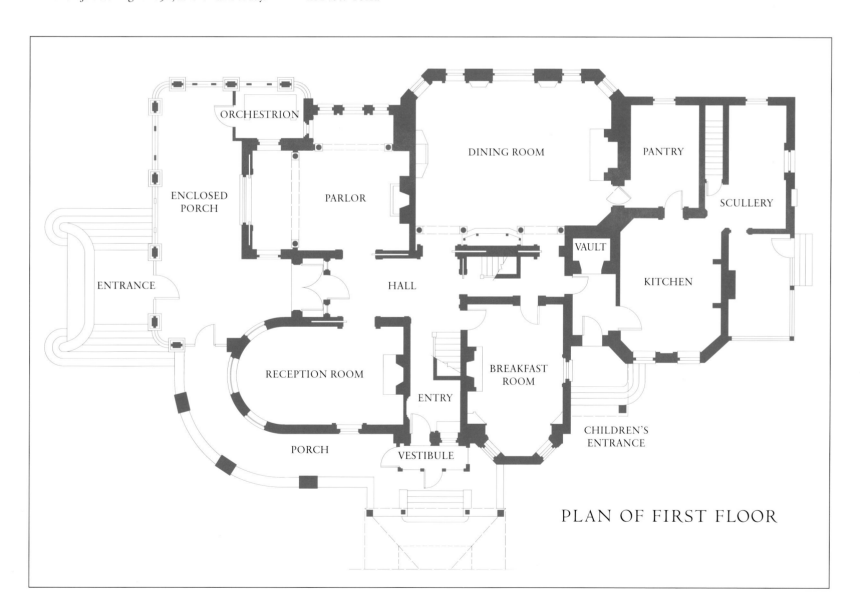

PLAN OF FIRST FLOOR

Helen also began organizing the Frick family archival records at Clayton. As a legal resident of Pennsylvania, she continued to live at Clayton for six months every year and to cast her vote in the basement of nearby Sterrett School, once when on crutches. While at Clayton she managed her philanthropy and spent hours organizing the inventories of her father's former homes and making scrapbooks and family albums to record her family history.

In 1981 for reasons of health and to insure that her will be probated in Pennsylvania, not New York, ninety-three-year-old Helen took up permanent residence at her beloved home. Her nurses remember every day pushing Helen around the house in her wheelchair as she remembered the past and contemplated Clayton's now safeguarded future. When she died on November 11, 1984 – thirty-three years after conceiving and implementing her house-museum plan – those charged with making an inventory of the paintings, decorative objects, furniture, and historic papers stored in Clayton's drawers and closets, as well as those people involved in the actual restoration of the house as a museum, said Clayton felt "as if [the Fricks] were going away for the weekend." Some twelve thousand items – furniture, linens, papers, books, games, and closets full of clothes – were found and catalogued by the museum staff. The New York architect overseeing Clayton's restoration, Thierry Despont, said: "It feels like a home. You can feel [the Fricks'] personalities and presence in these rooms."

During this six-year renovation, wallcovering dating from the 1940s and 1950s was removed from the breakfast-room walls, and painted and aluminum leaf strapwork from the 1890s was discovered. An invoice in the Frick Family Archives guided the staff to the textile firm in France that had made and could reproduce the curtains in Adelaide's bedroom. The library's stenciled jute wall covering, overlaid by a dark brown velvet, was removed and restored by an expert in Paris. And as restorers dug beneath Helen's pink wallcovering in the reception room, the beautifully painted frieze of roses on a trellis was uncovered.

Over two hundred skilled craftsmen from twenty-two firms in America and Europe were employed and $6 million spent. Describing the project's intent, Despont remarked: "We are trying to recapture the feeling, even the smell and the sounds of the house. We can have the music played that they played . . . and every clock will tick away, back in its place. We'll even have the famous telephone installed by Frick in 1883 outside his bedroom ringing now and then." "Frozen in time" is the way Despont summarized this Victorian masterpiece where even today visitors feel that long-deceased members of the Frick family could return at any moment.

On September 22, 1990, Clayton opened to the public with nearly all its original furniture and works of art. Almost a full century had passed since Henry Clay Frick and his wife, Adelaide, decorated their first home. One of the wealthiest young couples in America, the Fricks had seen a husband's distinguished career end, only to watch it start anew. They had seen their fortune skyrocket and their house renovated every ten years to keep pace with the latest fashion. But they had suffered the death of two children in one year, an assassin's attack, and the betrayal of business partners. The opulent Golden Era in architecture and interior design long since had been replaced by modernism's abstraction and unadorned architecture. But for the small, nondescript Italianate house turned a Loire Valley château, time stood still.

*Above:* THE CORNER OF PENN AND HOMEWOOD
AVENUES

The original wood fence surrounding Clayton was
replaced in the 1880s with one made of iron. As the
Frick's teenage helper, Annie Blumenschein Stephany,
remembers in her memoir, this new fence was black
with gold-leaf fleurs-de-lis. According to her, it was
"the finest fence in the East End and the only one like
it in Pittsburgh." This photograph probably dates from
the late 1890s. By then the roads had been improved
with sidewalks.

*Below and facing page:* THE PORCH

Before the porch was enclosed in 1899, it was used for lunch and for viewing the Fricks' private Fourth of July fireworks display. Afterward it became a family room where they enjoyed Christmas morning and, like many other Victorians, displayed plants from their greenhouse. When ninety-six-year-old Helen Clay Frick died at Clayton in 1984, her coffin was placed on the porch and her funeral service was held there.

The floor is a fleur-de-lis mosaic tile from the 1892 renovation, and the rattan furniture, evocative of the Far East, was purchased from Sperling Brothers in New York in 1899. The most interesting feature of the room, however, is the orchestrion (facing page), a ceiling-to-floor musical instrument that imitates a full orchestra: winds, brass, percussion, keyboard, and strings. A Victorian status symbol, it was selected by Andrew Carnegie when abroad during the 1892 Homestead Steel Strike. He described the orchestrion to Frick as "something that will give great pleasure, and be a marvel in Pittsburgh." On Carnegie's advice Frick purchased it for approximately $5,000 from Michael Welte & Sons in Germany and installed it in the parlor. Too heavy for the floor, however, in 1899 it was moved to a special compartment on the porch, supported by a cement wall in the basement. In 1904, the orchestrion was converted from a weight-driven system to one driven by electricity. Today the orchestrion is housed on the porch and plays for Clayton visitors.

Unlike the many front halls that are designed to impress, if not intimidate, visitors, Clayton's is warm and welcoming. The L-shaped room has rod-to-rod silk curtains at the front and side windows, accompanied by rust-red, appliquéd portieres *en suite* to the hall and rooms off the hall, and red carpeting by A. Kimbel & Sons. As can be seen today, the golden oak dado and the applied woodwork on the staircase brackets and hall paneling are typical of the Victorian period, creating a luxurious, textured backdrop for the Fricks' guests. The apricot-red faux-leather frieze, as well as the caisson of the coffered ceiling, is made of Lincrusta-Walton. This material was invented in 1877 in England by the son of the Frederick Walton who invented linoleum in 1863. A thick, heavily embossed material made of paper pulp and linseed oil mixed

in a vat and pressed into a mold, Lincrusta became fashionable in America in 1882. Used in 1892 by Osterling in the hall and parlor, the Lincrusta would have been applied like wallpaper and then painted or glazed in place to give the effect of tooled leather.

The two striped pedestal jardinières by the doorway are American, c. 1890s, and are glazed brown and yellow pottery. The carved oak chest held the orchestrion's numerous paper rolls from G. Baker-Troll & Company of Geneva, Switzerland, and the window grilles beyond – hinged to allow access to the window panes for cleaning – are black-painted brass. An 1892 carved oak settee by A. Kimbel & Sons can be seen inside the hall at the right. At the far end is an 1892 Theodore B. Starr long-case clock.

The reception room at the time of the Osterling renovation evidenced Henry Clay Frick's early interest in contemporary artists, particularly the Barbizon School. To the left of the mantel is *Crown of Flowers* by Jean-Baptiste-Camille Corot, now in the Baltimore Museum of Art, the Helen and Abram Eisenberg Collection. To its left is *Puy de Dome* by Jean-François Millet. To the right of the mantel is Narcisse-Virgile Diaz de la Peña's *The Pond of Vipers,* and below, to the right, is *The Washerwomen* by Charles-François Daubigny, now in the Frick Collection. Some of the more interesting objects in this c. 1900 photograph of the reception room are the classically inspired, Louis XVI−style onyx and gilt-bronze clock and candelabra on the mahogany mantel with an over-mirror. Frick purchased the set from Tiffany & Company in New York for $850 shortly after moving into the Monongahela House in 1880. They are among the few decorative objects from this period still in Frick's collections.

*Above:* Helen Frick, seated far right, during her 1908 debutante party.

*Left:* THE RECEPTION ROOM

Above the sofa in the reception room as decorated by Osterling in 1892 are more examples of Frick's early collecting efforts: *Shepherd Minding His Flock* (above left) and *La Fermière* (above right) by Jean-François Millet. On the bottom row from left to right are *La Rivière* by Jules Dupré, *Love's Caresses* by Narcisse-Virgile Diaz de la Peña, and *A Pasture in Normandy* by Constant Troyon, now in the Frick Collection. Helen returned the Millets to Clayton in anticipation of her house-museum (now the Frick Art and Historical Center). A crystal and silver two-handled cup can be seen on the center table. It was an 1895 Christmas gift to Adelaide from her husband.

In 1903 Cottier & Company changed the look of this room entirely, updating it to be consistent with the more restrained ideals of Edith Wharton. The mahogany mantel was replaced with one of green Italian marble, and the walls were covered in floor-to-ceiling gold and white damask. Green and gold velvet curtains graced the windows. And as one visitor commented at Helen's 1908 debut: "[All] was gold and white with tapestries and beautiful works of art." The off-white ceiling with gold highlights became a glazed aluminum relief ceiling with a green background, silver ribbons and sunbursts, red rosettes, and other gold-colored motifs — a result of Pittsburgh's advances in making affordable aluminum, considered a precious metal when first discovered.

In 1905, when the Fricks moved into 640 Fifth Avenue, they took all the reception-room furniture with them. Only a bronze statue, a vase, and two rugs dating from 1892 remained. In 1908, however, a new suite of furniture was purchased from Cottier & Company, probably in anticipation of Helen Frick's debutante party. Some pieces were upholstered in green and gold silk velvet, others in pink and green cut silk velvet.

*Above:* THE PARLOR

The parlor largely was used for entertaining. As did the reception room, it underwent many renovations over the years as styles changed and the Fricks endeavored to keep abreast of fashion. The overstuffed "Turkish" furniture of the 1880s was maintained, but updated in 1892 with red silk damask by D. S. Hess & Company. A narrow-loom, machine-made Bigelow carpet with a small pattern lay on the floor, and P. Hansen Hiss of Baltimore designed the classically inspired gilt walnut woodwork and columns — as well as the then fashionable glazed aluminum leaf ceiling with allegorical medallions — to Osterling's design. The 1892 renovation introduced the tripartite wall division with a wood dado, a striped wall covering for the filling, and a Lincrusta-Walton frieze similar to the one in the entrance hall. To enhance the luxurious feeling of this room, seven pairs of red velvet curtains with narrow gold borders frame the windows, while white needle lace curtains cover the glass. Like the reception room, the parlor has gold-plated metalwork.

In 1899, when the orchestrion was moved to the newly enclosed porch, a Steinway piano was added to the parlor. Far from a decorative addition, it served a real purpose: Helen was a serious piano student.

Above the piano is Jean-Marc Nattier's *Portrait of Elizabeth, Countess of Warwick.* Purchased in 1899, the painting represents one of the first Old Master acquisitions by Henry Clay Frick and it, as well as *Portrait of a Young Artist,* then considered to be by Rembrandt and placed above the sofa, is now in the Frick Collection. Of interest is the fact that in 1905 eight different paintings of inferior quality were listed as being in the parlor, probably because the Fricks took the better ones to the Vanderbilt house in New York or to their new summer home, Eagle Rock.

*Above:* THE PARLOR

In 1903 Cottier & Company redecorated the parlor in a simpler, more refined manner than the Osterling renovation of 1882. The chimneypiece was retained, but red Siena marble was installed for the fireplace surround, hearth, and fender. The Lincrusta-Walton frieze was replaced by one more in keeping with the new decor. Of deep pile, red silk plush with over-embroidery of silver thread framed in silver gimp and sewn with faceted mother-of-pearl sequins, it harmonized with the walls covered in embossed red velvet. As also was true in the hall, reception room, and breakfast room, the chandeliers were changed to bowl-shaped fixtures. Later generations of Fricks particularly

remember this room because of the happy family gatherings around the fireplace and the delicious teas that Helen Frick always served.

These c. 1900 photographs of Clayton show the many paintings and decorative objects the Fricks displayed in their parlor. The ewer in the center of the mantelpiece was purchased by the Fricks at the 1893 World's Columbian Exposition. Made expressly for this show by Coalport, the prizewinning ewer represented Coalport's newest technique: applying slivers of semiprecious stone to porcelain. Other decorative objects included a rococo, Louis XV–style chair, a large Sèvres oil lamp, French porcelain vases,

Bohemian glass, a Tiffany vase, a cranberry tyg with gold casing, and other pieces of Coalport and Royal Worcester porcelain.

The painting to the left of the mantel – *The Honorable Lucy Bing* by John Hoppner – is now in the Frick Collection. Above the mantel is displayed *Portrait of a Lady,* originally thought to be *Portrait of Mrs. Prado* by Sir Joshua Reynolds but now considered to be by Hugh Barron and possibly of Isabelle d'Almeida. It is now at the Corcoran Gallery of Art in the William A. Clark Collection. *Miss Mary Finch-Hatton* by George Romney, also in the Frick Collection, is to the right of the mantel.

*Above:* THE DINING ROOM

Unlike most Victorians, Adelaide and Henry Clay Frick did not dine separately from their children. Dinner was served in the Clayton dining room promptly at 6:30 P.M., often to Frick's favorite music from the orchestrion: "Ave Maria" and selections from *Tannhäuser, Martha,* and *William Tell.* Frick rarely talked business in the evenings and often reviewed Helen's homework when having dinner.

Clayton's dining room is entirely an 1892 creation by Frederick Osterling. The woodwork is Honduran mahogany, and all the furniture — the heavy, carved mahogany table (it could extend to over twenty feet) with Celtic interlace; arm and side chairs with green tooled-leather seats; sideboard; mahogany and green tooled-leather screen — was designed by Osterling and made by A. Kimbel & Sons. Osterling also designed the stained-glass transoms, the andirons, the silver-plated metalwork, and the rich, green plush curtains with leather strapwork, aluminum bosses, and silver thread appliqué. They too were made by Kimbel, as were many other items in this room: the matching portieres; a rich, terra-cotta-colored, stylized Oriental carpet and bright, matte-finished lighting fixtures. The silver-plated chandelier was manufactured by the Yale Company, now famous for its locks. But the tooled, painted and gilded leather polychromed frieze in green, ivory, red, and gold to match the curtains and portieres was made by C. Yandell & Company. The room, designed by Osterling to harmonize into a unified whole with all the elements working together — including the Bohemian glassware — remains almost unchanged to this day. Above the mantel is *The Last Gleanings* by Jules-Adolphe Breton. In 1906 Henry Clay Frick sold this painting to Henry E. Huntington, and it is now in the Henry E. Huntington Library and Art Gallery, San Marino, California. To the left of the mantel is *Les Premiers Pas* by Jozef Israëls, eventually returned to M. Knoedler & Company.

The painting seen through the doorway to the
entrance hall is *Chagrin d' Enfant* by Emile Friant.
Purchased by Frick in 1896, it is a poignant reminder
of the times when Martha's teenage companion,
Annie Blumenschein Stephany, held Martha in her
lap and consoled her as she suffered. To the right
of the dining-room door is *La Fenaison* by Leon
Augustin Lhermitte, also returned to M. Knoedler &
Company. As can be seen when visiting Clayton today,
however, the china included Dresden, Coalport,
Mintons, Worcester, and Limoges. Some egg cups
were made of silver; porringers came from Tiffany;
and oyster forks, berry spoons, and salt cellars came in
the form of swans. There were eleven different types
of stemware for formal dinners — all with Adelaide
Frick's gold monogram and seen in the cabinet.

*Left:* THE DINING ROOM

In this later photograph of the dining room, a
statue of Flora can be seen. According to Helen Frick's
note in a family album, the sculpture was a gift from
Andrew Carnegie and eventually was given to the
Phipps Conservatory. *Consolatrix Afflictorum* by
Pascal-Adolphe-Jean Dagnan-Bouveret — reserved by
Henry Clay Frick in 1898 and purchased in 1899 —
stands in front of the Osterling-designed Romanesque
fireplace. A reference to the Frick family mourning,
*Consolatrix* later was displayed at 640 Fifth Avenue
and at Eagle Rock but seems to have been placed in
storage when Frick died. After Helen's numerous,
unsuccessful attempts to sell the painting, or give it
away, *Consolatrix* was relegated to the basement of
the Frick Building. Upon Helen's death in 1984, the
mysterious painting was discovered and today can
be seen, authentically reframed, in its original position
in the Clayton dining room.

During the 1900 Christmas season the Fricks
entertained the newly married Andrew Mellons here,
and on July 4, 1902, they hosted an eight-course
luncheon for President Theodore Roosevelt, served
by twelve waiters from the Waldorf-Astoria Hotel in
New York. The massive centerpiece for this occasion
boasted 285 American Beauty roses shipped in from
Washington, D.C., and Chicago and orchids from the
greenhouse. The U.S. Marine Corps Band played
marches on the lawn and security was tight. Hordes
of detectives and policemen were on hand. Many
years later, in 1984, a quiet family reception following
Helen Frick's funeral service was held here.

47

*Facing page:* THE BREAKFAST ROOM, c. 1898

Unusual plasterwork and aluminum leaf tracery in ochre, russet, and pale olive coordinate with the woodwork and decorate the walls and ceiling. As in the reception room and parlor, the use of aluminum exemplifies the Fricks' desire to have not only the most fashionable decor in their home but also the most technologically advanced. Adelaide Frick chose the ochre color for the walls because the "pictures are brought out so much better." Although only needle lace curtains grace the windows, as in many other Clayton rooms, an elaborate oak parquet floor enhances the decorative feel.

Seen here is one of the Eastlake-inspired dining-room chairs with a matching high chair. Made by D. S. Hess & Company in 1882, the set was designed for the Fricks' former dining room and reused in the

breakfast room. Two paintings can be identified in these photographs: *Still Life with Apples and Roses* by Antoine Vollon to the left of the mantel and *Landscape with a Carriage* by Joseph R. Woodwell above the triangular corner cabinets with leaded glass fronts.

The breakfast room was used for Henry Clay Frick's poker games. His group included Andrew W. Mellon (later secretary of the treasury under Presidents Harding and Hoover) and Philander Knox (a U.S. senator, U.S. attorney general under McKinley, and secretary of state under Theodore Roosevelt). Helen Frick enjoyed organizing the poker chips but noted in her Clayton memoir that in the morning the smell of cigar smoke still hung heavily in the room.

*Above:* THE STAIR LANDING AND SECOND-FLOOR HALL

Originally the stair landing contained *Love in the Tower,* a four-panel stained-glass bay window made in 1882 for the newlywed Fricks by the Philadelphia firm A. Godwin & Company. In 1904, at the end of the Cottier refurbishing of Clayton, the panels were replaced by ones depicting four adolescent female figures referred to by Helen Frick as *The Four Virgins:* Miranda from Shakespeare's *Tempest;* Isabella from Keats's "The Pot of Basil"; Marguerite from Goethe's *Faust;* and Madelaine from Keats's "St. Agnes Eve." An electrified oil and candle chandelier hangs over the stair landing. The delicate wall stenciling dating from the 1892 Osterling renovation remains today.

*Above: Henry Clay Frick*, 1896, Théobald Chartran.

*Left:* HENRY CLAY FRICK'S BEDROOM

At the top of the stairs to the left – on the northwest corner of Clayton – is Henry Clay Frick's bedroom. A spartan, cold room, it connects with his wife's through a small hallway, now called the telephone room but probably Frick's dressing room in the 1890s when this photograph was taken. The bedroom is paneled in bird's-eye maple. The silk curtains are from A. Kimbel & Sons. The plain, rose-burgundy, plush upholstery; stenciled walls and ceiling; and narrow-loom, foliated carpet add warmth to this austere room. In July 1892, only a few months after returning to the entirely renovated Clayton and during the Homestead Steel Strike, Frick suffered a near-fatal attack by an assassin, Alexander Berkman. Despite his wounds, Frick continued to run the strike, and the Carnegie Steel Company, from this room. Also from this room a dangerously ill Frick and his wife, who also was near death from difficulties in childbirth, listened to the funeral service for Henry Clay Frick Jr., a son born during the strike. He was their second child to die within a year. In 1894, Frick ordered a new bedroom suite from P. Hansen Hiss – the firm responsible for much of the fine woodwork and flooring in the 1892 renovation. They provided a simple, massive, French Empire–style mahogany suite, still intact today. Above the headboard is *The Drawing Room* by Louis-Emile Adam, and to the left of the bed is an 1889 family portrait signed by an artist recorded only as Rosetti.

*Below:* HENRY CLAY FRICK'S BATHROOM

Located in a turret on the northeast corner of Henry Clay Frick's bedroom is the bathroom added in 1897 by Pittsburgh architects Alden & Harlow. As the place of pleasure that fashion now dictated, it has high, white-tile wainscoting, a classical plaster frieze, and a marble sink. The stained-glass dome and windows and curved, paneled door add to the luxury. The silver-plated bath fixtures and nickel-plated plumbing represent the latest technology of the day. Frick's maple medicine chest with double-mirrored doors still contains his medicine bottles.

*Right:* VIEW INTO THE TELEPHONE ROOM FROM HENRY CLAY FRICK'S BEDROOM

A large, silver pendulum clock, no longer at Clayton, can be seen on the east wall of Henry Clay Frick's bedroom. The speaking tube outlet to the right of the sofa was common in servant-serviced households at the time. Above the sofa, on either side of the clock, are copies of portraits by Théobald Chartran of the Frick daughters. From left to right are Martha (in an idealized, 1895 posthumous rendition) and Helen in 1896. The originals were displayed on either side of the library mantel. In 1883 the Fricks, who liked to be on the cutting edge of technology as well as fashion, rented a newly invented telephone from the Central District and Printing Telegraph Company in Pittsburgh. The phones still can be seen at Clayton and were used by Helen Frick until her death in 1984.

*Above:* Adelaide Howard Childs Frick, c. 1902.

*Left:* ADELAIDE HOWARD CHILDS FRICK'S
BEDROOM

Adelaide Frick's bedroom is in complete contrast to
her husband's austere room. Full of accessories holding personal meaning to Adelaide – and little changed
from the 1880s with the exception of the crimson
brocade curtains woven to order in 1892 in Lyons,
France, the silk capital of the world – the room is
warm, friendly, and welcoming. The life-size photograph of Martha, seen here as a reflection in the
mirror, just as Adelaide would have seen it when
lying in bed, is similar to the one on Adelaide's
bedside table and the one Frick placed over his
bedroom mantel. The red-painted walls and ceiling are
now fully restored with fifty-three cornflower rosettes,
and an elaborate molded frieze by Dewer & Clinton
encircles the room. Although the original frieze was
covered by wallpaper in 1911 and later, today the
room is fully restored to the 1880s. Adelaide Frick
insisted that her bedroom not be changed in the 1892
renovation, even though her husband's secretary
warned him, "Mrs. Frick's room is in such condition
that I know it is a great mistake not to put new paper
on the walls. I hope you will see fit to speak to Mrs.
Frick." Perhaps Adelaide's firmness on the subject
came from a need to feel secure. All her children were
born in this room, and during the 1892 renovation,
while still recovering from the death of Martha the
previous year, she was expecting her fourth child.

55

*Left:* ADELAIDE HOWARD CHILDS FRICK'S
BEDROOM

Adelaide's bedroom contains composite photographs
of the Fricks' two deceased children. One of Martha
is above the dressing table. It contains twenty-nine pictures, with one row for each year of Martha's life. In
addition, as this photograph reveals, when lying in bed
Adelaide also could see four posthumous photographs
of her infant son, Henry Clay Frick Jr., to her left, by
the door into the telephone room.

The entire suite of heavily carved walnut furniture
in Eastlake's Anglo-Oriental style is by D. S. Hess and
dates from the 1880s when the Fricks, as newlyweds,
may have shared a bedroom. To the left of the headboard are three small etchings by Jean-François
Rafaëlli and a circular frame with photographs of
Adelaide's family. Above the headboard is the *Head of
Christ* by Pascal-Adolphe-Jean Dagnan-Bouveret.

*Below:* ADELAIDE HOWARD CHILDS FRICK'S
BATHROOM

Adelaide's bathroom was installed in 1892 and never
redone. Both functional and beautiful, it has parlor-
sized stained-glass windows and woodwork worthy
of, and possibly from, a downstairs room. The elegant
and feminine tone is enhanced by a painted cove and
ceiling depicting such aquatic plants as rushes, grasses,
and irises taken from the stained glass; tall tile wainscoting; a fine yellow onyx washbasin; and a turn-of-
the-century bathtub and toilet. The chandelier, chest
of drawers, and small carpet all give the feeling of a
furnished room.

*Facing page and above:* HELEN CLAY FRICK'S
BEDROOM

In 1892, when Osterling completed his renovation of Clayton, Helen was three and a half years old. For her he created a sunny, cheerful room with hand-painted birds, butterflies, and flowers on the walls and ceiling. Little changed from the 1892 renovation to Helen's death in 1984, as curator Ellen Rosenthal notes: "Considering that [Helen] used the room for [the next] ninety-[three] years, it is astonishing that only one major redecoration and a few minor changes in furniture occurred in that time." Helen's own words as a nine-year-old perfectly describe the room where she lived and died: "My bedroom has three beds in it. One is Mademoiselle's. The other is mine. No one sleeps in the other. It is so pretty. There are flowers and birds painted on the ceiling and walls. If all the children had such a pretty room as mine, there would not be any of

them sad or unhappy." Sometime between 1900 and 1906, the smallest bed (probably meant for Henry Clay Frick Jr. because it has crib sides) was removed and the desk and some of the smaller objects replaced with others.

From left to right above the three beds (facing page above) are *Still Life with Flowers and Bird Cage* by V. Pangon; *Girl with a Lamb* by an unknown artist; and *Cats: The Burglars* by Le Roy. The latter painting is now in the collection of a Frick family descendant.

The east wall (facing page below) shows Henry Clay Frick's 1895 purchase of *Mischievous Girl* by Adolphe-William Bouguereau. Frick placed the painting in eight-year-old Helen's bedroom because it reminded him of his deceased daughter, "Rosebud," Martha. It covered a sentimental tribute to her — a

single, hand-painted, fallen rosebud from the 1892 renovation. Forty-seven years after her father purchased this portrait, Helen is thought to have given it to a family member. Since then it has passed through the auction houses and was sold at Sotheby's, New York, on February 12, 1997.

A portrait of Martha, Helen, and Childs Frick (above) is over the mantel. A posthumous photograph of Henry Clay Frick Jr. can be seen on the left corner of the mantel. Above the physician's iron standing scale to the left is *Still Life with Pink Roses* by Margaretha Roosenboom, while to the mantel's right is *Woman in a Dressing Gown* by Jean-François Rafaëlli.

*Above:* Helen Clay Frick, c. 1895.

*Left:* HELEN CLAY FRICK'S BEDROOM

The curtains in this c. 1900 photograph of Helen's bedroom are striped cotton, as are the slipcovers. The armchair, side chairs, and chaise longue all are upholstered in pink silk with a small pattern. The bedroom suite of golden oak furniture was purchased in 1892 from R. J. Horner & Company. Careful inspection of the left side of the dressing table shows a posthumous photograph of Henry Clay Frick Jr. being held by his nurse. The picture was taken in Helen's bedroom shortly after the baby died.

*Below:* THE BLUE GUEST ROOM

The Blue Guest Room is directly across the hall from Helen's bedroom. Cheerful in decor and tone, it has stenciled walls and ceiling, delicately hand-painted by A. Kimbel & Sons with blue festoons and pink flowers. Blue silk damask portieres with a small floral pattern, and curtains to match, frame the doors and windows. The furnishings were purchased out of a Matthew Brothers & Company catalogue. This well-known Milwaukee decorating and manufacturing concern supplied the woodwork and the strongly architectural, carved mahogany furniture with spiral turned columns in the French Renaissance style. The c. 1880s cut glass chandelier is a combination of six gas jets and six electric bulbs (added in the 1890s) and was made in Pittsburgh. Of the four paintings original to this room, three remain. One, to the right of the wardrobe, is *Milkmaid with Cows* – a blue painting on tile with clear overglaze from the school of Anton Mauve.

*Above:* THE BLUE GUEST ROOM

Many Frick guests used the Blue Room over the generations. Perhaps the most famous visitor to sleep here was President Theodore Roosevelt, who napped in the large bed following the 1902 luncheon in his honor. Of the three paintings over the bed, *Landscape with Three Men in a Boat* by Eugene S. Ghieny (left) and *Village Landscape* by G. M. Bogert (center) can be identified.

*Facing page and right:* THE LIBRARY

The second-floor library, like the dining room and the sitting room, is entirely the design of Frederick J. Osterling. With stenciled and painted green-brown jute wall fabric simulating antique tapestry, curtains of green-on-beige woven fabric with appliqué work and tassels framing the library windows, matching portieres, coffered ceilings, parquet floors, elaborate golden oak paneling, and handsome mahogany furniture, he created just what the Fricks wanted — an aesthetic yet homelike atmosphere. In the library, the Fricks could relax as a family, read, warm themselves by the gas-log fire, or entertain and discuss business and art with such close friends as Andrew Carnegie (until their fight in 1899), Philander Knox, and the Mellon brothers. Helen remembers her father as often "having the fidgets" after dinner and wrote in her Clayton memoir that she took him by the arm and walked him around the room, weaving in and out of the furniture, until he calmed and went peacefully to bed.

In typical high Victorian manner, the library was a storehouse of decorative objects including souvenirs from trips abroad; contemporary ceramics and glass; collections for display such as three then fashionable Rookwood Pottery vases; and framed photographs of family and friends. To the right of the door (facing page) are a c. 1900 marble statue entitled *Winter* by Cesare Lapini, a portrait of Childs Frick by Dagnan-Bouveret, and a portrait of Childs as a two-year-old by James Archer. Childs Frick inherited his Dagnan-Bouveret portrait and displayed it at his Clayton Estate on Long Island. On his death in 1965 the painting passed to Childs's son, Henry Clay Frick II, who recently has returned it to Clayton.

Over the mantel (above right) are *Portrait of Helen Frick,* 1896, by Théobald Chartran (left), *Christ at Emmaus* by Pascale-Adolphe-Jean Dagnan-Bouveret (center), and the 1895 posthumous portrait of Martha Frick (right), also by Chartran. On the floor to the right of the library fireplace is a Limoges cuspidor.

On the west wall (below right) is displayed *Little Red Riding Hood* by George Frederic Watts, now in the Birmingham Museum and Art Gallery in Birmingham, England; *The Dipper* by Jean-Charles Cazin; and *Portrait of Henry Clay Frick,* 1896, by Chartran. Childs Frick also inherited this portrait and displayed it at his Clayton Estate on Long Island. On his death it passed to one of his daughters and now is on loan to Clayton from a private trust.

*Left:* THE SITTING ROOM

The sitting room's arched windows are treated with intricately looped, cream-yellow silk damask curtains, fringed and with ball rosettes. All the furniture here and in the library is covered in black leather. The oak armchairs, center table, Henry Clay Frick's desk, and Adelaide's specially designed slant-front corner desk — somewhat inspired by Louis XIV — were custom-made from Osterling's design by A. Kimbel & Sons and date from 1892. Drawers were stuffed with game boards; card sets from Joseph Glanz in Vienna; monogrammed ivory dominos from Tiffany; and extra desk accessories.

Over Henry Clay Frick's desk is a marble sculpture entitled *Summer* by Cesare Lapini. Of the twenty-one original paintings in the sitting room many remain: from left to right are *Sunday Evening in a Miner's Village* by Jean-Charles Cazin, *Still Life with Yellow Roses* by Margaretha Roosenboom, and to the right of the arched window above the oak game table, *Fishermen's Houses, Venice* by Martin Rico y Ortega.

*Left:* The Sitting Room

The daybed on the south wall is covered in leather and oriental-patterned plush. To the left of the arched window by Adelaide's desk is *Landscape with Two Riders* by Francisco Domingo y Marques. To the right are R. W. van Boskerck's *Sussex Cottage* (above), a c. 1892 oil painting by Childs Frick of a white house with two gables (below), and to the right, *Watercolor of a Woman* by L. R. de Cuillion, *Still Life* by William Michael Harnett, and *Manon* by Gustave-Jean Jacquet.

Childs's bedroom remained unchanged from 1905, when he graduated from Princeton. Decorated in reddish brown embossed wallpaper with a brocade pattern, it has pine woodwork and a decidedly masculine feel. More important, the room conveys Childs Frick's early scientific interests. As a small boy he kept a pet raccoon and other woodland animals on the back porch of the playhouse; spent time identifying, trapping, and tagging animals; shot birds; and practiced marksmanship and taxidermy. The mounted head shown in the photograph on the facing page is an Asian brow-antlered deer, probably purchased by him as a boy.

Childs graduated from Princeton University in 1905, and by 1910, his childhood passions had metamorphosed into big game hunting in Africa, paleontology, horticulture, botany, and wildlife protection. He donated many of his African trophies to the Carnegie Museum of Natural History in Pittsburgh and to the American Museum of Natural History in New York. A gun belt filled with shotgun shells is draped over the left side of the desk chair, and a hat similar to the one Teddy Roosevelt wore on his African safaris can be

seen on another chair. A small gesture reveals Childs's sense of humor: he has balanced a rifle on the deer's horns.

Four rifles, three pistols, one dagger and sheath, five swords, and a shield with two axes and sword were found in this room. Above the bed can be identified the mounted head of a North American white-tailed deer as well as a Nubian-figural tie rack and an African mask. Silver-backed military brushes are on the large bureau, and Princeton pillows rest on the bed. Many of the pictures on the wall to the left of the bed are of his tutor, Clyde Augustus Duniway, who encouraged Childs's scientific pursuits and was instrumental in his learning to shoot. In 1930, as a result of his life-long interest in paleontology, natural history, and the conservation of natural resources, Childs became Honorary Curator of Late Tertiary and Quaternary Mammals at the American Museum of Natural History in New York. In 1942 he received an honorary doctorate in science from Princeton University.

The photograph of Childs Frick on the porch with his gun was taken c. 1898.

*Above and facing page:* THE PLAYROOM

The children's playroom was down the hall from Childs's bedroom. Helen kept her canaries here, as well as her "doll family." Often the Mellon brothers climbed the stairs to give Helen piggyback rides and have tea. Of the parties, Helen wrote: "[They] were delightful . . . I was fully prepared to serve refreshments which they were kind enough to taste or pretend to enjoy while they sat in chairs much too small to be comfortable and at a table that was far from the proper size." Of interest in this c. 1900 photograph, taken when Helen was about twelve years old, is the

symbolic way that she and her parents are expressing their mourning for Martha. Unbeknownst to the family, two-year-old Martha ingested a pin in 1887. She then entered a fatal decline that lasted four years, a decline that in her final months saw her unable to eat or drink. Her condition was complicated by the fact that aseptic techniques had not been discovered or x-ray technology invented. With peritonitis and septicemia setting in, Martha's life ended when her right side erupted in a stream of foul-smelling pus. Two-year-old Helen was witness to her sister's death. Here she has arranged her

dolls so that each one is a "sister" to another, and she has placed the single doll with fat cheeks at a highchair, pretending to eat. On the wall to the left is a picture of two sisters about five and two years old, the same ages as Martha and Helen at the time of Martha's death. The central picture is of a sad, older, lonely little girl.

This photograph of the playroom also foreshadows the direction Helen Frick's adult life would take. Apart from the fact that she would become her parents' life-long caretaker — particularly her father's — throughout her life Helen exhibited a special concern for

Reference Library in New York, both established by Helen after her father's death in 1919, and both a memorial to him. The New York library, in particular, became so comprehensive and so high-tech that on March 21, 1993 – nine years after Helen Frick's death – the *New York Times* noted that the library "serves . . . as the equivalent in art of . . . the Mayo Clinic [and] the Missing Persons Bureau."

*Below:* In this view of the playroom is another example of the Fricks' mourning – a copy of the Martha look-alike portrait in Helen's bedroom, Bouguereau's *Mischievous Girl,* is above the desk.

suffering girls. When in France during World War I and helping the Red Cross repatriate Belgian refugees, she organized an orphanage for undernourished refugee girls. During World War II she cared for seven British refugee girls who became as "daughters" to her – the children that she, a woman not permitted by her father to marry, never had. The bookcase filled with leatherbound volumes also foreshadows her art and historic preservation efforts when founding and developing the Henry Clay Frick Fine Arts Library at the University of Pittsburgh and the Frick Art

*Facing page:* THE LARGE GUEST ROOM

These third-floor rooms were decorated by Cottier
& Company in Clayton's 1903 refurbishing and show
the influence of the neoclassic decorating ideals pro-
claimed by Edith Wharton and Ogden Codman Jr.:
classical motifs, a single wallpaper from ceiling to
baseboard, an emphasis on stripes, neutral colors,
and as the mantel in the Large Guest Room shows,
painted woodwork. The carved mahogany bed in this
room, however, is in Eastlake's particular brand of
Victorian eclecticism — Greek anthemions, classical
urns, oriental flowers, and classical colonettes.
Probably retained from Osterling's 1892 renovation,
it was made *en suite* with the other furniture in this
room. *Woman with a Horse* by Charles Courtney
Curran is above the mantel, and a landscape by
Joseph R. Woodwell is to its right.

*Above:* THE SMALL GUEST ROOM

The wood mantel in the Small Guest Room also is
of classical proportion and style. The white wallpaper
with a gold fleur-de-lis motif — repeated in the fireplace
tile, frieze, ceiling, and vase on the mantel — bespeaks
Edith Wharton's preference for the French eighteenth-
century style and her tenet that a room should speak
in one voice. Another first for Clayton is the white
leaded-glass chandelier. The paintings and photographs displayed in this room and still in the Clayton
collection are a watercolor attributed to George
William Thomson entitled *The Old Mill* to the left
of the mantel; a photograph of Childs Frick riding in
a goat cart with Martha's dog, Brownie; and a photograph of Henry Clay Frick's father, John Wilson Frick
(1822–88).

*Facing page above:* MADEMOISELLE OGIZ'S ROOM

"Mellie," as Helen Frick called her beloved Swiss governess and tutor, was adored by the Frick family. She came to Clayton in the late 1890s, probably at the suggestion of the Frick family's friend and portraitist, Théobald Chartran. A well-educated woman in her own right, she was the person most responsible for Helen's becoming both a scholar and an art and historic preservationist. She gave Helen a superb education in the humanities, and when accompanying the Frick family on their many trips abroad, she was able to advance Helen's understanding of Europe and its culture. "Mellie," who also read to Adelaide Frick and kept her company when she was ill, forever remained a friend of the Frick family. In 1958, when seventy-year-old Helen took a great-niece on a tour of Italy, the two made a special stop in Geneva to visit the Ogiz family.

*Facing page below:* THE SEWING ROOM

This light and airy sewing room was located across the hall from Mademoiselle Ogiz's room. A sunny, happy place for attending to the Frick family's tailoring, dressmaking, and mending needs, the doll-filled room indicates that Helen Frick spent a lot of time here, perhaps embroidering the pillows she is known to have given her parents on Christmas. Additionally, the photograph foreshadows Helen's compassion for those less fortunate than she. In 1908 Helen Frick founded the Iron Rail, a fresh-air camp in Beverly, Massachusetts, for the women and girls working in Boston's textile and shoe mills.

*Above:* THE GYMNASIUM

Located on the fourth floor, the gymnasium (named for German secondary schools designed to prepare students for college) was where Helen Frick took her daily instruction from Mademoiselle Ogiz. In 1905, when Helen was seventeen, her father moved the family to New York, rented the Vanderbilt house at 640 Fifth Avenue, and enrolled Helen in Spence School. In an October 8, 1905, letter to Clayton's cook, Helen described the school as "tiny [and] *homely,*" a place "most bothersome and horrible." Apart from the fact that this was the first time Helen had experienced a large, competitive, educational environment outside the home – not to mention one that brought her in close contact with socially well-connected girls she did not know – Helen, who spoke French fluently, noted: "I hate the program . . . I am 'stuck' in with girls learning how to conjugate verbs . . . an awful come-down." When assigned Latin, not German as she had hoped, she complained: "The villains are making me take Caesar." Nevertheless, Helen adjusted and became an honor-roll student. When the restoration of Clayton as a house-museum began after Helen's death in 1984, those creating an inventory of the papers in the house discovered many of Helen's childhood essays and notebooks still tucked away in the desks shown in this c. 1900 photograph.

*Above:* THE PLAYHOUSE WITH THE GREENHOUSE BEYOND

Built in 1897, the children's playhouse contained miniature furniture, a bowling alley, and a photography laboratory for Childs. At the far left of the playhouse is the greenhouse, built in 1897 by Alden & Harlow. It contained Henry Clay Frick's prizewinning roses and chrysanthemums and in this way provided the Fricks with a necessary aspect of Victorian culture: bringing their plants indoors to add beauty to the home as well as growing exotic plants to show status, refinement, and culture. Since Frick loved to eat mushrooms, these too were grown in the greenhouse. In 1904 a hail storm broke every piece of glass and battered many of the plants, but the building was fully repaired, at a cost of $10,000, and soon reopened on Sundays to the public.

*Left:* The Clayton Cadets, organized by Childs when attending nearby Sterrett School, held practice drills on the second floor. The cadets wore navy blue wool uniforms in Civil War style made by Wanamaker and Brown of Philadelphia. Childs — pictured in the center holding a sword — was the commander. On Decoration Day the regiment took part in the Homewood Cemetery exercises honoring the war dead.

*Below:* THE STABLE

Henry Clay Frick, Adelaide, and their children were fine riders and often rode in Schenley Park. Adelaide drove a fast trotter called Fred M., a gift from Philander Knox. By age four, Helen could drive a goat cart; in her teenage years, she drove a two-seat, custom-made phaeton. Under her control were Countess and Violet – Welsh ponies presented to her by Pennsylvania Senator Simon Cameron. To her delight, the family coachman, James Elmore, often drove her dolls around the neighborhood. Childs became an expert polo player.

This stable was demolished in 1906 and the horses and carriages moved to Eagle Rock. But in 1959, when Helen Frick was renovating Clayton as a house-museum,

she built a carriage house for the family cars and carriages. Included in what is today considered one of the finest collections in the country are fifteen carriages including two sleighs, two broughams, a phaeton, a surrey, a wagonette for picnics, and two market wagons for servants. Also preserved by Helen are a 1914 Rolls-Royce and 1931 Lincoln. According to Henry Clay Frick's biographer George Harvey, Frick's "real hobby was speed, terrific speed . . . Motoring he found delightfully exhilarating unless hampered by road regulations, to which ultimately, after securing the most expertly daring chauffeur to be found in France, he paid little heed."

*Below:* FRICK PARK

For her 1908 debutante wish Helen Frick asked her
father to give the wooded ravine, open fields, and
thick forest adjacent to the southern portion of the
Clayton property to Pittsburgh's children as a park.
The land, known as the Gunn's Hill tract, formerly
belonged to the Wilkins family. When Frick died in
1919, his will stipulated that these 150 acres be
preserved, and thus they became Pittsburgh's first
"wilderness park." He endowed it with two million
dollars, and for the balance of their lives Helen and
Childs Frick oversaw the development, improvement,
and enlargement of Frick Park. In the 1930s, when
John Russell Pope was awarded the commission to
convert One East Seventieth Street into a public
facility, Childs and Helen engaged him to design the
French-style entrances for Frick Park. They also
engaged a Boston landscape architect, Guy Lowell,
as well as the Long Island firm of Innocenti & Webel,
to assist with the park's layout and design. Today
Frick Park covers nearly five hundred acres, and
improvements to its facilities and education
programs continue.

*Facing page:* CLAYTON, c. 1900

Visitors approaching Clayton today will see a house
little changed from this photograph. The house, therefore, stands as a tribute to the historic preservation
efforts of Helen Frick and is a graceful monument to
the high Victorian style popular in the Golden Era of
American domestic architecture. A modest example in
comparison to many millionaire houses of the day,
its architecture and interiors are nevertheless typical of
houses built by America's new industrialists. More
important, Clayton serves as a fascinating example of
the life that was lived by this wealthy, turn-of-the-century
Pittsburgh family. As such, Clayton is both a vital
resource for the study of American social history and
a poignant comment on what home meant to Henry
Clay Frick.

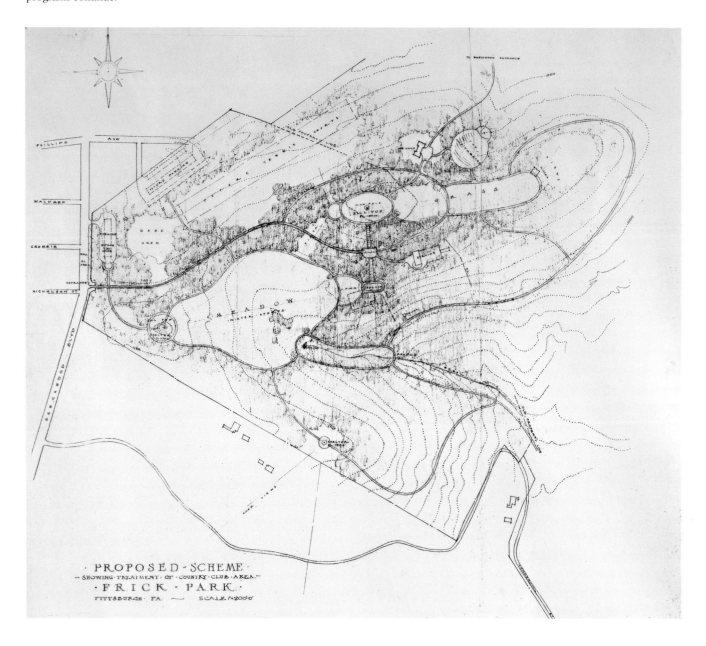

· PROPOSED · SCHEME ·
~ SHOWING · TREATMENT · OF · COUNTRY · CLUB · AREA ~
· FRICK · PARK ·
PITTSBURGH · PA · — · SCALE · 1"=200'-0'

*Following pages:* EAGLE ROCK, ENTRANCE FACADE

# CHAPTER II

# EAGLE ROCK

## A SUMMER RETREAT, BOSTON'S NORTH SHORE

*Right:* Henry Clay Frick, c. 1918, on the terrace facing his colossus.

*Facing page:* Eagle Rock, Henry Clay Frick's answer to the Vanderbilt summer "cottages" in Newport, Rhode Island.

SINCE 1900, HENRY CLAY FRICK had been spending an increased amount of time in New York monitoring the progress of U.S. Steel, and he had branched out still further by renting a house on the Robert S. Bradley estate in Prides Crossing, Massachusetts, for the summers. Here his teenage children could enjoy swimming, riding, coaching, and golfing. On Boston's North Shore, Helen could sharpen her driving skills on the many carriage trails, and Childs, then about to attend Princeton University, could practice polo, his favorite equine sport, at the Myopia Hunt Club.

More important, many close friends summered in this area. The painter Joseph R. Woodwell, Frick's friend and next-door neighbor in Pittsburgh, stayed at Magnolia, an American artist colony and fashion center locals deemed second only to Paris. Here Frick, a silent, somber man, could continue what had been one of his greatest pleasures when living at Clayton — visiting Woodwell's studio, enjoying his extroverted enthusiasm, listening to his advice about art, contemplating his comments about Frick's latest acquisitions, and reveling in his stories about the then modern French masters he had introduced to Frick.

The North Shore also hosted many of Frick's business associates, particularly railroad men from New York, Chicago, Detroit, St. Louis, Cleveland, and Pittsburgh. The list included such notables as Frick's friend Frederick H. Prince, who had enabled Andrew Carnegie to buy the railroad that connected his holdings in the Mesabi ore field on Lake Superior to his Pittsburgh mills. Later, when Frick was playing a pivotal role in the formation of U.S. Steel and acting as go-between for J. P. Morgan to secure John D. Rockefeller's holding in the Mesabi range, the existence of this railway gave Frick added leverage. Other equally prominent members of the railroad and shipping business with homes in the area included T. Jefferson Coolidge, who together with Frick was running the Atchison, Topeka, and Santa Fe; John Greenough, the railroad financier and merger expert; James McMillan, a Republican senator and Detroit rail and steamship man; and Henry C. Rouse, president of thirteen railroads.

Perhaps the most influential of these businessmen — as far as Frick's decision to summer on the North Shore was concerned — was "Judge" William H. Moore. A New Yorker, he was known for his railroad syndications and for stock watering — inflating stock prices and selling out before their value inevitably dropped. He was called "Judge" only because he was a keen judge of horses and of lucrative financial deals. In 1899 he had formed the Moore Syndicate with Frick, a consortium organized to take over Carnegie Steel and buy out Andrew Carnegie. Although the syndicate failed when it missed the option deadline by a few weeks, Moore and Frick had remained friends, united by their shared anger at Carnegie for pocketing the syndicate's one-million-dollar option fee rather than reopening the deal. In 1901 Moore purchased Eugene Thayer's house and in 1902 suggested to Frick that he purchase three nearby parcels on Hale Street overlooking the Atlantic Ocean. On his advice, Frick bought these properties, and although the fifty-acre site boasted Lookout Rock, a famous landmark, Frick named his new summer estate Eagle Rock, after the eagles nesting there.

Surrounded by men who were loyal to him and who ran the companies cementing America's infrastructure, as well as companies whose stock he held, Frick could not have chosen a more congenial place to build his summer residence. Nor could he have assembled a more illustrious team to create the sophisticated estate he desired. With the Codman-Wharton ethic taking a firm hold in architecture and interior design, he hired the Boston architectural firm owned by Arthur Little and Herbert W. C. Browne to design the house and outbuildings, as well as the driveway and grounds. Arthur Little — the project's principal architect — lived in nearby Beverly and had designed many distinguished houses in the area: the Robert S. Bradley house, "Judge" Moore's Rockmarge, Edwin Swift's Swiftmoore, and John T. Spauling's Sunset Rock. More important, Little and Browne were close friends with another Boston architect, Ogden Codman Jr., co-writer with Edith Wharton of *The Decoration of Houses,* the volume whose advocacy of a streamlined neoclassical style Frick had emulated in a recent Clayton renovation. Cottier & Company, the firm assisting with that work, now was commissioned to oversee Eagle Rock's decor, providing antique and reproduction French and English eighteenth-century furniture as well as porcelains, bronzes, rugs, tapestries, and andirons. Joseph Duveen, a nationally and internationally respected art dealer and decorator, who later would play an important role in shaping Frick's collection at One East Seventieth Street and would be knighted in 1919 by George V for his work on Buckingham Palace, also supplied Eagle Rock with treasures.

Thus, in 1902, when Frick took another step toward creating a new life for himself away from Pittsburgh, a revolutionary change in interior design also was taking place. The overly elaborate, heavily patterned, eclectic, late Victorian style, though splendid in its day, was deemed outdated and no longer representative of upper-class America's aesthetic taste. A return to classicism based on stringent, historically accurate designs from antiquity was the new decorative ideal; with the firm of Little & Browne on the cutting edge of this movement Frick could be assured that Eagle Rock would meet this new standard. Like Codman — the third member of the pioneering "Colonial Trinity" — Arthur Little respected the past and had first-hand knowledge of the grace and dignity of colonial and federal architectural styles. He and Browne made measured drawings of Boston's neoclassical buildings, grew up in historic houses of architectural importance, and studied the treatises and pattern books available to the original architects, builders, and clients. They understood that "the supreme excellence is simplicity."

By November 1902, all the drawings for the house, drive, courtyard, stable, automobile house, power house, gardener's cottage, and other outbuildings were complete and ready for estimates. Adelaide Frick examined the plans and lobbied for such things as a white marble terrace, radiators beneath the windows, and a steam plant to generate electricity. But Arthur Little felt a marble terrace would not be durable and insisted on forced-air heating for the main house and gas-operated engines for the power house. Adelaide, however, did persuade him to enlarge the front stairway to a width of six feet, to install a burglar and fireproof safe in her apartments, and to provide a lavatory in the stable for the "outside men."

From 1902 to 1905, Henry Clay Frick and Adelaide monitored every aspect of Eagle Rock's development and carefully scrutinized each and every architectural invoice. As was Frick's habit, he quibbled endlessly about money and costs. On January 21, 1905, he wrote Little & Browne: "I want nothing but first class material put in the work you are having done for me, as I am under the impression that is what I am paying for." And on May 22, 1905, he warned: "I want everything properly done and if mistakes are made I want them corrected."

Frick was equally exacting about the external appearance of Eagle Rock. On November 3, 1905, he expressed to Arthur Little his scorn for New York's most prominent architects and, most surprisingly, the much celebrated author Edith Wharton: "We will have all in grass without any walks whatever through it. I want the place kept simple as possible. That suits my taste, and as to whether it would be approved by Messrs. McKim, Mead and White, Messrs. Carrère and Hastings, or Mrs. Edith Wharton does not matter to me." And again on November 27, 1905: "After looking at the two photographs sent me showing how you had planned the layout of the terrace on the ocean side and also the descent from the house to Hale Street, I was rather alarmed. While it probably is beautiful it is far too elaborate to suit my taste, as I have always explained to you."

*Above:* Proposed design for Eagle Rock by Little & Browne, c. 1904.

The determined industrialist also was adamant about the simplicity of the interior designs. Although less than six weeks before he had disavowed the influence of Edith Wharton's stringent decorating principles, on December 13, 1905, he now wrote Little of the Wharton-like feeling he desired: "It seems impossible to impress upon you our great desire to have the wood finish in our house severely simple . . . I have frequently told you that we want everything in connection with the house made of the best materials, but we want it severely plain, and I trust you will now be governed accordingly."

As the construction of Eagle Rock progressed, Henry Clay Frick's departure from Pittsburgh moved forward as well. He rented William H. Vanderbilt's New York house at 640 Fifth Avenue, the residence he had coveted ever since he first saw it in 1880 when, as a new millionaire, Frick had said to his friend and banker, Andrew Mellon, "It is all I shall ever want." Now, twenty-five years later, he had this wish. And as Duveen and Cottier & Company began decorating that residence, houses were burnishing a whole new self-image for Henry Clay Frick. The industrialist now lived in the most prestigious of the New York Vanderbilt houses and was building Eagle Rock, a mansion challenging the more elaborate of that family's summer "cottages," most notably the Breakers in Newport, Rhode Island.

When the Frick family moved into Eagle Rock during the summer of 1906, the moment was a defining one for its patriarch, as newspapers noted. Not only had they remarked that Frick, with his just completed Allegheny Building in Pittsburgh casting its long shadow on the Carnegie Building, seemed to be insulting Carnegie yet again, they now christened Eagle Rock "the grandest mansion north of Newport." The statistics certainly were up to the Vanderbilts' standards. Three hundred local workers alone were engaged for the grading and stonework, and in two months, forty-eight thousand yards of fill and loam — amounting to two or three trains a day or 1,650 car loads — rolled in from West Peabody on a special train using a private spur. For the twenty-five-acre site spanning Hale Street, Thistle Street, and Prides Crossing Center, fifty or more maple trees were planted, and when fully landscaped, Eagle Rock boasted a naturalistic, romantic design with expansive lawns, serpentine stone walls, lush woodland, and shrub gardens — all planted with winding approaches and spectacular vistas.

If anyone wondered about the statement Henry Clay Frick was making at Eagle Rock, the iron fence on Hale Street with granite posts inscribed "Eagle Rock" gave clear indication. One hundred feet long and costing $100,000, the fence was the longest and most expensive ever built in the area, while behind it lay one of the most extraordinary estates on Boston's North Shore. After passing through the gate, the long, curving drive stretched from Hale Street to a massive forecourt surrounded by more decorative iron fencing and brick piers topped with urns and other sculpture. Then came the entrance portico with six limestone Ionic columns. Fabricated entirely of brick, the four-story mansion — the most massive house built on the North Shore — had a columned bow front and was just the statement of power Frick sought. Said to resemble the White House, Eagle Rock in fact outdid the White House: it was thirty feet longer. Not incidentally, its construction costs of $1,050,049.14 set a record for the North Shore.

The house — with an automatic power house that provided electricity and two ten-ton water tanks in the attic that were needed because the town water supply provided insufficient pressure — contained 104 rooms, most with private baths, and more for guests and servants than the family. The main rooms all were decorated in the severe neoclassic style with plain walls and the emphasis on simplicity Frick demanded. Whether or not Frick cared about Edith Wharton, she would have been pleased.

Glazed bronze doors provided a 25-foot opening into a 60-foot-long entrance hall; beyond were matching doors opening onto a large terrace (131 feet long and 28 feet wide) overlooking the Atlantic Ocean. Adding to the splendor of the house were hand-carved marble mantels chosen by Frick in Italy; a grand staircase with black and gold marble columns and architraves; a brass railing; and six-foot-wide marble steps as requested by Adelaide. Italian window grilles, a $50,000 Aeolian pipe organ playable from three different consoles, and a 35-foot-square drawing room made a graceful impression, as did the music room, den, library, breakfast room, glassed-in loggia, and silver-plated plumbing fixtures in every bathroom. Important porcelains and bronzes soon were to come, as would paintings from Frick's growing art

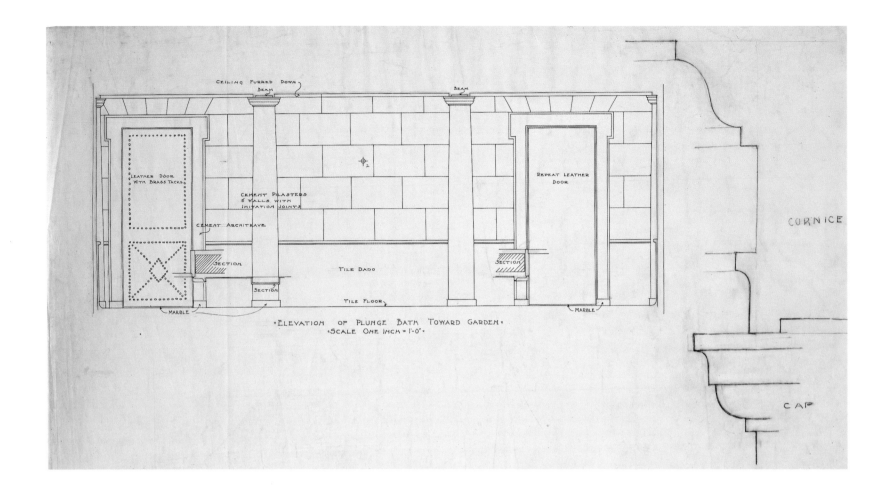

The labels visible in the drawing include: CEILING FURRED DOWN, BEAM, BEAM, LEATHER DOOR WITH BRASS TACKS, CEMENT PILASTERS & WALLS WITH IMITATION JOINTS, REPEAT LEATHER DOOR, CORNICE, CEMENT ARCHITRAVE, SECTION, SECTION, SECTION, TILE DADO, SECTION, CAP, MARBLE, TILE FLOOR, MARBLE, ·ELEVATION OF PLUNGE BATH TOWARD GARDEN· ·SCALE ONE INCH = 1'-0"·

*Above:* Elevation of the plunge bath by Little & Browne.

collection – all meant to harmonize with his newly acquired antique and reproduction eighteenth-century French and English furniture. With the help of Little & Browne, Cottier & Company, and Duveen, Eagle Rock set a high standard. A letter of August 2, 1905, from the architects to Henry Clay Frick in Paris notes their attention to detail:

> Enclosed you will find Caldwell's estimate for electric fixtures, as selected by Mrs. Frick, amounting to $18,270.84. Please cable us [if] we shall accept this, so we can start the work along, as it will take some little time to get the fixtures. Caldwell is always slow on special designs like this.
>
> We have also received from Russell & Erwin Company estimates on the hardware selected by Mrs. Frick amounting to $10,575.00. This is for all French hardware made in France and finished in French gilt.
>
> We have been over the stable hardware with Mr. Richmond, representing Joseph Woodwell & Company, and we have accepted their estimate as Mrs. Frick desired, as it came within the allowance.

Additionally, many of Cottier's porcelains, jardinieres, and vases previously purchased by the Fricks for Clayton were sent to Eagle Rock in 1906, and as Joseph Duveen wrote to Frick on August 26, 1906, his work on behalf of the house continued as well: "I have several andirons here, and they will be shipped very shortly. I also have the small tables for the dining room nearly finished, and they will be sent to you in good time."

Even the basement reflected the grandeur and perfection of Eagle Rock. Below ground rested a one-acre, tiled, Grecian-style plunge bath with fluted columns of artificial limestone, marble dado, and molded pilasters and architraves, together with temperature control, pipes for either salt or fresh water, and two sets of dressing and toilet rooms. According to the *New York Times*, the pool was necessary because, as Frick said, "Physicians have recommended salt water bathing for Mrs. Frick."

The basement also housed Henry Clay Frick's office; a billiard room with seventeenth-century Jacobean oak paneling, possibly from Chastleton Manor in England (later reinstalled by Helen Frick in the Frick Art Museum at Clayton); an unpacking room; a wine room; the bellows room for the organ; the servants' dining room; a hotel-size kitchen; the butcher's room; dumbwaiters; and the servants' elevators to the fourth floor done in white Tiffany tile. In addition, still remaining on this Atlantic side of the property is the garage for Frick's automobiles, more beautiful and larger than most neighboring houses.

On the other side of Hale Street still stands the vast, 150-foot-long, two-story stable. Behind it also remains the house for the Westmoreland, Henry Clay Frick's private railroad car. In front of the stable are the former gardener's cottage and the foundations for the tennis court, vegetable garden, formal rose garden, parterre Victorian garden, and rock garden designed by Olmsted Brothers.

*Below right:* The Westmoreland Railway Car.

When Henry Clay Frick moved into Eagle Rock in 1906, he was the largest individual stockholder of railroads in America. Just before Christmas in 1910, the Pullman Company delivered his private railway car, the Westmoreland, to Eagle Rock. Named for the Pennsylvania county of Frick's birth, it was the second all-steel railway car in America – George Pullman had received the first. It weighed eighty-three tons, cost $39,656, and required $12,280 in annual upkeep and a staff of two. Eighty-two feet long and ten feet wide, it contained a kitchen, pantry, servants' quarters, toilet room, four private suites, an observation room, running water, central heat, refrigeration, a telephone, and electricity generated from the car wheels and stored in batteries. The furniture was built in, and although upholstered largely in red satin, Adelaide's upholstery was pink and Helen's pale green. There was no bedroom for Childs because he was on safari in Africa and living on his own. The eight-foot dining-room table seated ten people, and the Mintons china, with "Westmoreland" monogrammed in gilt, glistened, as did the engraved silver and silver-monogrammed writing paper.

The car was stored in a house behind the stables and was connected to the main line by a short spur that still exists. The Westmoreland could be attached to any train, and often these trains made special stops for the owners of private railway cars. When Henry Clay Frick died in New York on December 2, 1919, the Westmoreland was draped in black and transported his remains to Pittsburgh for burial. The railway car returned to Eagle Rock, and a few years later, Adelaide Frick offered it to a friend for his use. After her death in 1931, Helen lent it to presidential candidate Wendell Willkie for his whistle-stop tour of the country and then to her friend Charles Graham. In 1967 she had the railway car destroyed. In a letter of July 1, 1964, to her cousin James B. Stevenson, who wanted to borrow the car, Helen wrote of the Westmoreland's imminent demise: "The reason is that [Graham's] taste is far different from my father's and I would not wish to have it connected with the family as it looks now. Furthermore, it would always be connected with 'Charles Graham' as he has used it for so many years – and I wouldn't care for this either . . . It was perhaps a mistake on my part – & this is confidential – to allow Mr. Graham to have it – but I had no possible way of keeping it, & this seemed to be my only way of solving one of the many problems at that time."

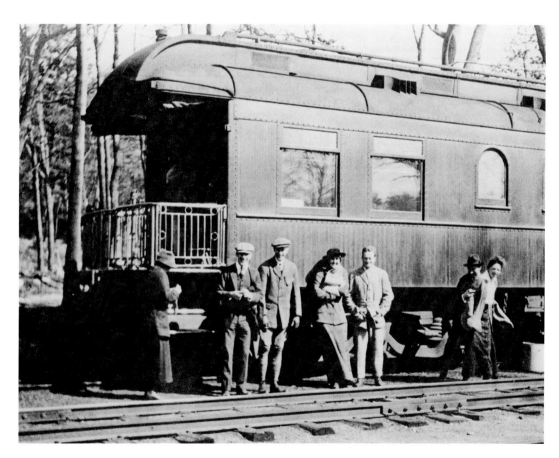

*Above:* Henry Clay Frick, c. 1918, enjoying his right-of-way to the Atlantic beach.

Only one thing was missing — a right-of-way to the Atlantic beach. So Frick offered his neighbor, Catherine Peabody Loring, one million dollars for access. But the Boston-born Peabody turned him down, saying: "Goodness! What in the world would I do with a million dollars?" Although the Fricks eventually obtained their right-of-way, and the two families shared the cost of maintaining the retaining wall between the properties, and descendants of the two families married, Loring's initial response typified the reaction of old Bostonian families to the invasion of new wealth on their shores. They made their discomfort abundantly clear when the Fricks hosted an organ recital, concert, and cotillion to celebrate Eagle Rock's opening in the summer of 1906. According to family legend, none of the North Shore elite came to the party.

Nevertheless, whether rejected by some or accepted by others, the Fricks shortly made Eagle Rock their favorite residence, a place where they could forget their cares, a transitional place as they shifted from midwesterners to easterners, a place with a life of its own. In 1906 all the horses and carriages at Clayton were shipped to Prides Crossing, and by 1908, the Frick family was fully entrenched in Eagle Rock life. Although Frick recently had purchased a large site in New York City where the Lenox Library stood, for $2.4 million, he had done this merely as a real estate investment, not with the idea of building a permanent home for his art collection. Adelaide, who inevitably suffered from one malady or another, thrived on the ocean air at Eagle Rock; Childs, now a year out of Princeton and uncomfortable in the business world, still loved polo; Helen, now a young lady of twenty, continued to enjoy driving her Welsh ponies around the countryside and had started a new project – the Iron Rail, a summer retreat in nearby Beverly for young women working in Boston's textile and shoe mills. Frick himself was busy combining his art collections at 640 Fifth Avenue and Clayton with the one at Eagle Rock. On May 11, 1911, a letter from Frick's primary art advisor and great friend Roland Knoedler indicates the extraordinary lengths taken to transport Frick's paintings from New York to Massachusetts: "These we have placed in a steel car of the N.Y.C. & H. R. No. 2764 and we are shipping them by American Express to Prides Crossing where our men will be on hand in the morning to unload and rehang the pictures as per your instructions." In an astonishing remark, however, Knoedler noted that the multimillion-dollar collection was "not insured in transit."

Knoedler was accustomed to the way Frick handled his money and art – willing to pay large prices for paintings, but tight-fisted with other expenses. And Knoedler also was accustomed to the rigors of hanging pictures for Frick. In 1904 Frick had advised the art dealer:

> I have given instructions to Holroyd to have your men here ship to you, to be placed in my apartments in New York the Gainsborough [*Mrs. Charles Hatchett*] and the Hoppner [*The Honorable Lucy Byng*] portraits.
>
> I should like the Gainsborough hung near the door, on one side of the Corot [possibly the recently acquired *Boatman of Mortefontaine*] and the Hoppner on the other side of the Corot.
>
> This will make it necessary for you to remove the two other Corots [possibly *Ville d'Avray, The Pond,* or *Couronne de Fleur*] I have in my apartments, and which you would better take to your store.

When William Howard Taft was elected president of the United States in March 1908, Eagle Rock assumed a political air. Frick always had been a man behind the scenes in Republican government, and with Taft's election he took a personal interest in seeing the new president happily summering in the Prides Crossing area. Most likely Frick's close friend Philander Knox – former counsel for the Carnegie Steel Company, U.S. attorney general, U.S. senator from Pennsylvania, and now Taft's secretary of state – called on Frick to help with this project. On October 10, 1910, Frick wrote Andrew Carnegie II, the industrialist's nephew who lived in nearby Manchester: "The President is anxious to lease your house . . . and has been informed you are willing to lease . . . He does not feel he can afford [your price] . . . I will make good any agreement he makes with you."

Whether or not Taft rented this particular house is unknown, but the president did come to the North Shore, as did many national and international dignitaries and Republican officials. Prides Crossing long had been called "Boston's Riviera." Now it was known as "Taft's Summer Capital." And Taft, as well as other prominent politicians, was a regular guest at Eagle Rock for dinner, poker, bridge, or Russian bank. Adelaide lunched with Mrs. Taft, and since Henry Clay Frick and Taft were avid golfers, they often played together at the Myopia Hunt Club. As Frick's biographer George Harvey notes in *Henry Clay Frick: The Man,* Frick "enjoyed special privileges, and all stood aside when the good-natured warning was passed forward, 'Look out, Mr. Frick is coming!'"

By December 1911, Henry Clay Frick was so pleased with his life at Eagle Rock that he intended to build an art gallery on Eagle Rock's east wing. Confiding his plan to a North Shore neighbor, he said, "[It] will be the mecca for the world's best known artists, and the pride of Summer visitors, including President Taft, who spends his Summers less than a mile away." According to the *New York Times*, which reported the story, the gallery would be "the finest private art gallery in the world, to exceed in value of paintings and construction that of Mrs. John L. Gardner in Boston." The multimillion-dollar, two-story addition of "gray stone and facing brick, matching the mansion," was expected to have an interior scheme "similar to that of the first floor of the house, the floor of which is marble mosaic in elaborate designs. The staircases are to be architraves, the rails and steps probably being of imported marble with a grillwork of gold." And Daniel H. Burnham, the Chicago architect who had designed the never-realized house on Pittsburgh's Gunn's Hill, the Frick and Allegheny Buildings, and the large granite monument for the Frick family plot at the Homewood Cemetery near Clayton, as well as New York's Flatiron Building at Madison Square (a wedge-shaped building that was one of the first steel-framed structures in New York, a symbol of the new skyscraper age) and the newly opened Hotel Rector, was to be the architect.

When Burnham received the commission from Frick, he immediately traveled abroad for inspiration. As he later explained to his wealthy client: "It was necessary for me to make a special study of the picture galleries and of palaces containing them, and I dropped other things and went abroad for the special purpose of studying the sort of thing I was to undertake. I saw and analyzed the principal things in this country and Europe, taking careful notes and studied all the works on the subject." In fact, Burnham had a compelling need for this immersion. Frick also was contemplating building a house for his art collection on the New York site and had asked Burnham to draw plans for this possibility as well.

As the *New York Times* broke the story about an Eagle Rock gallery, however, it had no idea that Frick was considering other options, nor did the press know that Burnham's plans for the Eagle Rock gallery had not yet been accepted. Frick had sent them to P. A. B. Widener, a Philadelphia business and art-collecting friend, for study. A fellow director of U.S. Steel, he had as his lawyer an impassioned art-collecting mentor, John A. Johnson, who also was the person who successfully had extricated Frick's $15 million fortune from Carnegie Steel in 1900. A kindred spirit in another way, Widener, like Frick, solicited the advice of scholars and dealers but ultimately made his own selections where art was concerned. Within his vast collection were such masterpieces as *The Dead Toreador* by Edouard Manet (in 1914 Frick would acquire *The Bullfight*, the top half of the original painting by Manet that once included both *The Bullfight* and *The Dead Toreador*), three of the seven famous Van Dycks from the collection of the Cattaneo family from Genoa (Frick owned two: *Ottaviano Canevari* and *Marchesa Giovanna Cattaneo*), as well as superb Rembrandts, Corots, Constables, and Gainsboroughs, among others. All were exhibited in his home, Lynnewood Hall, where Widener lived with his art, as did the Fricks, in a palatial but "homelike" setting. After scrutinizing Burnham's plans for the Eagle Rock gallery, however, Widener advised Frick against them.

Outraged, on January 2, 1912, Burnham wrote Henry Clay Frick, "As [the Eagle Rock gallery] stands it is a far better thing than Mr. Widener's. And, when it is built every Art Museum man will realize it." In the same letter he complained that Widener had said that he "would no more think of retaining [him] for a picture gallery than he would think of retaining anyone else for a great building." Still hopeful of saving the commission, Burnham switched to flattery: "I do not know what effect this may have had on your mind. I presume it had none whatever, as you are a man who forms his own judgment on the facts and not on what some-one else may say." On January 8, Frick explained his concerns to his sixty-six-year-old architect:

> I know Mr. Widener has a very high opinion of your ability as an all-around architect, but he thinks your strong point is great buildings.
>
> I am very undecided about the Prides Crossing addition, and also the house on the Lenox Library site, and it was for that reason I thought it would be better to settle with you, and if I decide in the future to use your design for the Prides Crossing house, or your design for the New York house, it could be taken up.
>
> If I build one, I will not build both, and may later reach the conclusion to build a New York house and leave Prides Crossing alone.
>
> While your design for the New York house is monumental, it seems to me too much so. I think if I ever build on the New York site, it will be a much smaller house, and arrange to leave a great deal of ground around it on all sides.

Frick had made his decision. Wanting to make New York a more permanent residence, he decided to give up his Vanderbilt rental and build a New York house for himself, his family, and his paintings. He would not build a gallery at Eagle Rock. And then, in a final stroke, Frick shut out Burnham altogether by hiring the prominent New York firm Carrère & Hastings for the New York home.

That summer of 1912 Frick gave another large party at Eagle Rock, inviting everyone from the local villagers to Boston's high society and the North Shore elite. Although the art gallery was not to become a reality, the Fricks now were accepted members of the community and everyone came. In the afternoon, the townspeople roamed the house and grounds and enjoyed a three-hour concert by John Philip Sousa. In the evening, Japanese lanterns strung across the terrace were lit, and after dinner and an organ concert by Archer Gibson, the summer residents and Bostonians danced until long past midnight.

Although by now the Fricks had broken ground at One East Seventieth Street and would move into the new house late in 1914, Eagle Rock remained an important part of Frick family life. Frick continued to move his art collection there in the summers, and in 1914–15, while he was recovering from a severe attack of inflammatory rheumatism, the house underwent a $35,000 renovation, including a new third-floor bedroom for Frick. With a stupendous ocean view, it promised what he needed, absolute quiet. The family's rooms and those for their guests were on the floor below. In addition, the porch off Helen's second-floor bedroom was enclosed as a writing room so she could work more efficiently on her Iron Rail project and on the provenance of her father's paintings. Various rugs and items of furniture were repaired, and the prominent American decorator Elsie de Wolfe, who was then playing a significant role in the decoration of One East Seventieth Street's second- and third-floor bedrooms, also helped with the refurbishing of Eagle Rock.

When the Frick family moved into their permanent New York residence in November 1914, Europe was at war and Frick still was suffering from inflammatory rheumatism. Burdened by pain, he nevertheless pursued more building projects in Pittsburgh (yet without Burnham) — the vast William Penn Hotel and the adjacent Union Arcade. But Eagle Rock was not forgotten. In 1916 Frick purchased many valuable porcelains and almost the entire collection of important Renaissance and Baroque bronze statuettes from the Morgan estate sale. These he divided between One East Seventieth Street and Eagle Rock — not necessarily saving the best pieces for New York.

By 1917, when America entered the war, though Eagle Rock was filled with important art works and decorative objects, the mood in the house became somber. Normally rocking with the laughter, noise, and confusion of family and guests, the house went silent. Childs, who had married in 1913 and now was the father of both a two-year-old and newborn daughter, was commissioned a first lieutenant in the Signal Corps and departed for California with his wife and children. Helen went to France with the Red Cross to help repatriate Belgian refugees. But both soon returned — Helen to New York in 1918, whereupon she immediately went to Eagle Rock. There she rejoined her parents and furthered her war effort by making a Red Cross fundraising movie for the young men from the North Shore still fighting in Europe's trenches. Entitled *Home Fires,* the movie was meant to give them hope and remind them of home. It showed tennis matches between ladies of prominent North Shore families, hunting and golfing scenes, polo matches, and whippet racing at Ipswich. When the war ended, Childs returned with his family — now including a third daughter. The silence was over and Eagle Rock came alive as three generations of family once again summered at their seaside retreat.

When Henry Clay Frick died in 1919, Adelaide Frick inherited the property. Noting that she had waived her right to a $68 million widow's dower and would accept instead only $5 million so that her husband could accomplish his philanthropic dreams, Adelaide asked the estate to pay for needed renovations to the house. The trustees agreed, and for the balance of Adelaide's life, Eagle Rock remained the Frick family's summer compound. Childs took a personal interest in the plantings on the property and introduced specimen trees from around the world, much as he was doing at his own estate on Long Island. Upon Adelaide's death at Eagle Rock in 1931, Helen inherited the neoclassic marvel and continued to invite her brother's family to enjoy its many pleasures. But in 1938, perhaps tired of living alone in the wing where she, her father, and her mother had spent their time together, Helen decided to downsize. She demolished the four-story wing containing the salt-water swimming pool, billiard room, drawing room, den, oak room, and the family's former private quarters. But in a carefully planned

*Above:* Henry Clay Frick with his children and grand-children after World War I. From left to right are Frick; his granddaughter Adelaide; his daughter-in-law Frances holding her daughter Martha; his grand-daughter Frances; and his son Childs.

and meticulously orchestrated effort, Helen saved virtually all of the exterior and interior architectural elements. She then hired Innocenti & Webel — the renowned Long Island land-scape architecture firm then drawing up plans for Frick Park in Pittsburgh and assisting Childs Frick with the landscaping of his Long Island estate — to design what she called "The Little Garden" — a small garden pool and tea house on the former wing's foundations.

By the 1940s, Childs's children were grown, married, and raising children of their own. Helen, now in her fifties, also enjoyed having this fourth generation of Fricks at Eagle Rock, and when World War II struck, Helen decided to invite refugee British girls to stay there. Hoping to be sent at least one hundred girls, she turned the stables into a dormitory. In the end, only seven girls came, largely because the Germans torpedoed a boat carrying refugee chil-dren and the British halted the relief effort. When her girls arrived, they moved into specially prepared rooms in Eagle Rock — not in the stables — and were given toys, books, and entire new wardrobes. Most important, English dishes were served and English customs observed.

The British girls remained devoted to each other and to their "Aunt Helen" for the remainder of Helen's ninety-six years. And for many years after the war, Eagle Rock continued to be used and enjoyed by them, Helen's nieces and nephews, and the fourth generation of Fricks. As these great-nieces and great-nephews grew to college age, those who attended Boston universities spent their weekends at Eagle Rock enjoying waltzes in the hall, organ concerts, and parties on the Atlantic beach.

By 1969, however, eighty-one-year-old Helen Frick had tired of maintaining her father's former summer house. Apart from the fact that the house required an enormous amount of time, energy, and expensive upkeep — and those demands were duplicated in Clayton and Westmoreland Farm — she no longer was involved in the Iron Rail and had few friends left on the North Shore. Moreover, although Helen had enjoyed driving her ponies as a child and had

*Above:* The Little Garden, c. 1946, as designed by Innocenti & Webel.

*Facing page:* In a photograph by Helen Frick, one of her great-nieces romps on the lawn.

happily entertained family and friends at Eagle Rock, and knew the house was of architectural importance, she nevertheless always had considered it pretentious. In 1963 she had given some of its paintings, furniture, porcelains, tapestries, and bronzes to her Henry Clay Frick Fine Arts Building at the University of Pittsburgh, a cloister in the Italian Renaissance style complete with a small art gallery. But following her unfortunate policy argument with the university and its seizure of the building in 1967, Helen had removed her Eagle Rock collection and had begun designing a new museum for the collection at the Clayton site in Pittsburgh.

In 1969, with her treasures back in hand and deeply involved in the Frick Art Museum then under construction, Helen found a unique way to preserve Eagle Rock and personalize her new museum. She decided to demolish the colossus slowly, almost brick by brick, so she could preserve its history by re-creating parts of it in her museum. As the *Beverly Times* noted, the crew would dismantle one room a month "with the care given to the cutting of a precious diamond." As the paper further explained, "It is Miss Frick's wish that this work be done with extreme care to preserve as much as possible of her father's possessions."

As the house came down, she gave the Frick Art Museum the paneling from the billiard room and also sent her father's bedroom furniture from One East Seventieth Street, then housed at Eagle Rock, to the museum. She brought the Eagle Rock cars and carriages to the new carriage house at Clayton and, to ensure that the Eagle Rock site remain in the Frick family, gave the land to a great-niece who always had loved and enjoyed the property. This great-niece built her own house on Eagle Rock's foundations, using many of the architectural elements salvaged from the 1938 demolition and the 1969 razing. Plumbing fixtures, bookcases, doors, doorknobs, hinges, paneling, rugs, furniture, and marble wood floors and mantels, as well as porcelains and light fixtures, reappeared in the new house, and many others were distributed to Frick family members.

Today the property is no longer in the Frick family. But thanks to Helen's efforts, Eagle Rock did not vanish without a trace. Its architectural and decorative elements are scattered throughout the family and the historic Clayton site. The house, therefore, is embedded in the memory and hearts of all who enjoyed the romance and pleasure of this Georgian Revival palace on Boston's North Shore. However grand, the Frick family simply knew it as home.

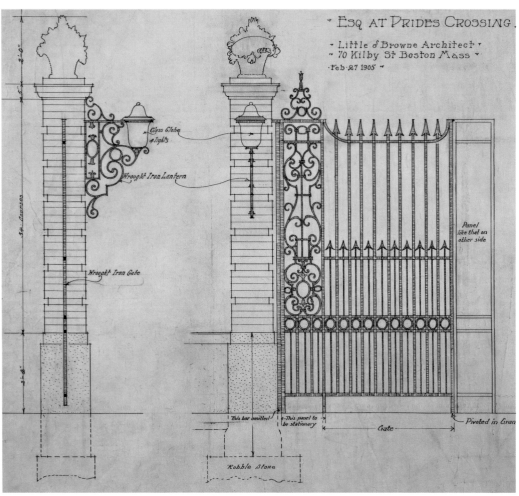

*Facing page, above, and right:* THE DRIVEWAY

The Eagle Rock driveway came off Hale Street, straight to the base of the archway and stairs at the bottom of the tree-studded bluff. The main drive then curved around the bluff to the right, up the hill, and behind the trees where the house was located. The back drive wound around to the left in the same fashion.

The drawing (left) of Eagle Rock's fence by Little & Browne is a fine example of grace and delicacy in design. Now a historic landmark, the fence remains the longest ever built in the area. It cost $100,000 and extended for one hundred feet. Sections on the stable side of Hale Street were given as scrap iron by Helen Frick in the 1940s for the war effort. Other sections were installed on the Clayton site in Pittsburgh.

The drawing of the driveway lampposts (right) illustrates Little & Browne's ability to create a simple yet dramatic effect.

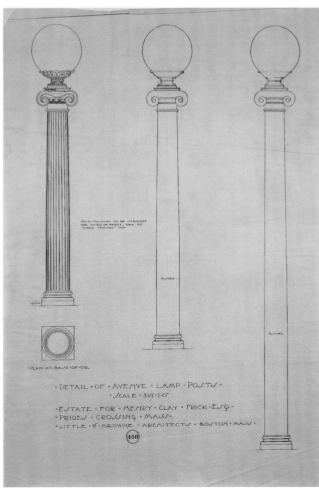

*Facing page:* The Forecourt Fence and Gate

Little & Browne created a harmonious relationship between monumental architectural elements and formal landscape design.

*Below:* Drawing of the forecourt fence and gate by Little & Browne.

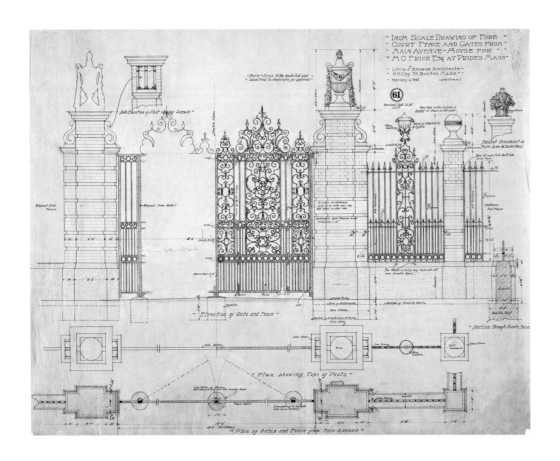

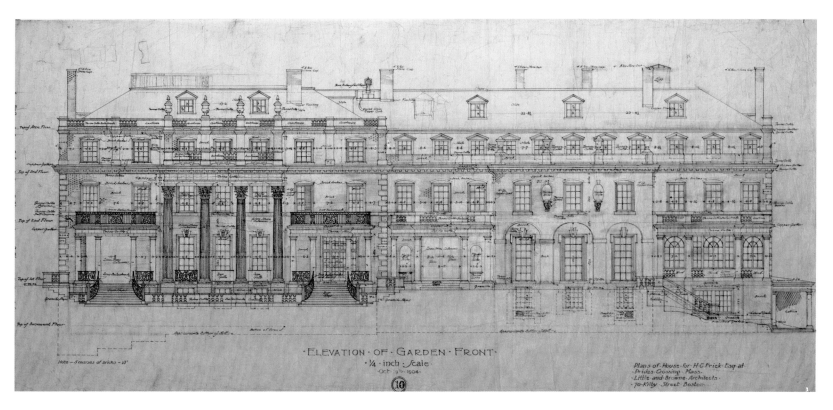

·ELEVATION·OF·GARDEN·FRONT·
·¼·inch·Scale·
·Oct·9ᵗʰ·1904·

Plans of House for H C Frick Esq at
Pride's Crossing Mass
Little and Browne Architects
70 Kilby Street Boston

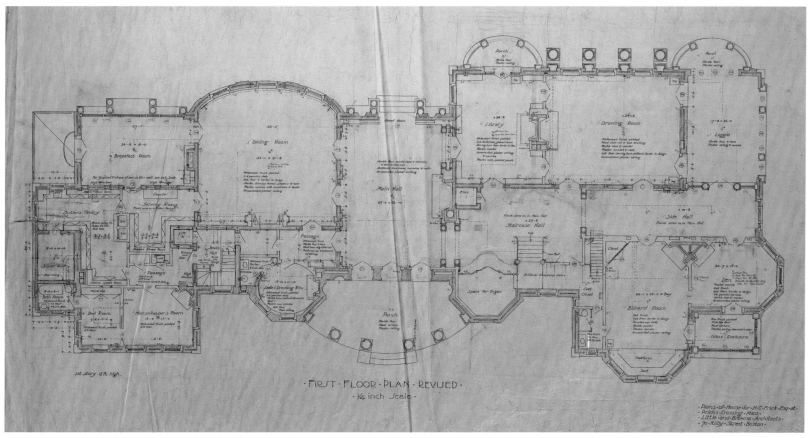

·FIRST·FLOOR·PLAN·REVISED·
·¼·inch·Scale·

Plans of House for H C Frick Esq at
Pride's Crossing Mass
Little and Browne Architects
70 Kilby Street Boston

*Facing page:* The family wing, c. 1918, later the site of
"The Little Garden."

*Above:* Elevation of the garden front by Little & Browne.

*Below:* The first-floor plan, revised, by Little & Browne.
All of the rooms to the right of the staircase hall and library
were demolished in 1938, and the site became "The Little
Garden."

*Left:* THE ENTRANCE HALL

The sixty-foot-long entrance hall was central to life at Eagle Rock. Decorated with violet breccia marble columns and an intricate marble mosaic floor, it was filled with Renaissance Revival furniture. Frick read the daily papers – nearly all those printed in Boston and New York – while sitting beneath these marble columns and before the massive fireplace. Helen remembered that as he turned the pages, her father could be heard from one end of the house to the other, and when he was through reading, she could hear him throw the papers on the floor. At 9:00 every morning the valet, Oscar, brought his hobnail golf shoes and outfitted Frick as he sat on a stool at the foot of the large table. Before leaving for his round of morning golf, Frick always glanced at the barometer in the front vestibule, and after golf he took a short nap either in his room or on the hall sofa. At odd moments throughout the day he would play solitaire here, and Helen remembers that he was very deliberate, rarely missed a move, and often became frustrated saying, "If I don't make it this time, I'll never play again" or "I'll eat my hat." The hall also was where the Fricks and their guests enjoyed playing Russian bank, bridge, and poker. The family took evening coffee here as well, and Frick, who limited himself to four cigars a day, had his fourth and last before playing more card games and retiring for the night.

On the long table can be seen two of the important bronze statuettes from the Morgan estate: an inkstand supported by three putti from the workshop of either Niccolo Roccatagliata or Giuseppe de Levis and *An Old Man Riding a Goat* by Ferdinando Tacca.

The painting over the mantel is a 1916 purchase by Henry Clay Frick entitled *Two Windmills*, sometimes referred to as *Dutch Landscape*, by Jacobus Hendrikus Maris and eventually returned to M. Knoedler & Company. The portrait of Henry Clay Frick is probably posthumous. *A Regatta on the Grand Canal* by the Venetian Francesco Guardi is partially blocked by the lamp on the center table. Purchased by Frick in 1913, *Regatta* is now exhibited in the main reading room of the Frick Art Reference Library in New York with its companion, *View on the Cannaregio Canal.*

107

*Below and facing page:* THE ENTRANCE HALL

The entrance hall elevation by Little & Browne shows the corner to the left of the mantel where the Fricks played cards. A photograph of the entrance hall, c. 1918, shows the Fricks playing double solitaire in this corner beneath an unidentified landscape painting. From left to right are Adelaide Frick; probably her brother, James Childs; Henry Clay Frick; probably Mary Childs; Helen Clay Frick; and Fido.

*Facing page, right, and below:* THE GRAND
STAIRCASE

Four flights of marble stairs began near the organ
alcove in the entrance hall. The black-painted brass
railing was custom-made for the house by Little &
Browne. The only painting in this photograph remaining in the Frick collections is *The French Gardens of
Venice* by Félix Ziem. Today it can be seen at the
Clayton house-museum in Pittsburgh, now a part of
the Frick Art and Historical Center. At one time some
nineteen engravings after Sir Joshua Reynolds, George
Romney, Sir Henry Raeburn, John Hoppner, Thomas
Gainsborough, and Sir Anthony Van Dyck graced the
walls of the second-floor hall. The first section draw-
ing by Little & Browne shows the grand staircase hall.
The other shows the entrance hall and grand staircase.

*Following pages:* The entrance hall looking toward the
grand staircase.

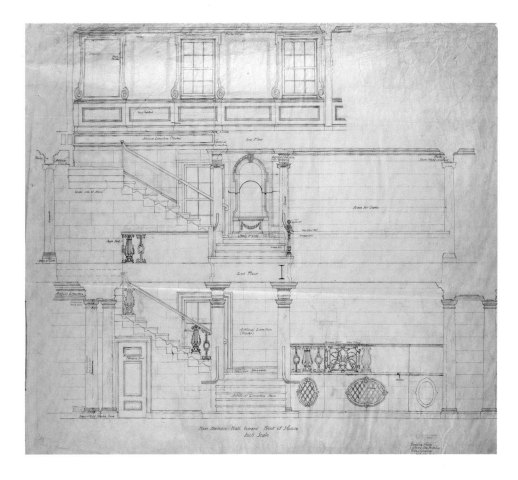

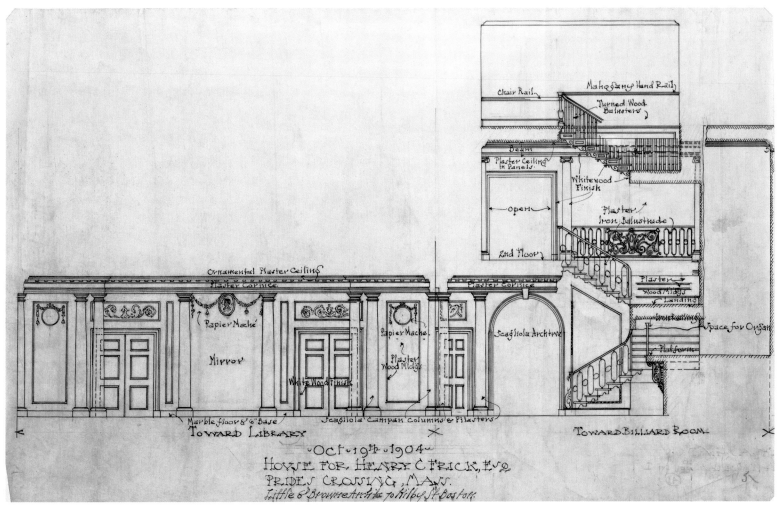

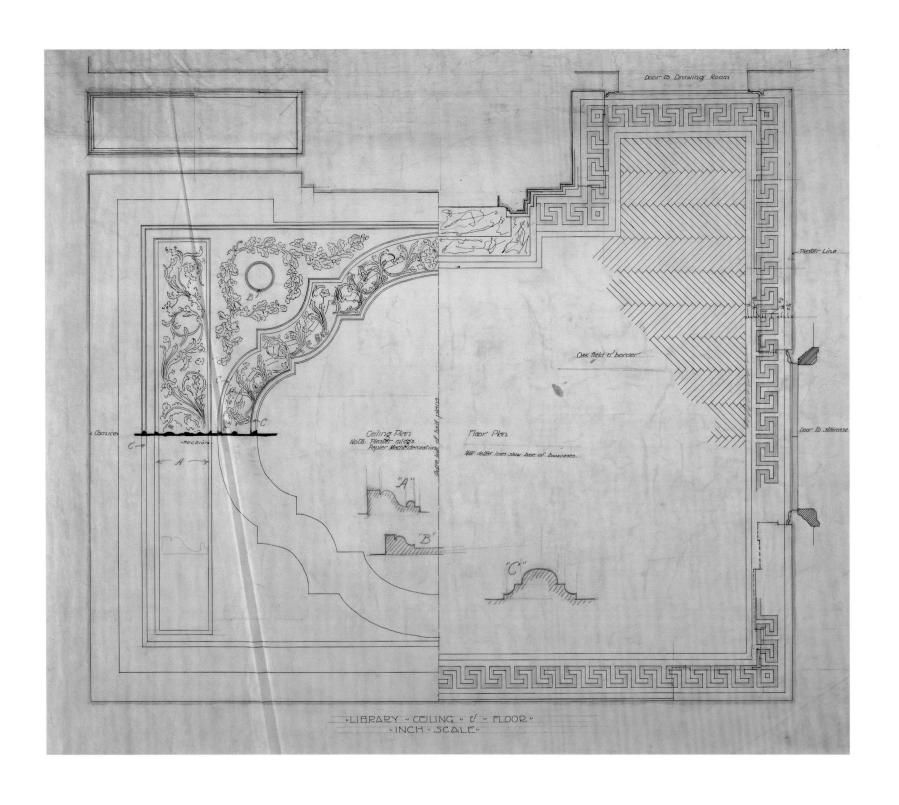

Door to Drawing Room

Plaster Line

Oak field & border

Door to staircase

Ceiling Plan
Note: Plaster mldgs.
Papier Maché decorations

Floor Plan
Note dotted lines show base of bookcases.

Cornice

Section

"A"

"B"

"C"

·LIBRARY · CEILING · & · FLOOR·
·INCH · SCALE·

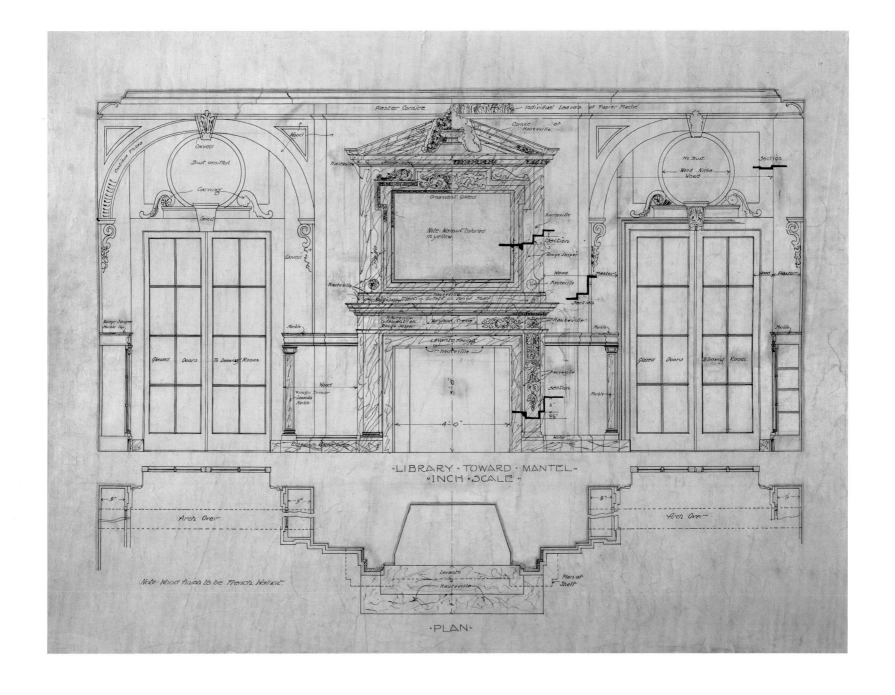

·LIBRARY·TOWARD·MANTEL·
·INCH·SCALE·

·PLAN·

*Facing page and above:* THE LIBRARY

No photographs of the Eagle Rock library appear to exist. These drawings by Little & Browne — a rendering of the library ceiling and floor and an elevation — indicate, however, that the room was impressive. If Frick incorporated these plans, or merely employed some of their elements, the library would have been consistent in all respects with other Eagle Rock rooms. Inventories show that the paintings displayed in this room were those from Clayton, Pittsburgh, by Jean-Charles Cazin, Théodore Rousseau, and Narcisse-Virgile Diaz de la Peña.

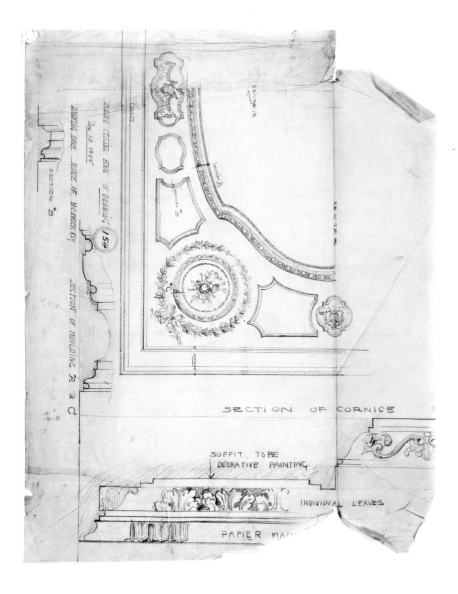

*Above and facing page:* THE DRAWING ROOM

Henry Clay Frick often played solitaire in this room in the early hours of the morning when he could not sleep. The furniture is largely Louis XVI. The writing table is attributed to the celebrated eighteenth-century Parisian cabinetmaker Martin Carlin. It was purchased for $35,000 by Joseph Duveen for the Fricks at a 1915 J. Pierpont Morgan estate sale in New York. Upon it rests a pair of early sixteenth-century bronze Neptune inkstands from the workshop of Severo Calzetta of Ravenna, purchased by Duveen from a 1916 Morgan estate sale. A sixteenth-century bronze statuette, also from the 1916 Morgan sale, is displayed on the commode. Of Mars or Perseus, it is attributed to Francesco Segala. Helen Frick sent all the bronzes, as well as the Carlin writing table, to Pittsburgh in 1970. She placed the writing table in the reception room at Clayton in anticipation of the house-museum and gave the bronzes to the Frick Art Museum.

This room was demolished in 1938 when the family wing was razed. The only painting remaining in Henry Clay Frick's New York or Pittsburgh collections is the portrait over the mantel by Arthur Devis depicting Sir Joshua Vanneck and his family of Roehampton House, Putney. Bought in 1916, it now is displayed in the Frick Art Museum in Pittsburgh. The tapestry fire screen originally belonged to a suite of furniture owned by the dukes of Devonshire and was purchased by Frick in 1914. Helen Frick gave it to the Frick Collection in 1953, where it rejoined the original suite. Also of note in this room is the small Chinese porcelain punch bowl of the Qianlong period, on the commode to the left of the writing table. One of a pair, it is of Rose du Barry with a lotus motif in turquoise. The bowls are now in the Frick Art Museum in Pittsburgh.

The rendering (above) by Little & Browne, c. 1904, shows the drawing-room ceiling.

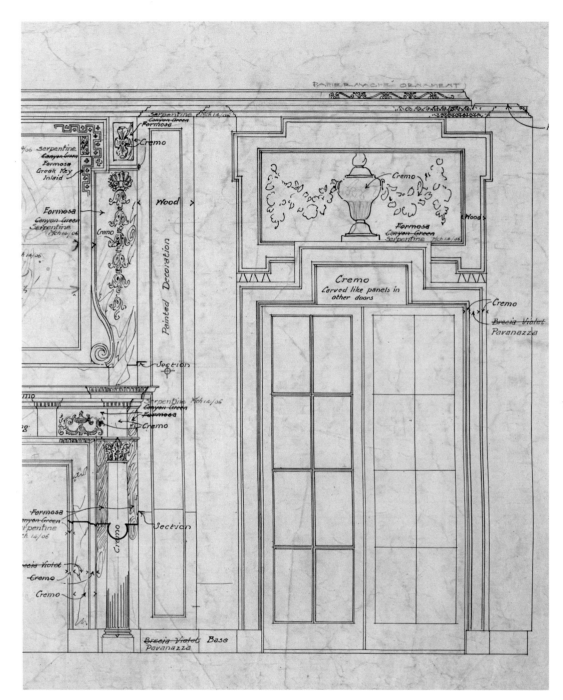

The following labels appear on the architectural drawing:

PAPIER MACHE ORNAMENT

Serpentine Canyon Green Formosa

Cremo

06 Serpentine Canyon Green Formosa Greek Key Inlaid

Formosa Canyon Green Serpentine Mch 14/06

Cremo

Wood

Painted Decoration

Cremo

Section

Serpentine Mch 14/06 Canyon Green Formosa

Cremo

Cremo

Formosa Canyon Green Serpentine Mch 14/06

Formosa Canyon Green Serpentine Mch 14/06

Cremo

Cremo

Brecia Violet Cremo

Cremo

Section

Brecia Violet Pavanazza Base

Cremo
Carved like panels in
other doors

Cremo

Brecia Violet
Pavanazza

*Left:* THE DRAWING ROOM

Elevation of the drawing room facing the
dining room, Little & Browne.

*Facing page:* THE DINING ROOM

The original elevations for the dining room by Little
& Browne — looking toward the mantel and toward
the hall — show a more elaborate design than used by
Frick. Although no photographs of the original dining
room appear to exist, images dating from 1938 and
1950 show that Frick eliminated the pilasters and
columns, as well as the over-mantel and ornamental
reliefs above the doors.

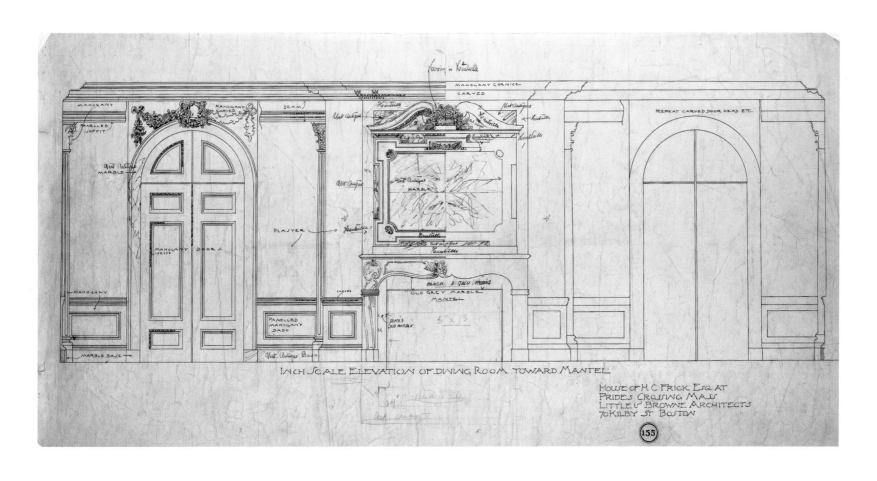

INCH SCALE ELEVATION OF DINING ROOM TOWARD MANTEL

HOUSE OF H. C. FRICK ESQ AT
PRIDES CROSSING MASS
LITTLE & BROWNE ARCHITECTS
70 KILBY ST BOSTON

155

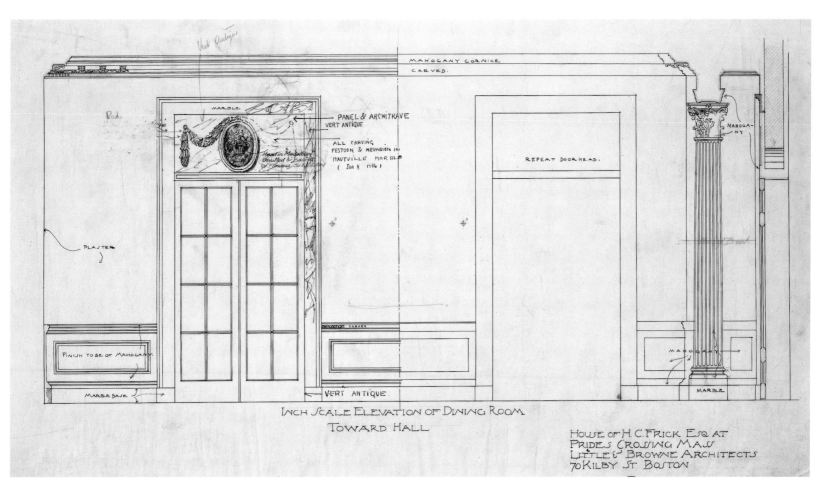

INCH SCALE ELEVATION OF DINING ROOM.
TOWARD HALL

HOUSE OF H. C. FRICK ESQ AT
PRIDES CROSSING MASS
LITTLE & BROWNE ARCHITECTS
70 KILBY ST BOSTON

*Right:* THE DINING ROOM AS THE LIVING ROOM, c. 1938

In 1938, when Helen Frick demolished the family wing, this room, originally the Frick's dining room, became Helen Frick's living room. According to family legend, the paneling came from the house of Dick Turpin, England's notorious eighteenth-century robber, the real Robin Hood. The Steinway piano and bench were designed for the Fricks in the Louis XVI manner by Duveen. The double-domed, George I japanned secretary with mirrored doors originally was purchased for Henry Clay Frick's bedroom at One East Seventieth Street. Helen took it to Eagle Rock after Adelaide Frick's death in 1931 and then gave it to the Frick Art Museum, Pittsburgh. It is now on loan to the Metropolitan Museum of Art in New York and can be seen in the English Gallery.

Three portraits in this photograph are also at the Frick Art Museum, Pittsburgh. From left to right they are: *Richard Brinsley Sheridan* by Thomas Gainsborough, *Princess Sophia, Daughter of George III* by John Hoppner, and over the mantel, *Marquise de Blaizel,* once considered a work by Sir Thomas Lawrence but now attributed to the School of David. The full-length portrait of a young gentleman is *Sir Griffeth Boynton* by Francis Cotes. It is no longer in the Frick collections.

Helen Frick celebrated her thirtieth birthday in 1918, the year Frick purchased the Hoppner portrait. Ironically, since Frick would not permit Helen to marry, she, like Sophia, died a spinster.

*Right:* THE DINING ROOM ARRANGED AS HELEN
FRICK'S LIVING AND DINING AREA, c. 1950

In the 1950s, Helen Frick closed the breakfast room
and converted this room to a combination living and
dining room. Later, in 1969, when Helen Frick razed
Eagle Rock, she offered the dining table to President
Richard Nixon for his personal use in the White
House. Since the offer was made with seating restrictions, the Nixon family politely refused. The table now
belongs to a family member. The painting over the
mantel, purchased in 1918, is a Dutch interior by Dirk
Hals, a brother and pupil of Frans Hals; it is no longer
in the Frick collections. The large portrait over the
Chippendale-style serving table, *Alexander Allan* by Sir
Henry Raeburn, is now in the Frick Collection and
also was a 1918 acquisition. The portrait to the right
of the mantel is of Lady Cecil Rice by Sir Joshua
Reynolds. It is now on the second floor of the Frick
Collection. Most of the furniture for the dining room
was custom-designed by Duveen. The four-panel, gilt-
wood tapestry screen is thought to have been made
from the borders of a large tapestry — probably eighteenth-century Brussels. It has a beige background with
a blue and rose design and now is in the Frick Art
Museum in Pittsburgh.

   The vegetable garden at Eagle Rock supplied the
Frick family with such delicacies as fresh asparagus,
corn, peaches, grapes, and spinach. Frick called
spinach "the broom of the stomach" and would
consume four ears of corn at one meal. He had distinct eating habits, such as pushing his food back and
a little away from himself. With precision he would
mix a small glass of whiskey with a tall glass of water
and ice. Hundreds of cases of Old Overholt whiskey
were stored in the basement, together with a large
collection of wine both homemade and imported.
After dinner, Frick always enjoyed a rare, old, golden-
toned chartreuse.

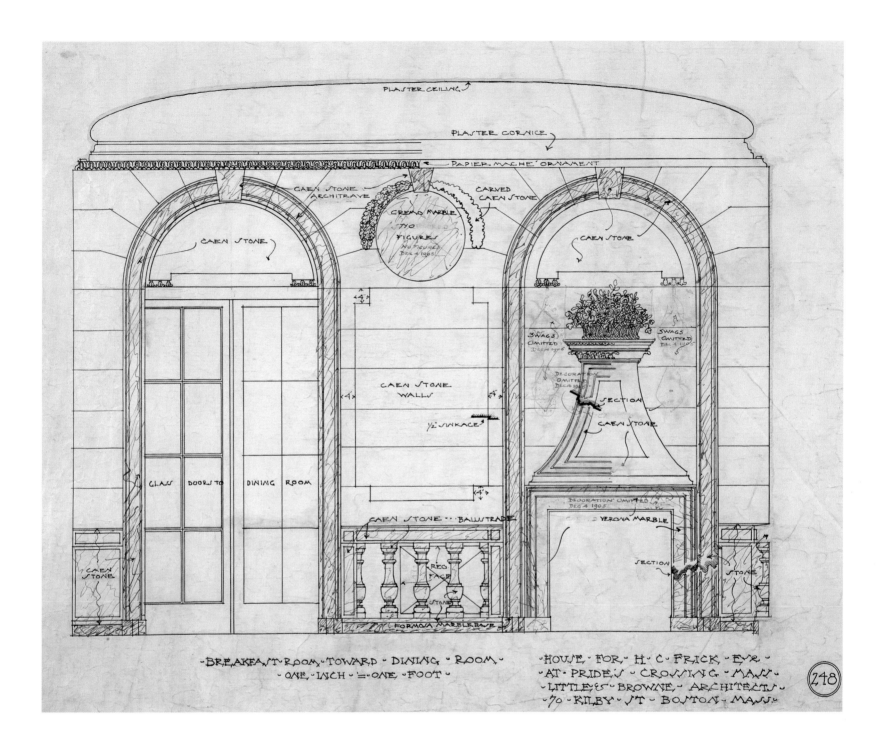

The drawing bears the following annotations:

PLASTER CEILING

PLASTER CORNICE

PAPIER-MACHE ORNAMENT

CAEN STONE ARCHITRAVE

CARVED CAEN STONE

CREMO MARBLE TWO FIGURES

CAEN STONE

CAEN STONE

SWAGS OMITTED

SWAGS OMITTED

CAEN STONE WALLS

DECORATION OMITTED

SECTION

½ SINKAGE

CAEN STONE

GLASS DOORS TO DINING ROOM

CAEN STONE BALUSTRADE

DECORATION OMITTED DEC 1905

VERONA MARBLE

CAEN STONE

REG FACE STONE

SECTION

CAEN STONE

FORMOSA MARBLE BASE

STONE

-BREAKFAST-ROOM-TOWARD-DINING-ROOM- -ONE-INCH-=-ONE-FOOT-

-HOUSE-FOR-H·C·FRICK-ESQ- -AT-PRIDE'S-CROSSING-MASS- -LITTLE·&·BROWNE-ARCHITECTS- -70-KILBY-ST-BOSTON-MASS-

248

*Facing page and above:* THE BREAKFAST ROOM

Breakfast was Henry Clay Frick's favorite meal. He was fond of eating rare steak with butter and plenty of salt and pepper, as well as stewed chicken on waffles, fresh mackerel, eggs, and bacon. He made his own coffee in what Helen called his "new toy" — a glass percolator. Often Frick's two eldest grandchildren would join him in the breakfast room just as he finished his meal. Once two-year-old Frances entered before her grandfather and took his seat. When Frick came in he said, "Well, well, look who's sitting in my chair"; since Frances would not budge, Frick was obliged to sit elsewhere.

The glass-enclosed breakfast room had a geometric pattern in the marble floor and a neoclassical chimney-piece and ceiling. It overlooked the terrace and was finished in Caen stone. The Chippendale-style mirror originally was purchased for Henry Clay Frick's bedroom at One East Seventieth Street and came to Eagle Rock after Adelaide's death in 1931. It is now in the Frick Art Museum. Beneath it is a seventeenth-century bronze statuette of a charging bull, also in the Frick Art Museum. The small console tables were original to the room and probably were the ones mentioned by Duveen in his letter to Henry Clay Frick

of August 26, 1906. In the 1950s the dining table and chairs seen in this photograph were moved to Helen Frick's combination living and dining room. The breakfast room then was closed to the family and used by Eagle Rock's caretakers.

The c. 1904 elevation of the breakfast room looking toward the dining room (above), by Little & Browne, shows that, with the exception of the balustrade along the wall, the finished room exactly followed the architects' design.

*Following pages:* THE STABLE

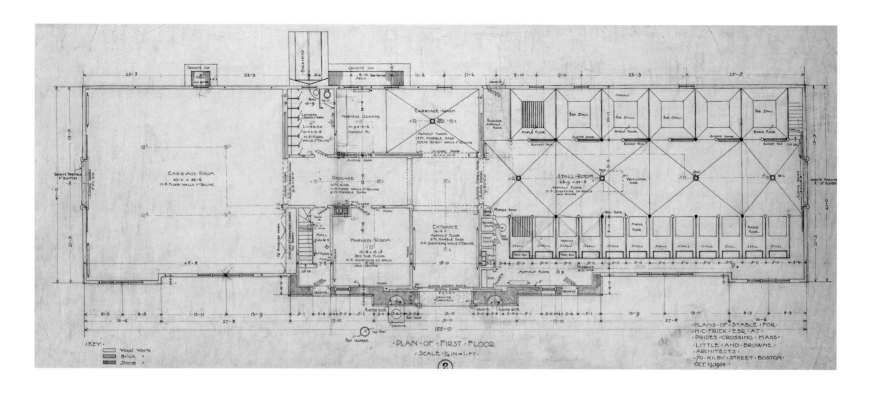

PLAN·OF·FIRST·FLOOR
·SCALE·¼ IN = 1·FT·

PLANS·OF·STABLE·FOR·
H·C·FRICK·ESQ·AT·
PRIDES·CROSSING·MASS·
LITTLE·AND·BROWNE·
ARCHITECTS·
·70·KILBY·STREET·BOSTON·
·OCT·19,1904·

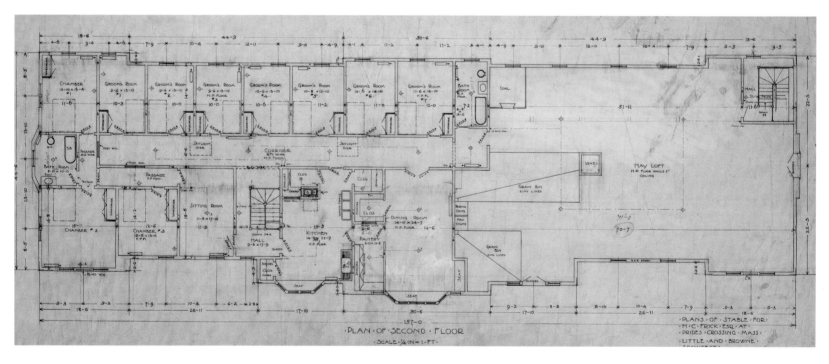

PLAN·OF·SECOND·FLOOR
·SCALE·¼ IN = 1·FT·

PLANS·OF·STABLE·FOR·
H·C·FRICK·ESQ·AT·
PRIDES·CROSSING·MASS·
LITTLE·AND·BROWNE·

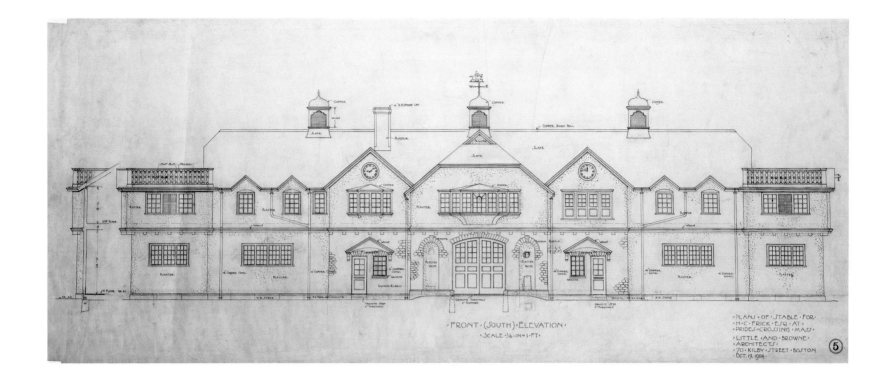

·FRONT·(SOUTH)·ELEVATION·
·SCALE·¼·IN·=·1·FT·

·PLANS·OF·STABLE·FOR·
·H·C·FRICK·ESQ·AT·
·PRIDES·CROSSING·MASS·
·LITTLE·AND·BROWNE·
·ARCHITECTS·
·70·KILBY·STREET·BOSTON·
·OCT·19·1904·
⑤

*Facing page, above, and right:* THE STABLE

These plans and elevations by Little & Browne — the first-floor plan, second-floor plan, front elevation, and east and west elevations — show that the stable was an extremely large building with more than enough room to house the stable help, horses, and carriages. According to Helen's note in a family album, the horses and carriages were brought to Eagle Rock from Clayton in 1906 when the family moved to the East Coast. Frick rode every day when at Eagle Rock, and his wife, daughter, and son all were expert riders. In the 1950s, Helen sold the stable property to Eleonora Sears of Boston for her Thoroughbred horses. At this time Helen built the carriage house at Clayton and returned the cars and carriages to Clayton, their original home, so they could be exhibited on the house-museum site. In the 1970s, Princess Anne and her then husband, Captain Mark Phillips, were guests of honor at a dance held in the stables. The royal couple were competing in the Ledyard Horse Trials in Hamilton, Massachusetts.

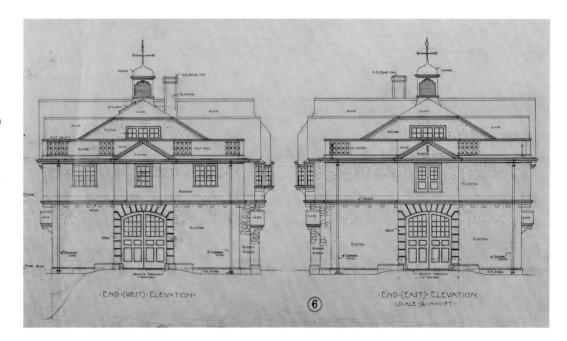

·END·(WEST)·ELEVATION·

·END·(EAST)·ELEVATION·
·SCALE·¼·IN·=·1·FT·
⑥

*Above:* THE EAGLE ROCK OUTBUILDINGS

The photograph of the Eagle Rock property across Hale Street from the main house shows the scale of the estate. The stable is to the left, the gardens are in the center, and the gardener's cottage is to the right.

*Facing page:* The front elevation of the automobile house by Little & Browne (located on the same side of Hale Street as the main house) reveals that it, like the stable, was larger than most houses in the area.

*Right:* Front elevation of the gardener's cottage, Little & Browne.

*Facing page:* THE TRELLIS GARDEN AND FOUNTAIN

*Below:* Henry Clay Frick riding out at Eagle Rock.

*Following pages:* ONE EAST SEVENTIETH STREET,
NOW THE FRICK COLLECTION, C. 1931

# CHAPTER III

# ONE
# EAST SEVENTIETH
# STREET

### THE NEW YORK CITY RESIDENCE, THE FRICK COLLECTION

*Facing page:* THE ENTRANCE HALL, c. 1931

This photograph of the original entrance hall to One East Seventieth Street shows the decorative iron grillework on the vestibule doors made by the master metalworker Samuel Yellin for $7,850. According to a March 30, 1914 list of contractors for One East Seventieth Street, the wrought-iron stair railing was designed by White, Allom & Company, for $9,500. A long-case régulateur clock, purchased by Frick in 1915, is deemed one of the most sumptuous of its kind. Its movement and dial are signed by Ferdinand Berthoud. The case is stamped by Balthazar Lieutaud, and the bronzes are signed by Philippe Caffiéri. The marble bust once was believed to be a portrait of Louis XIV and ascribed to Antoine Coysevox.

*Right: Henry Clay Frick* by John Christen Johansen.

IN THE SUMMER OF 1906, when Henry Clay Frick moved into Eagle Rock — intending it to become the Frick family's summer compound — he also purchased one of the last remaining prestigious pieces of real estate in New York. Located at Fifth Avenue and Seventieth Street, the property (home to a private library that later would be subsumed in the much-anticipated New York Public Library) stretched the entire block front on Fifth Avenue. Legend says that in his continuing building war and acts of revenge against his former partner, Andrew Carnegie, Frick now intended to build a house that would make Carnegie's Fifth Avenue residence "look like a miner's shack." Initially, however, Frick had no such resolve, or at least was in no hurry: he was happily dividing his time between Eagle Rock and the Vanderbilts' 640 Fifth Avenue. Moreover, he had agreed to delay the closing until 1911 to give the library time to move its collection to the New York Public Library, then under construction. Relieved by Frick's gesture, the executive committee of the New York Public Library noted its "high appreciation of the liberal and public spirited manner in which [Frick] ha[d] dealt with this subject."

*Above:* Proposed design of One East Seventieth Street by Daniel H. Burnham, c. 1912.

When Henry Clay Frick finally did take title to the New York property in 1911, he began considering his options — adding an art gallery to Eagle Rock and incorporating it into the Frick family home, or building a house on the New York site where all the rooms would display his art collection. As he weighed these alternatives, Frick engaged his Chicago architect friend, Daniel H. Burnham, to make proposals for both ventures, before eventually deciding in favor of a permanent residence in New York. In this, he very certainly was guided by the memory of his visit as a young man, over thirty years earlier, to the great museums in Europe and later to the Wallace Collection, a three-generation family collection given to the city of London after Lady Wallace's death in 1897. Ever since his 1880 trip, Frick had harbored the hope that he someday could create a collection for the benefit of his countrymen. Like Lady Wallace and perhaps inspired by her gift of the Wallace Collection, Frick intended that One East Seventieth Street and its treasures be used for the public benefit as the Frick Collection on his death. Additionally, his friend the noted Boston collector Isabella Stewart Gardner — the first American to establish the idea of housing great artworks in a palatial setting that also served as a private residence — already had made plans to leave Fenway Court, her Venetian palazzo, to the public on her death. Frick, undoubtedly struck by Gardner's house-museum concept, and fueled by the importance of Lady Wallace's gift to London, concluded that his Frick Collection should be housed in New York, America's financial and art center.

After discharging Burnham, who died in Heidelberg, Germany, a few months after learning he had lost the Frick commission, Frick engaged Thomas Hastings as the architect for his New York house. Hastings had studied at the Ecole Nationale Supérieure des Beaux Arts in Paris and later had formed a partnership with John Merven Carrère. Their firm, Carrère & Hastings, had become one of the foremost architectural firms in New York, and at the time of Frick's commission, it just had completed the classically inspired New York Public Library — one of the finest examples of heroic Beaux Arts architecture in America and the firm's first large urban commission.

The Beaux Arts style in America began in the 1880s and had reached a pinnacle by 1912. Although based on classicism and the integration of the various arts, the style was far more exuberant than the neoclassicism preached by the "Colonial Trinity" of Ogden Codman Jr., Arthur Little, and Herbert W. C. Browne. While the Beaux Arts tradition drew on everything from Roman architecture to the Renaissance for embellishment and visual delight, as did the followers of Codman and Edith Wharton, it placed less emphasis on historical accuracy. According to the architectural historian Pauline Metcalf, Codman sought to refine the Beaux Arts standard prevalent in America since the 1880s; indeed, his style was a reaction against it. Therefore, he "loudly denounced the work of . . . Thomas Hastings which reflected [his] Ecole training in Paris by accentuating some forms and details of classical sources, but without necessarily following the original scale."

To Codman, Little, and Browne, Henry Clay Frick's use of a Beaux Arts architect may have seemed a backward step — particularly so soon after having built the more avant-garde Eagle Rock. But this time Frick's need was not so much for a house on the cutting edge of style and fashion as it was for a building that in housing his family and art collection would symbolize the integration of his cultural refinement with his wealth, power, and social standing. This would be his last personal statement, the one that would outlive him. He wanted, therefore, something that was going to synthesize and define him; a final, personal, graceful, humanizing monument to his wisdom, depth, and triumph. Thus, Codman's stripped-down severity was not going to be helpful in immortalizing the man whose name and reputation were, at least as far as much of America's working class was concerned, infamous.

Although Frick initially did not tell Hastings that he intended to give the New York house and his art collection to the public on his death, privately he indicated just how One East Seventieth Street would serve his needs. He said to a friend that he wanted this house to be his monument. And as far as the sense of monumentality was concerned, there was no more capable or prestigious Beaux Arts architect in America than Thomas Hastings to realize Frick's dream. By June 1912 — only five months after releasing Burnham — the architectural drawings were complete and a model made. Frick's secretary, James Howard Bridge, wrote Frick on July 13, 1912, that the ultimate purpose of the house was still a well-kept secret:

I spent a delightful hour with Mr. Hastings & caught much of his enthusiasm. He is a wonderful combination of idealism & practicability — a personified blend of the artistic & useful. At first I thought him governed solely by instinct, his "feeling" for the beauties of his art was so spontaneous; but soon I discovered that every detail of his conception had a scientific basis & that the placing of even a window-ledge must conform to the laws of light and shade. That he is putting his soul into this undertaking is obvious, & he frankly called it the "chance of a lifetime." This after designing the New York Library, which most architects would regard as the culmination of a successful career.

By careful questioning I found he had aimed to make a beautiful and comfortable home, with a picture gallery & organ annexes; and he appeared to have no suspicion that eventually it might be more. As you had chosen to limit his understanding of what was required, I did not feel at liberty to do more than "suppose" the building were subsequently to be used as a museum; and I found with a few alterations it could be easily adapted to this end.

At the same time, the museum idea does not seem to be of very great importance just now. The thing is to have a worthy & homey residence for yourself. During the next twenty years, you will have lots of time to develop ideas for public work. The home as planned promises to be just that — a home, inside. Exteriorly it will be impressive & beautiful because of its simplicity which by a hairs breath escapes severity.

Prior to approving Hastings's design for a neoclassic, Indiana limestone house in the popular French eighteenth-century style, Frick asked the architect to take the plans to P. A. B. Widener, saying that his Philadelphia friend, fellow collector, and business associate "seems quite anxious to see the plans and would like so much for you to go to his house." Widener must have approved, for Hastings won the Frick commission. But Hastings would have a hard time with his client. The three-story, fifty-one-foot-high residence, with a terraced garden on Fifth Avenue to soften the urban feeling, would be one of the most expensive ever built in New York, costing an estimated three million dollars.

Although Frick was accustomed to spending large sums of money to get what he wanted, he continued his practice of keeping a sharp eye on expenses, as well as on the details of each building project. If he frequently quibbled over prices and was abrupt with those working for him, he became more so with Hastings, who complained to James Howard Bridge: "I go to see him and talk until I am nervous. When I stop talking he gazes at me in silence in the most disconcerting way. Then I make a few more remarks, which are always received in silence; and when I come away I am exhausted of all nervous energy."

By May 1913 construction of One East Seventieth Street was well under way. About half the first-floor arches were in; some of the porte cochère stones had been placed; and the steel roof for the West Gallery was about to be fabricated. In addition, the tilework, floors, and walls of the basement were nearly complete, as were the specifications for the electrical work and plumbing, and the details of the kitchen and pantry plans were almost ready to be submitted to Adelaide Frick for her approval. By July the steel was in place for the gallery roof, ready for the installation of the arches and glass skylight. All the main cornices on the dining-room wing

*Facing page:* One East Seventieth Street
The West Gallery (above) and the inner courtyard (below) under construction in 1913.

were complete. The porte cochère had reached the third story, and the excavation for the Seventieth Street retaining wall was about to begin. On July 17, 1913, D. B. Kinch, who supervised the construction, wrote Frick's other secretary, Mr. McElroy, "We sure are going fast, and when you think we have not worked one hour of overtime, it looks that much better." On August 15, however, he did admit, "Sometimes I wonder why the foremen don't tell me to go to ——, but they don't, so there you are."

But progress did slow at times. Once a railroad car loaded with steel for the third-floor beams and lintels for the doors got lost, and another time a construction worker was killed on the job. Adelaide asked for the details of dozens of things, including her bedroom and closet. Although she undoubtedly changed her mind about some things and rejected others, Kinch reported, she "was just as nice as ever & we settled the detail on every room in the house."

The entire team was giving One East Seventieth Street their all and took a proprietary interest in watching the house take form. In mid-July 1913, Kinch wrote to Frick, "One of the men from Knoedler's [Frick's close friend and art dealer largely responsible for Frick's collection] was at the house this afternoon . . . and he expressed himself that [the art gallery] was a beautifully proportioned room . . . Mr. Hastings was amazed to see how far the work had progressed, and of course was very enthusiastic about it. [The house] is only beginning to show its real lines now, and it is going to be very quiet, and by far, the best." Enthralled, he beamed: "[It] sure is a darling." And in August, Kinch wrote McElroy that he was "so busy with [his] big baby down here, [he] simply worr[ied] if away, even for a day."

And the best it was to be. In August 1913, on the advice of Joseph Duveen, Frick announced that he had commissioned Sir Charles Allom for the interior decoration of all rooms on the first floor, as well as for the second-floor breakfast room and Frick's private sitting room. The son of an architect and grandson of two well-known artists, Allom had served such magnates as P. A. B. Widener and William Randolph Hearst, and more important, he was then Britain's leading decorator — by far the most acclaimed Frick had used to date. Edward VII had commissioned him in 1907 to banish Victorian stuffiness from Buckingham Palace and redecorate it in the lighter, more cheerful French manner. When Edward died in 1910, Allom's yachting companion assumed the throne as George V. His wife, Queen Mary, had a love of history and an eye for quality and set about adding important pieces to the royal collection. She initiated a system of labeling and cataloguing the royal palaces' inventory, rearranged the furniture and decorative objects in Buckingham Palace, and reassembled sets of chairs long separated. A memorandum in the Royal Archives written by Sir Charles Allom in 1913 shows that he had been in charge of this latest Buckingham Palace redecoration as well.

When Frick selected him, Allom maintained offices in London, Montreal, and New York. Although his quote for the interior decoration of One East Seventieth Street exceeded the estimates of others by $300,000, perhaps because of Allom's recent knighthood, a fashion-conscious Henry Clay Frick accepted the bid. During the summer of 1913, however, Allom proved himself to his American client. Charles S. Carstairs, one of Frick's closest friends and art advisors (the first to promote the sale of Old Masters in M. Knoedler & Company), suggested to Allom that the east wall of the drawing room (now the Fragonard Room) would be improved by the removal of the door to the left of the mantel. Although it was designed to open onto the South Hall, a similar door to the right of the mantel already had been removed. Allom advised removing the door and sealing the wall, and instead placing a new door in the south wall to improve the flow between the drawing room and the dining room. The change was made, and Carstairs advised Frick on July 11, 1913: "I think Allom is extremely interested and anxious to make [the house] the finest thing he has ever done, and so long as he keeps that in mind I am sure it will be a success."

Frick may have wanted a "royal residence," but nothing as elaborate as Buckingham Palace. In a June 24, 1913, letter to Allom — written before the Frick–Allom commission was announced — Frick cautioned him to use economy and restraint: "Please see that ceilings are almost plain. From what I see Mr. Hastings is favoring too much carving. Please impress upon him my earnest desire to avoid anything elaborate and show him this."

In the meantime, construction continued at a pace that astounded everybody. Soon the plumbing in the house was tested and the plastering on the second and third floors imminent, and in September, Kinch was delighted to be "so far ahead of the architects." He boasted to McElroy that Hastings had asked him, "Why start plastering so soon & I said for moral effect." Earlier he had bragged: "Gee, if Hastings would have given me plans in time, I would have the house 90% completed by January 1st, 1914." In December, Frick again reminded Allom, as he did Hastings, to use restraint: "We desire a comfortable, well arranged home, simple, in good taste, and not ostentatious." Frick must have been pleased with the results, for in March 1914 he was toying with the idea of paying Allom more: "I think the various percentages named are low and I trust after we are through I will feel like revising them upward to some extent."

More than ever, taste remained a matter of great concern for Henry Clay Frick. About the time he engaged Sir Charles Allom, he also hired Elsie de Wolfe — a former actress turned America's self-proclaimed first professional interior decorator. She recently had published a best-selling book, *The House in Good Taste,* a volume similar in theory to Edith Wharton and Ogden Codman Jr.'s *The Decoration of Houses.* It was less stringent and less philosophical than theirs — a more chatty, personal treatise, advocating simplicity, suitability, and proportion. It also promoted a perspective directed at "modern women [who] demanded simplified living" and included gossipy references to de Wolfe's own houses and apartments, most of them remodeled and decorated by her mentor and collaborator Ogden Codman. In her book, she also laid down an aesthetic that called for air and light. She insisted on practicality, advocated the use of good chintzes (printed English cotton) instead of inferior silks and damasks, and encouraged the use of chinoiserie, stripes, leopard skin, pale walls, and trompe l'oeil — all to be accompanied by French and English eighteenth-century antique and reproduction furniture.

Emphatically anti-Victorian in her approach, de Wolfe's unapologetically fresh style could be seen in her successful 1906 redecoration of New York's Colony Club, a building designed by Stanford White. The commission was noteworthy not only because it was for the first exclusively female club in New York but also for the first nonresidential establishment in America to be designed by a professional interior decorator. Smart, businesslike, and well-connected socially to such members of the Colony Club's board of governors as Thomas Hastings's wife and J. P. Morgan's youngest daughter, Anne, Elsie was the talk of New York.

With Sir Charles Allom working on the first-floor interior, Frick gave de Wolfe responsibility for the decoration and furnishing of fourteen rooms comprising most of the second and third floors. Part of her appeal was that she acted as a buffer between her clients and the dealers. She was therefore an invaluable asset for Frick, who was pursued by every known dealer. More important, she preferred to buy largely from individuals and estates. But there were other qualities about de Wolfe that also must have appealed to Frick: she was efficient, organized, and firm. When Frick asked to see an alternative set of plans for the second- and third-floor rooms, de Wolfe countered, "Mr. Frick, when I draw up a set of plans there is no second choice. There is only what I show you. The best."

Although speculation exists that de Wolfe was engaged by Frick in part to help launch Helen in New York society, such was not the case. At the time de Wolfe entered the Frick family scene, twenty-five-year-old Helen was well beyond "launching" age — and not in need of a launch of any kind. She was working for the Red Cross in New York, managing her Iron Rail

*Below left:* One of a pair of small, eighteenth-century console tables with supporting figures of Nubians purchased in 1914 by Elsie de Wolfe through Jacques Seligmann.

*Below right:* One of a pair of small corner cupboards attributed to Martin Carlin, also purchased in 1914 by Elsie de Wolfe through Jacques Seligmann.

project for girls working in Boston's textile and shoe factories, and researching the provenance of her father's art collection. Furthermore, Helen never had an interest in New York society, and in any case Frick expected her to dedicate herself to his interests.

Whatever Frick's additional intentions might have been in hiring New York's most socially connected decorator, and much as Frick was impressed with de Wolfe, he supervised her with the same firm hand as others in his employ. In March 1914, when presented with a bill in excess of what he had anticipated, Frick made his position clear: "Our understanding was that I am to pay you 10% above cost for anything you may from time to time purchase for my house, you at all times making the closest bargain possible. This, however, does not apply to anything you make for me in your own establishment, like curtains, etc.; in that case you are to furnish an estimate and have my authorization in writing before you commence work. I expect your estimate to be reasonable and based on giving you a good profit, but I am averse to paying any one an exorbitant profit." He also had to mediate among members of the One East Seventieth Street team. In one instance, he had to calm the excitable Thomas Hastings who "admitted he lost his temper and agreed to work . . . in every way possible to carry out [Miss de Wolfe's] ideas." Frick wrote de Wolfe after the meeting and said that all were "agreed to see that matters went along harmoniously so that the result would be all right and [she] could have no excuse for saying [Hastings] had embarrassed [her] and destroyed the scheme as originally planned by [her] for all the rooms."

Another time Frick tried to temper what had turned into an escalating competition between Elsie de Wolfe and Sir Charles Allom. Although de Wolfe had fourteen bedrooms and numerous baths to work with — and the budget to make them as luxurious and comfortable as she could — in a letter dated March 20, 1914, she announced that she wanted more. In trying to take "Mr. Frick's Room" from Allom, an ambitious de Wolfe claimed she had "such a wonderful scheme . . . [for the] room at the end of the Gallery." As for the ladies' reception room — also Allom's domain — while de Wolfe admitted this "sounds conceited, but it's true," she wrote Frick, "I hope I shall surely do the ladies reception room — I know much more about this than any mere man can do!!" She further pressed Frick to reassign her his second-floor private sitting room and breakfast room:

> Though it is not in my scheme of creation to fight for work, and I am, believe me, not writing now, impelled by any monetary consideration, I feel that all my scheme as planned should go together, and that it will be the greatest mistake if these rooms are not carried out by one person. To take two of the principal rooms right out breaks the harmony, and certainly, White-Allom & Co., with all the big downstairs rooms to their credit, should be willing to waive any imaginary claim they may feel they have on the upstairs portion of the house.

Pressing him still further, de Wolfe begged, "*Please,* my dear Mr. Frick, tell White-Allom that you wish me to do those two rooms on 'my' floor and to confine their energies to the downstairs portion."

In the end, Frick released only the ladies' reception room. Allom kept "Mr. Frick's Room" at the end of the West Gallery and the second-floor private sitting room and breakfast room. Undaunted, in the spring of 1914 de Wolfe went to Paris with Frick in order to buy furniture for her assigned rooms from the residence of the late Sir John Murray Scott. As the longtime secretary for Lady Wallace, Scott had inherited part of the French decorative arts collection assembled by the fourth marquess of Hertford and his son, Sir Richard Wallace. Although the will was being challenged and Scott's house at 2, rue Laffitte was sealed by court order, the contents had been consigned to the French art dealer Jacques Seligmann pending the outcome of the lawsuit. In perhaps her greatest and most successful performance as an actress, the normally ultra-chic de Wolfe dressed herself in a drab suit and entered Scott's house with Seligmann disguised as his secretary. After making some selections, she contacted Frick and persuaded him to delay his morning golf game outside Paris at Saint-Cloud Country Club so he could inspect the items. Frick spent a hasty half hour in the house and, according to de Wolfe, spent three million dollars on pieces acquired mostly for the ladies' reception room, the second-floor hall, Frick's bedroom, Helen's bedroom, Adelaide's bedroom, and her connecting private sitting room or boudoir (now the Boucher Room).

While large numbers of antiques and paintings continued to be purchased by the Fricks from de Wolfe, Allom, Duveen, Roland Knoedler, and a variety of other dealers, Hastings was

*Below:* Design for the center table-desk of the library by White, Allom & Company, c. 1913–14.

completing the structural work on One East Seventieth Street. The pediment sculptures by Attilio Piccirilli were finished, and the sub-basement and basement were nearly ready. The floors on the first level were almost done, as were those in Adelaide's boudoir, bedroom, and closets. Those in Helen's bedroom were about to be laid, and the last of the Allom-designed bookcases were being installed in the library. The woodwork in what then was known as Mr. Frick's Room (now the Enamel Room) had been completed. And the Allom-designed bookcases, as well as one of Frick's special art concerns — the overmantel in his second-floor sitting room custom designed for El Greco's *Purification of the Temple* — were already in place.

But on March 6, 1914, the already fast pace needed to accelerate. George Vanderbilt, landlord of 640 Fifth Avenue, died, and Frick's tenancy came to an abrupt close. As required by the terms of the lease agreement, Frick had to vacate the house in favor of its new owners, Cornelius and Grace Vanderbilt. He began pushing his team for an October occupancy of One East Seventieth Street, and Adelaide started coming to the house twice a day to check on various matters. As soon as the third floor was finished, she began sending the family's belongings over for storage. Although delighted with the progress of the house, she requested many changes, such as wooden doors to go with Samuel Yellin's iron grille vestibule doors with glass panes. Of her many other requests, Kinch said they "all . . . shall be done but some are going to be rather difficult & rather expensive."

Ever concerned that the comfortable, family atmosphere of his new house not be sacrificed to ornamentation, on March 24, 1914, Frick again reminded Allom, "I do hope we will not make any mistake in having a livable, homelike house and in the best of taste; we depend on you largely that such will be the result." And yet when he returned from Europe later that spring, he found he had no cause for concern; he was, in fact, delighted with the house. On June 3, 1914, he wrote Knoedler in Paris: "Went almost immediately to the new house which I found had progressed marvelously. The picture gallery is going to be a dream; I like its proportions immensely."

He seemed happy with Elsie de Wolfe as well. In the nearly seventy-nine letters in the Frick Family Archives written to this lady of taste, Henry Clay Frick's compliments abound: "Delighted to hear of the bureau for my daughter's room, also the table, and the mantel . . ." "Mrs. Frick is delighted with the bed as shown in the photograph." But the money-conscious Frick also chided: "I have told [Mrs. Frick] that you have cost me a fortune in providing things to make her apartments most attractive." He advised the decorator, "I should also think you might secure better prices, Take your time — you know time is money!" Then, playing to her ego and desire for future work he dangled this carrot: "We will go slow in securing furniture for the first floor. I hope to consult you, in whose taste I have the greatest confidence." Finally he wished her a "happy summer" and wrote, "am delighted that you are improving in your bargaining capacity — that is all you need to make you perfect!"

By June 1914, the Fricks had moved the last of their personal belongings from 640 Fifth Avenue to One East Seventieth Street. They turned their residence of the last nine years over to Cornelius and Grace Vanderbilt and anticipated spending a quiet summer at Eagle Rock with

their friends and their art collection. The Fricks hoped to be in their New York house by October, but in July everything seemed to suddenly unravel. Hastings lost his temper with Elsie de Wolfe's assistant. Frick's sister-in-law and beloved family companion, Martha Howard Childs, died of pancreatic cancer. Frick himself suffered a near-fatal attack of inflammatory rheumatism, an illness that had plagued him from childhood and once again left him bedridden and entirely helpless. And to top it all, war broke out in Europe.

Additionally, Frick was feeling the stress of two other building projects, both adjacent to the Frick Building in Pittsburgh and scheduled to open in the spring of 1916: the six-million-dollar, twenty-story, thousand-room, classically inspired, Renaissance-style William Penn Hotel, and the ten-story Gothic Revival shopping mall called the Union Arcade. Like the Frick Building, these new structures would face Grant Street and would cover an entire city block. For the hotel Frick engaged the respected Pittsburgh firm of Janssen & Abbott, hoping to construct the most modern hotel of the day — one that would bring foreign visitors to Pittsburgh. Certainly, it would be among the most visually splendid, with its lobby ceiling of sixty-five octagonal coffers patterned on the palace of Fontainebleau, its richly paneled Italian Room for dining, and a Renaissance-style ballroom with gilt reliefs. Bedridden as he was, Frick only could dream about the new hotel — dream of the seven-room State Suite he hoped to reserve for himself on opening night; dream of how he would lure the chef from the Plaza Hotel, the maitre d'hôtel from the Savoy in London, and the chief clerk from the Bellevue-Stratford in Philadelphia to his William Penn.

As for the Union Arcade — a structure that would evoke northern French and Flemish Gothic of the fifteenth century — Frick had pressed a retired and partly deaf Frederick Osterling back into service to accomplish what would be the largest enclosed shopping arcade in the world. Seriously incapacitated as Frick was, however, he only could hope that this, like the hotel, would be as glamorous a building as he wanted. Perhaps it would be his answer to architect Cass Gilbert's recently opened Gothic Revival Woolworth Building in New York. And maybe, as nurses carried him to and from his bathroom and as he pondered the possibility of life as a cripple, Frick was sustained by the knowledge that his hotel, shopping arcade, and office building would be connected to each other by side doorways.

By the end of September a still suffering Henry Clay Frick became increasingly argumentative and angry. He remained plagued by inflamed joints, atrophying muscles, high fever, sweating, diarrhea, and other gastrointestinal disorders associated with inflammatory rheumatism. Still helpless and threatened with permanent lameness, he seemed to take out his pain and frustration on Sir Charles Allom, writing on September 29: "You are very much behind on all contracts with me. What are you going to do about it?" He complained: "There are a number of things you certainly could have completed by this time that are not done, — the railing around the stairs, doors, etc., etc. I do not know how you are getting along with the electric light fixture, but the work is certainly dragging and has been." Although still confined to his bed after eight weeks and, as he described, "only able to move around with difficulty," he nevertheless reported to Allom, "I am glad to say that I am well again, and will see that things are pushed

*Facing page:* The William Penn Hotel, Pittsburgh, 1914.

from now on." But Frick wasn't the least bit well. And with a salvo that indicated the extent of his anger at Allom, Frick complained: "Rather surprised that you pestered me about the beginning of my illness for money, when there was nothing coming to you – that is, nothing due."

A month later, on October 21, 1914, Frick again cabled Allom: "Your failure to make good on any contracts is causing us much trouble and inconvenience. When do you expect to give them your personal supervision?" And one week later, he exploded: "Simply outrageous unbusinesslike your dilatory manner completing contracts with me. First contract in many respects notably hardware for doors not even heard of. War excuse absurd."

When moving day arrived on November 16, 1914, however, Frick seemed to put his physical issues and complaints concerning Allom aside, at least temporarily, as he took part in the excitement and activity. Traditionally, Frick personally oversaw the unwrapping process and the placement of every new acquisition, carefully noted the date of the acquisition and the date of each artwork's arrival or departure when transferred from one of his houses to another, and always recorded where each painting was displayed. He now directed the men from Knoedler's and Duveen's as they hung the pictures about the Gallery and in the other rooms on the first floor.

Nevertheless, only one week later, he once again was fuming over Allom's unfulfilled contracts. Allom had written Frick a stern letter on October 30, in his defense, explaining the delays and tweaking, as carefully as he dared, his client's apparent inability to respect wartime emergencies:

> Certain doors could only be ordered considerably after our contract, and some of the locks of these doors are absolutely abnormal . . . a lock in some cases works fully 1 ft. higher on one side of the door than on the other. This has meant these special locks being made by hand, but as I told you in the cable, locksmiths have been taken off to make rifles, and nothing in the world that we could do could have affected that, any more than we or you could have stopped the war had we desired to do so.

Patriotically, he reminded Frick:

> I can tell you that it is just wonderful that this country [England] is proceeding with its work as it is, when it has at least 2 million men under arms, with equipment having to be made for them at forced pressure. It has not only taken men from normal employment, but it has taken material, money, and has even interfered with the shipping of goods . . . The share which France has taken in your house, has naturally caused delay, for which I am sure you cannot blame me.
>
> It is in a way just as unfortunate to me as it is to you, you by not being able to get your home as quickly as you had hoped, while I am being discredited for reasons absolutely beyond my control . . . and conditions have arisen which as you know are those which void, together with so-called Acts of God, liabilities of Insurance Policies and other contracts from holding good all over the world.

*Facing page:* The Union Arcade, now the Union Trust Building, Pittsburgh, 1914.

But acts of God were not plausible excuses for Henry Clay Frick. On November 17, he responded to White, Allom & Company in London:

Your Mr. Allom's letter of October 30th has been received. It is perfectly absurd for him to write me that he is innocent of any neglect. The unsatisfactory condition of all of the contracts I have with you is simply deplorable. From what I saw of the management of your establishment while I was in London, I feared just such a result.

Here we are now on the seventeenth of November with not even your first contract completed, all of which was to be done by April fifteenth last, and your contract for various furnishings is in the same, if not worse condition. These locks should have been completed by April fifteenth, long before any war was thought of; you showed no foresight.

If you think I am going to permit you to treat me in this manner you are badly mistaken. I regret exceedingly that I did not give Miss de Wolfe the furnishing of my entire house; her work is practically done, and absolutely satisfactory.

The following day, Frick wrote Allom directly: "Don't you think it rather absurd to ask for payment . . . in view of the condition of your work? It is now the 18th of November and many doors are without locks; the door entering this room for instance, (the office in the rear of the art gallery), is without a lock; it certainly must be a simple lock and nothing complicated about

*Below left:* A bed and work table with trellis marquetry by Martin Carlin, purchased in 1914 by Elsie de Wolfe through Jacques Seligmann and used by Adelaide Frick in her boudoir. The top section of this remarkable piece is removable for use as a bed table. It also contains a mirror, an adjustable bookrest, and storage compartments.

*Below right:* Writing table with mahogany veneer by Jean-Henri Riesener, also purchased in 1914 by Elsie de Wolfe through Jacques Seligmann and used by Adelaide Frick in her boudoir.

it, and illustrates the inefficiency of your organization." He further admonished Allom: "You are just now finishing putting in the backs of the fire-places, etc. How the war could have affected the finishing up of work of this character which should have been completed by April 15th last, I do not understand."

Frick went on to complain that the table for the breakfast room, which they had used at 640 Fifth Avenue, had not been "put in good order . . . and we had to secure another table for that room." Moreover, "You have not delivered a particle of furniture for my sitting room on the second floor, part of which was to be done here out of material taken from our art gallery at 640 Fifth Avenue." Furious, he asked, "What excuse do you make for this?" He continued: "We are without chandeliers . . . So far as I know you have not delivered one article of furniture contracted for . . . If anyone can point out a more flagrant case of non-fulfillment of contract, I would like to know it." In a parting shot, he concluded, "If you have any organization it seems to me it needs a thorough overhauling. The inconvenience and damage you have put us to is hardly to be estimated in dollars and cents."

In addition, since Allom had requested payment for certain items, Frick replied, "It seems to me it would be very unsafe to pay your firm for the furnishings before they are delivered." He commented on the fact that although he received a cable that Allom was sailing from London "to give this work his personal attention . . . [Mr. Allom] so far as I am advised . . . has not sailed yet."

Frick then turned his attention to Elsie de Wolfe. On Christmas Eve 1914, to assuage her concern that unsuitable objects were being placed in the house, he assured her, "It is true there are some things now being placed in the house that are unsatisfactory, but that is only tempo-rary, — they will be worked out as we find the right things to take their places." Always playing to de Wolfe's vanity by complimenting her on her "wonderfully good taste," Frick questioned her on the date of purchase of a fine Louis XVI commode and the price of some carved, gilt side chairs, and also chastised her, "you are still all wrong on values, and the shrewd art dealer is always around to take advantage of that, — a little weakness of yours."

Finally, on February 8, 1915, Frick felt compelled to clarify their financial arrangements: "I am willing to pay you five (5%) percent upon any item purchased below or up to twenty-five thousand ($25,000) dollars, and upon such sum by which it may exceed that sum, — but not to exceed fifty thousand ($50,000) dollars — the sum of three percent (3%); and upon any sum by which it may exceed fifty thousand ($50,000) dollars, two and one-half (2½%) percent. Where the purchases of a set of rugs, vases or suite of furniture, etc., the set to count as one item . . . any and all purchases to have my approval in writing." In the same letter he instructed that she "undertake not to accept directly or indirectly any commission, trade discount, cash discount or any other remuneration of any kind, other than your fee from me, and will use all your knowledge and means to purchase to my advantage, both artistically and financially; any and all purchases to have my approval in writing."

Upset because she felt Frick did not trust her, de Wolfe was quick to express her concern. Frick was equally quick to reassure: "That we desire to check your bill and get all the information we could for our records . . . in order to have a complete history of what goes into this house, should not have left on your mind the impression that you were in an atmosphere of distrust . . . In justice to myself, I must say that I do not think you in the whole course of your business have been entrusted so fully as you have in this transaction. Why you are so unduly sensitive is a mystery to me, for the reason that it seems to me I have been frankness itself." In this same letter of March 15, 1915, Frick continued to pander and chastise in his habitual way: "Your taste is unquestionable, but you certainly are a very poor buyer, and it is rarely that I have found that you secured anything much less than the price asked you, and your experience really should have taught you ere this, that great discounts can be secured, especially where the customer is willing to pay cash."

Even so, Frick was more than willing to pay top dollar when circumstances required it. Just weeks earlier, he had paid Duveen $1.25 million for Jean-Honoré Fragonard's panels *The Progress of Love,* from J. P. Morgan's estate sale. The works originally had been commissioned in 1771 by Madame du Barry for a new dining pavilion in the garden of her château at Louveciennes. The purchase of these elaborate panels also required that Frick remodel the recently completed drawing room. Determined to have the finest French room possible, Frick reminded Duveen that the panels were to be put in place "without charge" and gave him a deadline: "Much as I wish Fragonard Room perfect success in every detail In pure French style and when finished to be beyond the criticism of any French expert I must beg of you have room completely fixed here by November First at very latest and I think by unremitting attention and your personal attendance in Paris from time to time you will accomplish this." Additionally, as vanloads of furniture arrived from Duveen, Frick wrote a hasty letter to Elsie de Wolfe about Adelaide's bedroom: "Please arrange to have that room completed in blue as per your samples. If Mrs. Frick does not like it after it is finished we will change it."

Although few architects and decorators could have so swiftly completed a building of such magnitude and importance as One East Seventieth Street, particularly during wartime, Frick seemed unappreciative and unable to compliment when deserved. Angry at Thomas Hastings, on June 2, 1915, he wrote a stinging letter, spiking a compliment with criticism: "I think the house cost me a great deal more money than it should have on account of your office not having been properly organized, the plans and specifications properly and promptly made. [I] do not find fault with you on that account, because very artistic [people are] generally very poor business men." And in this same letter he quibbled: "If you will remember, you led me to believe the house would not cost over $1,000,000 to $1,300,000, and I am sure it should have been built for at least $250,000 less than it cost had it been properly looked after. All the same we are enjoying it, and there are many features for which we are indebted to you. I think it is a great monument to you, but it is only because I restrained you from excess ornamentation." And in March 1916, he continued to insult. Furious over Hastings's invoice (possibly for the anticipated sculpture gallery), Frick wrote: "I am in receipt of your absurd bill . . . I have some imagination, but it is not sufficient to take in this situation. I do not know how many draughtsmen you have continually employed for the time you mention, but their brain power must have been at a low ebb; they certainly were not overworking themselves."

But everyone was working very hard for Henry Clay Frick. After his purchase of the $500,000 François Boucher panels entitled *The Arts and Sciences,* Duveen had to redo Adelaide Frick's boudoir, already decorated by de Wolfe. The Pittsburgh projects also were nearing completion. Frick rented space in the Oliver Building so he could monitor the progress of the William Penn Hotel and the Union Arcade. On March 9, 1916, after delays caused by strikes — and Frick's counsel to his subordinates to "do very little talking and keep [their] eye on the ball" — the William Penn Hotel opened its doors. Initially, 625 men worked on the steel riveting alone, and this number increased to 700 as work progressed. The building — the first three stories were made of granite faced in Indiana limestone and the upper stories of red brick with terra-cotta ornamentation — was hailed by *National Architect* magazine as "not only abreast of, but ahead of the times." Among other amenities, each room boasted a private bathroom, a telephone, furniture in the Louis XVI and Adam styles, and an electric clock attached to a master timepiece that gave Western Union time. One hundred and fifteen miles of electric wiring snaked through the walls, while the telephone switchboard measured fifty-four feet in length, the largest between New York and Chicago. Other delights included an in-house bakery and a hotel staff of nine hundred. To celebrate the opening, Henry Clay Frick spent the night in the seven-room State Suite, as he had hoped.

Although the Union Arcade was meant to have its opening two months after the William Penn Hotel's, it still was under construction at that time. In 1915, even though Frick was fretting about Allom's job performance, he evidently still trusted and admired Allom's aesthetic taste and judgment. Frick had passed on to Osterling a suggestion from Allom and Duveen that he install dormer windows above the roofline to add height to the building without harming its character. Osterling agreed to the change, and although doing so caused some construction delays, more were caused by Osterling's negligence. He had not hired enough assistants, and those he had hired were working part time on other projects. As a result, when the Union Arcade opened on April 1, 1917, it did so fifteen months behind schedule. Frick refused to pay Osterling the $321,325 architect's fee, but four years later Osterling filed suit against Frick's estate for the money. In 1925 the Pennsylvania Supreme Court upheld a lower court's ruling that Osterling indeed had been negligent and should receive only $109,406.75 plus interest for his efforts.

Legal wrangling aside, the building was hailed as a visual and architectural wonder. The largest arcade in the world — and certainly the finest large-scale interior in Pittsburgh — it then was considered a modern expression of the bustling, burgher culture of fifteenth-century northern France and Flanders. The cathedral-like arcade with penthouse towers still contains the main corridor lined with white, terra-cotta galleries; intricate mosaic ceilings; a ten-story rotunda with a circular skylight made of stained glass; four open light courts; and hundreds of shops and office suites. And Frick, now fully recovered from his illness, undoubtedly enjoyed having his twin Pittsburgh projects complete and relished the cachet of walking through his glamorous hotel to the Union Arcade and the Frick Building.

While these new buildings were being celebrated in Pittsburgh, One East Seventieth Street was making news in New York. America by now had entered the war, and when French Field Marshal Joffré came to New York to enlist financial support for his nation's war effort, the Fricks, who had traveled extensively in France and were passionate about its art and culture, moved into the Ritz Hotel so Joffré and his entourage could stay in their house. Frick hosted a dinner at One East Seventieth Street in his honor, and on his departure, Joffré presented Adelaide with a basket of her favorite flowers, American Beauty roses. Later the Fricks offered their home as a first-aid station if such was to become necessary, and after the war, Helen hosted a party on the Fifth Avenue lawn for wounded veterans and their families.

Unfortunately, after all the painstaking attention lavished to such result, Henry Clay Frick would not have long to enjoy his beautiful house, the William Penn Hotel, or the Union Arcade. Within two and a half years of the arcade's opening, and having lived only five years at One East Seventieth Street, Frick contracted ptomaine poisoning. The November 1919 attack either was caused by, or aggravated by, the lobster he ate for lunch — a delicacy that never agreed with him. The attack led to heart failure, and as the month wore on, he entered a fatal decline. During what turned out to be the last month of his life, Frick wandered through the galleries at One East Seventieth Street carrying his blue quilt. Often he gently touched the portrait subjects as if they were children, not paint on a canvas. Bedridden during his final days, Frick, who had spent the last few months updating his account with Duveen, sensed that he was dying and instructed the dealer to remove over one million dollars worth of artworks he had on approval. A few days later, at two A.M. on December 2, 1919, Henry Clay Frick died in his sleep, never having seen his collection without the extra Duveen items, never having seen his final creation. After a short service in the Living Hall and Fragonard Room, his body was placed in the Westmoreland railroad car and taken to Pittsburgh for burial in Homewood Cemetery, near Clayton.

As had been his custom in virtually every aspect of the design and construction of this last great house, Frick took care to arrange for the details governing its use and maintenance upon his death. Four years before, on June 24, 1915, Frick executed his will formalizing his plan to leave One East Seventieth Street and his art collection for the public benefit. He endowed the house and collection with $15 million (today this endowment totals over $300 million) and stipulated that it open to the public as the Frick Collection after Adelaide's death. When she died at Eagle Rock in 1931, their son Childs became president of the board of trustees, John D. Rockefeller Jr. became its chairman, and Helen Frick, although angry and insulted that she had not been given a position on the executive committee (she had been a part of her father's collecting efforts since the age of eight and had been appointed a trustee of the Frick Collection by her father as had her brother and Rockefeller), nevertheless was granted chairmanship of the Art Acquisitions Committee. Then, following a limited design competition, New York's leading architect of the 1930s, John Russell Pope, who was trained at the Ecole des

*Right:* Treasures in the West Gallery awaiting storage in the new vault, May 1933.

Beaux Arts, received the commission to convert the house from a family home into a public facility. In this, Pope was continuing in the Frick tradition of architects who were both classically trained and impressively credentialed. Already Pope had designed the Duveen wing of the British Museum in London and a new sculpture hall for the Tate Gallery. Also among his many commissions were the American Battle Monument at Montfaucon, France, as well as the American Museum of Natural History in New York, the Baltimore Museum of Art, and four prominent buildings in Washington, D.C.: the Temple of the Scottish Rite, the National Gallery, the Jefferson Memorial, and the National Archives.

After chandeliers, furniture, paintings, and porcelains were wrapped in thickly padded white sheeting, construction began on the vault where the many priceless objects would be stored. To prevent theft, all the passageways between the basement and first floor, the stairs, elevators, and corridors were sealed. When the vault was completed, the passageways were opened but resealed once the treasures were placed inside. Four years of drilling through solid granite then commenced, and as the carriageway between Seventieth and Seventy-first Streets and porte cochère were demolished, Pope's Garden Court and the circular Music Room to the east began to take shape. On the south side, the front door – originally perpendicular to Seventieth Street – was moved to face the street. The original pediment by Sherry E. Fry was placed above the new front door, which opened into the new large entrance hall with the Garden Court beyond. On the north side, Henry Clay Frick's business office on Seventy-first

Street and a small building that housed the Frick Art Reference Library were incorporated into the present-day East Gallery and the Oval Room. Helen's library was moved to another house next door that Pope remodeled. The stairway leading from the business office to the basement bowling alley — with its fine iron banisters, marble stairs, and carved wood ceiling — was offered to the University of Pittsburgh's Cathedral of Learning, home of the Henry Clay Frick Fine Arts Department founded by Helen Frick in 1927.

When the Frick Collection opened to the public on Monday, December 16, 1935, policemen and plainclothes detectives surrounded the building and placed themselves strategically around the galleries. A roped pathway guided the visitors through the first-floor rooms, which the press hailed as "a legacy of beauty" with quality "unsurpassed anywhere."

During World War II, the Frick Collection, and especially the Garden Court, became a favorite haunt of those seeking solitude and comfort, although many of the most valuable paintings were removed to a specially constructed, bomb-proof vault in the basement and various windows were boarded up. After the war, the paintings were returned to their galleries. Since Frick's death in 1919, the trustees have increased the number of paintings in the collection by one-third, yet the collection and house feel unaltered. The Pope renovation and additions in 1977 of a reception hall, exhibition galleries on a lower floor, and a garden designed by Russell Page on the Seventieth Street side only have served to enhance what can at once be understood as Henry Clay Frick's last and finest home, as well as his greatest philanthropic gift.

*Left:* Five of Henry Clay Frick's fourteen great-grandchildren dabble in the Garden Court pool on the twentieth anniversary of the opening of the Frick Collection to the public.

*Facing page:* ENTRANCE TO THE CARRIAGEWAY

According to a March 30, 1914 list of contractors for One East Seventieth Street, this driveway gate and a similar one on Seventy-first Street were designed by Carrère & Hastings and fabricated by John Williams, Inc., of New York City, for $13,970. At the time of the Frick commission in 1914, the Williams forge had been in operation for over forty years and largely manufactured the designs of firms such as Carrère & Hastings; McKim, Mead & White; Richard Morris Hunt; Cass Gilbert; Little & Browne; Cottier & Company; and Horace Trumbauer. Work by the Williams concern was familiar to Frick: Horace Trumbauer's design for P. A. B. Widener's cast-bronze entrance doors, vestibule doors, and stair railing; and L. Marcott & Company's cast bronze entrance doors at 640 Fifth Avenue, the Vanderbilt house Frick rented from 1905 until he moved into One East Seventieth Street. These driveway gates were dismantled during the John Russell Pope renovation in 1931–35 and were used by the Childs Fricks in their Long Island garden. Both gates returned to the Frick Collection in the 1970s when Russell Page created the Seventieth Street garden. The smaller gate was used for the new garden. The other was consigned to P. A. Fiebiger, Inc., of New York, for sale.

Sherry Edmundson Fry sculpted the porte cochère pediment. In the 1931–35 renovation, the porte cochère, carriageway, and inner court were demolished and replaced by a new entrance hall with the original Fry portico, the Garden Court, the Music Room, the Oval Room, and the East Gallery.

*Following pages:* The original floor plans by Thomas Hastings for One East Seventieth Street.

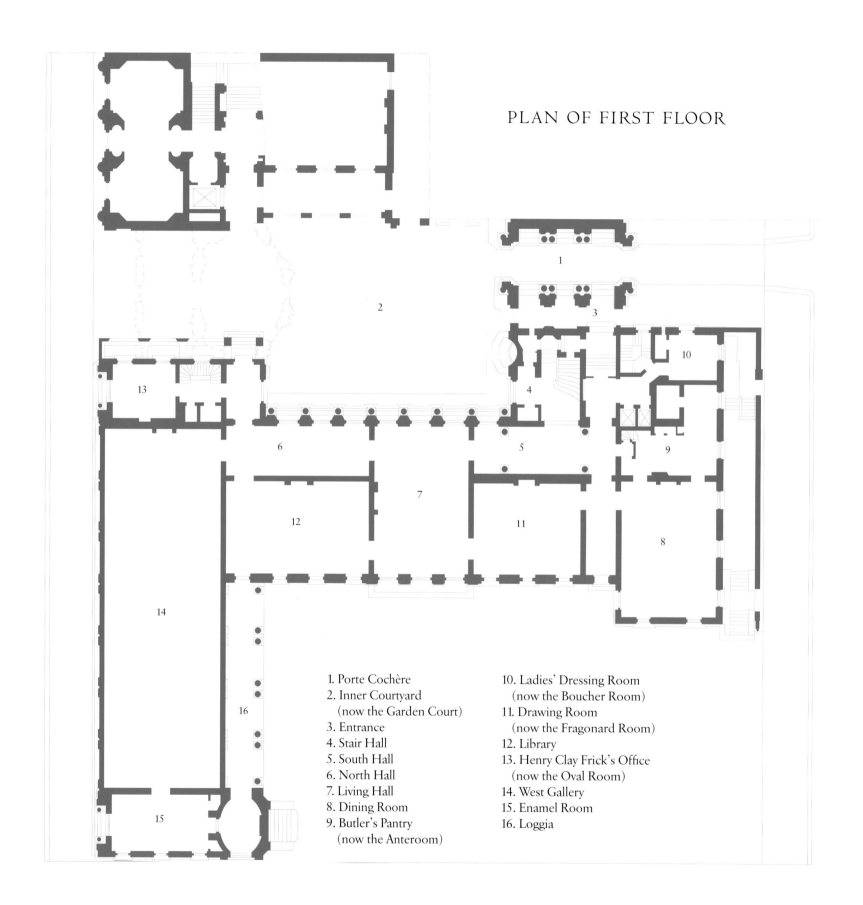

PLAN OF FIRST FLOOR

1. Porte Cochère
2. Inner Courtyard
   (now the Garden Court)
3. Entrance
4. Stair Hall
5. South Hall
6. North Hall
7. Living Hall
8. Dining Room
9. Butler's Pantry
   (now the Anteroom)
10. Ladies' Dressing Room
    (now the Boucher Room)
11. Drawing Room
    (now the Fragonard Room)
12. Library
13. Henry Clay Frick's Office
    (now the Oval Room)
14. West Gallery
15. Enamel Room
16. Loggia

PLAN OF SECOND FLOOR

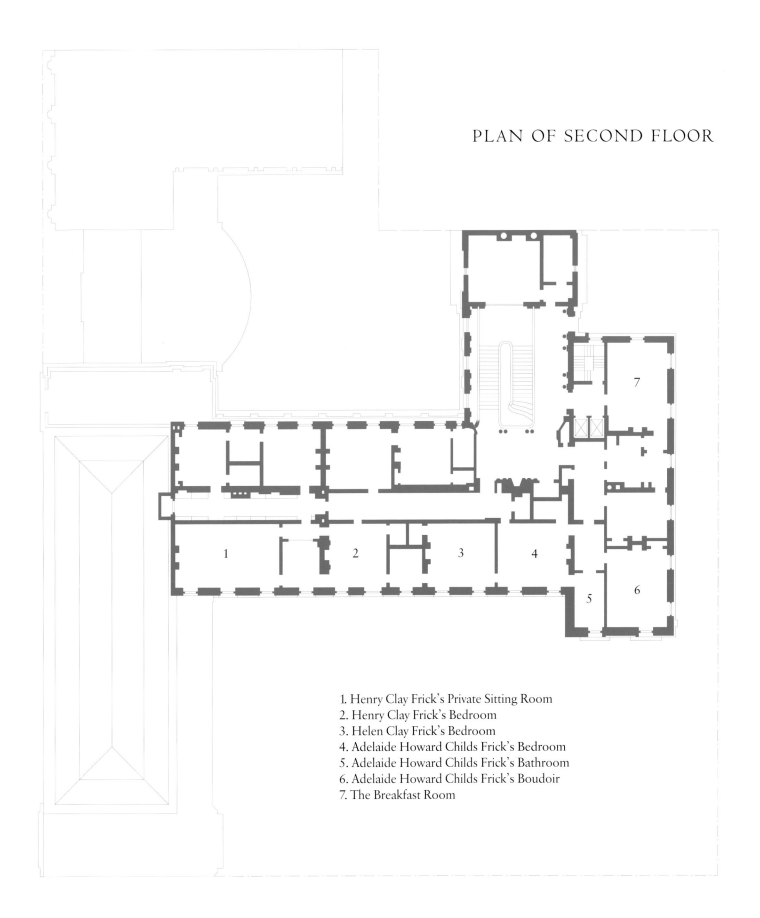

1. Henry Clay Frick's Private Sitting Room
2. Henry Clay Frick's Bedroom
3. Helen Clay Frick's Bedroom
4. Adelaide Howard Childs Frick's Bedroom
5. Adelaide Howard Childs Frick's Bathroom
6. Adelaide Howard Childs Frick's Boudoir
7. The Breakfast Room

*Above and facing page:* THE INNER COURTYARD

The garden vase by Jean-Louis Lemoyne was central to the inner courtyard (now the Garden Court) and represents Henry Clay Frick's first sculpture purchase for One East Seventieth Street. The decorative lattice-work, designed by Carrère & Hastings, was dismantled during the 1931–35 renovation and reworked by architects Newton P. Bevin and Harry O. Milliken into a thirty-foot-high garden pavilion for the Childs Fricks. According to a list of the scrap value of items from the Frick Collection dated January 8, 1934, the Fricks also took the carved marble, stonework, and decorative ornament from the porte cochère and inner court to their Long Island estate.

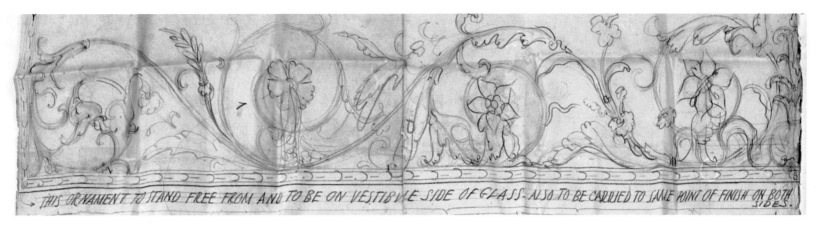

THIS ORNAMENT TO STAND FREE FROM AND TO BE ON VESTIBULE SIDE OF GLASS. ALSO TO BE CARRIED TO SAME POINT OF FINISH ON BOTH SIDES.

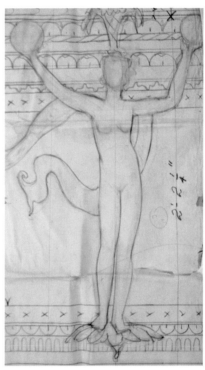

*Facing page:* INTERIOR AND EXTERIOR VESTIBULE DOORS

The wrought-iron grillework on the inner vestibule door and exterior entrance door to One East Seventieth Street was the work of Samuel Yellin. Born in Poland in 1885, Yellin became a master smith by age seventeen. Inspired by the work of medieval and Renaissance craftsmen, he traveled through Europe and studied the history and tradition of ironwork. After emigrating to America in 1906, he established a forge in Philadelphia and in 1911 won his first major commission — the entrance gates for J. P. Morgan's Long Island residence. At the time of the Frick commission in 1913, Yellin was yet to be recognized as the outstanding metal artist of his day. Nor had he yet become the foremost authority on decorative ironwork in the world. In 1913 Yellin largely was teaching metalworking at the Philadelphia Museum School of Industrial Art and satisfying commissions, for reasonable fees, for decorative ironwork in the Philadelphia area. As he labored, he was developing an ornamental style that fit the monumental decoration in architecture then reaching its height in America — a style that soon caught the attention of prominent New York architects such as Cass Gilbert and Carrère & Hastings. By the 1920s, he owned one of the largest collections of antique wrought iron in the world, as well as etchings, paintings, tapestries, and a comprehensive library. Important sources of inspiration for his designs, these collections reinforced one of his many convictions: "It is necessary, that a metalworker

in particular, if he is to deserve the name of craftsman, should not only be able to use the hammer and other tools, but be able to design and understand the history of this noble craft." Yellin further claimed: "A smith cannot busy himself with iron alone, but must be on familiar terms with all his brother crafts at least so far as to understand their close affiliation." By the 1930s, demand for Yellin's work had soared and his forge had become the largest metalworking establishment in the world, employing over two hundred craftsmen from all over the world. Among his many commissions were the Federal Reserve Bank, as well as IBM and the Pierpont Morgan Library in New York; the National Cathedral and Dumbarton Oaks in Washington, D.C.; Yale University; Princeton University; and the University of Pittsburgh. Private clients included R. B. Mellon, A. B. Mellon, Theodore Pitcairn, Harry du Pont, H. H. Flagler, and the Rockefellers.

*This page:* Drawings such as these for the One East Seventieth Street entrance and inner vestibule doors were hung on the wall so Samuel Yellin could check every detail. Those for the Frick commission measure twenty-five by five feet. They served as a guide for Yellin and his craftsmen as they hammered out the work at the anvil. In these details of the inner vestibule door drawings are a crest of flowers, a lintel with a female figure similar to that in Botticelli's *Birth of Venus*, and a decorative door handle.

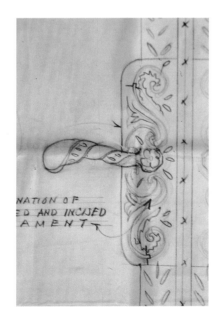

NATION OF
ED AND INCISED
AMENT

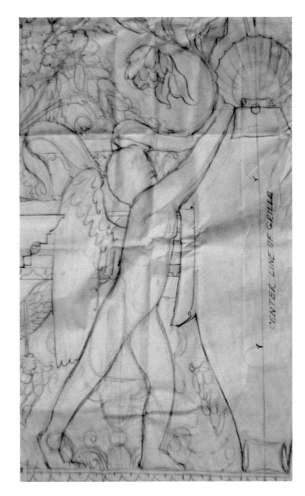

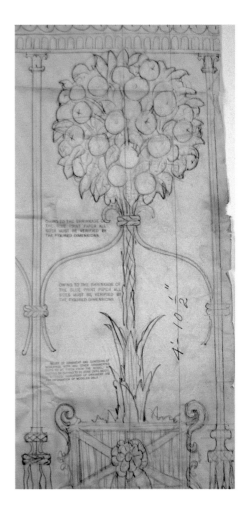

*Facing page and above left:* EXTERIOR ENTRANCE DOOR

Before starting a project, Yellin tried to understand his client's interests and personality. Equally important, Yellin insisted: "What I make must be real, as the material itself." The boy and girl angels above the entrance vestibule door suggest that Yellin may have understood the Fricks' preoccupation with the deaths of their two small children, Martha and Henry Clay Frick Jr. He also seems to have had knowledge of Frick's experience of Martha's lifesaving apparition. The lunette motif of grapes, seeds, and roses alludes to death and resurrection and becomes all the more poignant in knowing that the Fricks affectionately called Martha "Rosebud." References to these deaths can be seen elsewhere in the house. Statues of four children, possible references to the two who lived and the two who died, are above the organ screen, as well as in the pediments surrounding One East Seventieth Street, and in symbolic references within many of Frick's art purchases.

*Above right:* Detail, topiary tree.

*Below right:* Detail, door pull.

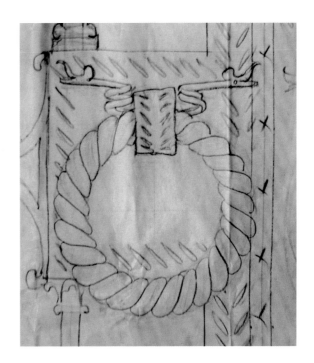

*Above:* The lunette, exterior entrance door.

*Below left:* "Sketch in Iron" for the lunette.

*Below right:* Detail, Cupid's head from full-size drawing of the lunette.

Samuel Yellin described himself as "born with a hammer in [his] hand." Passionate about iron — "a dead metal . . . fun to bring . . . to life" — he nevertheless referred to himself as a blacksmith, not an artist. In confessing his great love of iron, he said: "It is the stuff of which the earth is made. And you can make anything you will. It eloquently responds to the hand, at the bidding of the imagination." As such, Yellin worked iron with "a hammer for a pencil and the red hot iron for the drawing paper." Rather than first making a clay model of his proposed design, he forged what he called "sketches in iron," such as these for the griffin motif above the exterior door opening and the grape motif for the interior vestibule door kick-plate. He insisted: "Iron cannot be modeled in clay . . . Metal can only be suggested on paper, but the actual life, character, and beauty depends on its making. The very best way of working is to make sketches in the actual iron on the anvil and let them serve as the inspiration and character of the work contemplated. Then the drawing can be made . . . There is only one way to make good decorative ironwork and that is with the hammer at the anvil, for in the heat of creation and under the spell of the hammer, the whole conception of a composition is often transformed." Thus, Yellin began a project by forging a sample design directly at the anvil. Then full-size shop drawings were made — fully accurate down to the last bolt or rivet — and hung on the walls of his forge. In this way he could see the project as it would look installed and could study it while he worked. A proponent of the tenets of John Ruskin, William Morris, and Charles Locke Eastlake, Yellin insisted that his work be honest, that joinery be visible, and that the techniques used in crafting the work not be concealed. "The effect of a piece of work," he said, "must be the undisguised appearance of its material and workmanship . . . all of my work is honestly and simply done . . . and the nature of the material is truthfully expressed both in handling and finish."

Henry Clay Frick, a man whose eye for beauty and whose quest to have only the finest and most fashionable in his residences, certainly would have appreciated Samuel Yellin's principles and his craftsmanship — not to mention his drive for perfection. Indeed, "blacksmith" Yellin once described his resolve in terms that Frick would have embraced: "When I go to rest at night, I can hardly sleep because my mind is aswarm with visions of all the gates and grilles and locks and keys I want to do. I verily believe I shall take my hammer with me when I go, and at the gate of Heaven, if I am denied admission, I shall forge my own key."

*Left:* VIEW OF THE GRAND STAIRCASE

At the lower level are the organ console, the Berthoud long-case clock, and *Cologne: The Arrival of a Packet Boat: Evening* by Joseph Mallord William Turner. *The Ocean* by James Abbott McNeill Whistler and *Mother and Children* by Pierre-Auguste Renoir are on the second-floor landing.

*Right:* THE ORGAN CONSOLE, rendering by White, Allom & Company.

The Aeolian pipe organ was installed in 1914. In the fall of 1915, however, the $100,000 organ console designed by Christopher Wren, from a house called the Rows in Chester, England, and marble pedestals for the organ screen still had not been delivered. A letter from Thomas Hastings's office to Henry Clay Frick said that Hastings wanted "this work . . . to be artistically on a par with the best examples of [Frick's] paintings and other art treasures; [so he] cannot afford to hurry the artist in his modeling and endanger the value of the resulting product." In 1915 Frick bought a pair of eighteenth-century French lapis lazuli candelabrum vases with seated female musicians to place beneath the organ screen.

Archer Gibson, the highest salaried organist in America, played for Henry Clay Frick at Eagle Rock and at One East Seventieth Street. Frick purportedly paid him an annual salary of $15,000.

*Right:* THE SOUTH HALL

When the Frick family moved into One East Seventieth Street in November 1914, Henry Clay Frick instructed Roland Knoedler to place his newly acquired *Cologne: The Arrival of a Packet Boat: Evening* and *The Harbor of Dieppe* by Turner in the South Hall. Knoedler did as Frick asked and told him that he had covered the paintings to protect them from construction dust.

*Left:* THE DINING ROOM

The Frick family usually ate lunch and dinner here, and Henry Clay Frick hosted about two formal dinners a week in this room – including the lobster luncheon that initiated his fatal decline. Food was prepared in the hotel-size kitchen in the basement and sent up to the butler's pantry (now the anteroom) in a dumbwaiter. In recent years the Frick Collection has used the dining room for fund-raising dinners.

The painting over the mantel is *The Ladies Sarah and Catherine Bligh* by John Hoppner. The French mantel clock (c. 1765–70) depicts the Triumph of Love over Time and is signed by Ferdinand Berthoud, the same horologist who made the long-case clock at the foot of the staircase. The Louis XVI–style furniture for this room was designed by the London firm of White, Allom & Company.

*Right:* THE DINING ROOM

In this southwest view of the dining room, from left to right are exhibited *Charlotte, Lady Milnes* by George Romney, *Anne, Countess of Clanbrassil* by Sir Anthony Van Dyck, and another Romney – *Countess of Warwick and Her Children.* The Hoppner portrait above the mantel and Romney's *Countess of Warwick* are the only paintings in this room that still hang where Frick placed them.

The silver-gilt wine coolers (c. 1802–4) bear the arms and crest of the earls of Ashburnham; the other two (c. 1811) are by Benjamin and James Smith. Yet to be placed in the dining room are the sensational pair of tall porcelain vases (probably Qianlong) with *famille rose* decoration. Originally at Eagle Rock, they were given to the Frick Collection by Helen Frick in 1958 and can be seen in the southwest and northwest corners of the room.

*Left:* THE FRAGONARD ROOM

The late Paul Mellon remembered having tea as a small boy in this room with Henry Clay Frick and his father, Andrew Mellon, the first overnight guest at One East Seventieth Street. At that time the room was known as the drawing room, and it was in the early eighteenth-century French style. As such, it had a painted wainscot with walls covered in figured red velvet. Large paintings by François Boucher, on approval from Duveen, were displayed. But in 1915 the Boucher paintings were returned and the room entirely remodeled to accommodate the fourteen grand-scale panels entitled *The Progress of Love.* Purchased from the estate of J. P. Morgan by Frick, the panels initially were commissioned from Jean-Honoré Fragonard (thus today's name, the Fragonard Room) by Madame du Barry, mistress of Louis XV, for her garden pavilion at Louveciennes. Rejected by her, they then were installed in a house owned by Fragonard's cousin and later decorated the London residence of J. P. Morgan. On purchasing the Fragonard panels, Frick also spent five million dollars through Duveen for items such as the chimneypiece, furniture, porcelains, and sculpture. They were meant both to complement the Fragonard panels and ensure that the room would be "beyond the criticism of any French expert." When Frick died in 1919, a short service was held for him in this room and the adjoining Living Hall.

The many decorative objects include a marble bust on the mantel by Jean-Antoine Houdon of the comtesse du Cayla dressed as a bacchante, a pair of commodes by Pierre Dupré on either side of the mantel, a French center table with marquetry of trelliswork and quatrefoils upon which rests a Sèvres potpourri vase shaped like a masted ship (one of only a dozen such extant examples), and to the left of this table, a small gilt-bronze guéridon (tripod table) with Sèvres porcelain plaques — a fine example of the Louis XVI period attributed to Martin Carlin. The commode on the south wall is by Gilles Joubert and Roger Lacroix. Purchased for the Fragonard Room in 1915, it was made for Madame Victoire, the daughter of Louis XV; it holds a terra-cotta sculpture by Clodion entitled *Satyr with Two Bacchantes.* To the right of the commode is a c. 1785 French, gilt-bronze guéridon with a lapis lazuli top, bought for this room in 1915.

179

*Right:* THE FRAGONARD ROOM

The pair of console tables on the west wall are of interest. The table on the right is by Jean-Henri Riesener, while the one on the left is a nineteenth-century copy. They display four *famille rose* Qianlong jars, purchased in 1916 for this room. In 1918 Frick bought the Louis XV canapé and fauteuils with Beauvais tapestry covers, by Nicolas Heurtaut, to replace the original suite, deemed too large for the renovated room.

*Right:* THE LIVING HALL

Of all the rooms in the house, the oak-paneled Living Hall perhaps has changed the least from the time Henry Clay Frick and his family lived in One East Seventieth Street. The Fricks retired to this warm, elegant, but spacious room for after-dinner coffee. Often they played cards, read, or just talked about such things as the day's events, their newest acquisition, or the suffragette movement. After the 1931 renovation, John D. Rockefeller Jr. (appointed a trustee of the Frick Collection by the terms of Henry Clay Frick's will and chairman of the Frick Collection board of trustees) wanted to replace the family's early twentieth-century sofa and armchairs in the Louis XIV style with finer pieces. Although Rockefeller had offered advice to Frick about the construction of Eagle Rock and One East Seventieth Street, Helen Frick felt that in this case he was encroaching on Frick family territory. She prevented the removal of the furniture and battled with him, and her brother Childs, for nearly forty years on acquisition policy and Rockefeller's intended bequest to the Frick Collection of his art objects. Although a 1948 court ruling gave the Frick Collection the right to accept the Rockefeller gifts, and other gifts from the public, Helen, a scholar and collector in her own right, as well as a vital part of her father's highly personal collecting decisions from the age of eight, was infuriated. She believed that the Rockefeller objects did not meet the high standard set by her father and felt that Rockefeller's artworks would destroy the sanctity, purity, and genius of her father's one-man effort. When Rockefeller died in 1960, and his artworks entered the collection, Helen, then in her seventies, resigned as a trustee. She, however, largely had succeeded in thwarting Childs's and Rockefeller's plans: only three of the hundreds of Rockefeller items entered the collection, and one of the most appealing aspects of the Frick Collection remains the all-Frick, homelike atmosphere that Helen fought so hard to preserve.

The paintings are displayed today exactly as Frick originally placed them. *St. Jerome* by El Greco is over the mantel, flanked by two portraits by Hans Holbein the Younger: *Sir Thomas More* on the left and *Thomas Cromwell* on the right (note the photograph of Henry Clay Frick beneath the painting).

Among the many sumptuous decorative objects still in place from when the Fricks lived at One East Seventieth Street is a pair of chests flanking the mantel. Each has a rare panel of Japanese lacquer with asymmetrical designs created by two members of the famous Van Reisen Burgh French cabinetmaking family — Bernard II and Bernard III. A marquetry bureau plat from the workshop of André-Charles Boulle can be seen behind the sofa. The central sculpture is an eighteenth-century copy of a bronze marine nymph by Stoldo Lorenzi, now in the Studiolo of the Palazzo Vecchio in Florence.

*Left:* THE LIVING HALL

In the center of the south wall of the Living Hall is *St. Francis in the Desert* by Giovanni Bellini, a magnificent painting known to have been one of Frick's favorites. Frick could be found sitting in a chair, alternately reading and gazing at it. To the left of the Bellini is *Portrait of a Man in a Red Cap* and to the right, *Portrait of Pietro Aretino,* both by Titian.

Against the south wall stands a pair of nineteenth-century commodes en tombeau that are English copies of André-Charles Boulle's "sarcophagus" or tomb chests at Versailles. There is a photograph of Henry Clay Frick on the right commode. Against the east wall is a pair of octagonal pedestals from the workshop of Boulle, each holding a superb porcelain covered jar (probably Qianlong) with *famille rose* decoration on a black ground. Upon the large, moss green carpet with a floral border lies a smaller, orange-red Persian rug from the second half of the sixteenth century.

185

*Facing page:* THE NORTH HALL

The North Hall feels empty in this c. 1931 photograph largely because the many posthumous additions to Frick's collection are yet to be made. In fact, one-third of the paintings in the Frick Collection were added after Frick's death. Still to come in the North Hall are such treasures as *Portrait of the Comtesse d'Haussonville* by Jean-Auguste-Dominique Ingres and *The Portal of Valenciennes* by Jean-Antoine Watteau. The former painting is now exhibited above the blue marble console table. Purchased by Frick in 1915, the table, according to *The Frick Collection: A Tour,* was "one of the costliest and most magnificent pieces of furniture produced in France in the late eighteenth century." It was made by François-Joseph Belanger, Jean-François-Thérèse Chalgrin, and Pierre Gouthière for the duchesse de Mazarin expressly for the grand salon of her Paris house on the quai Malaquais.

The various portrait busts include the 1922 bust of Henry Clay Frick by the American sculptor Malvina Hoffman, given to the Frick Collection by Helen Frick in 1935. The marble figures on either side of the doorway also were purchased by Helen. With monumental works of the Italian Renaissance a great rarity, the figures were deemed by her advisor to be "absolutely wonderful . . . unbelievably rare." Even more exciting, they were sold to the collection as the work of the famed Italian painter Simone Martini, who was "unknown" as a sculptor. Within four years, however, the marbles were found to be fakes made by the master copyist Alceo Dossena and sold as originals by an Italian dealer named Volpi. This purchase was a rare mistake on Helen's part, but she found herself in good company. When the news of the forgeries broke in 1928, the list of others who had been duped included the Metropolitan Museum of Art and the Cleveland Art Museum, as well as museums in Munich and Berlin. So other collectors would not be similarly deceived, Helen gathered photographs of all the Dossena forgeries for her fledgling Frick Art Reference Library — then located in a building where the Frick Collection East Gallery is today. On February 8, 1933, the director of the Frick Collection, Mortimer Clapp, offered the fakes "for study purposes" to the University of Pittsburgh. They are now on view in the Henry Clay Frick Fine Arts Building, an Italian Renaissance cloister built by Helen in the early 1960s to house the Nicholas Lochoff frescoes — facsimiles of Italian Renaissance originals — sold to Helen as such by Bernard Berenson.

*Above:* FIFTH AVENUE GARDEN

The windows of the Living Hall and library look out toward Central Park across the terrace designed by Thomas Hastings. Unique to Fifth Avenue houses, the recessed terrace gives One East Seventieth Street a pastoral feel. A black-and-white mosaic path made of river pebbles connecting the Fifth Avenue wings at the south and north is most likely a reference to Henry Clay Frick's Masonic ties. In the Masonic tradition, a candidate for the Third Degree or Master Mason swears his oath on a black-and-white mosaic path. Only a Master Mason may walk on this path — symbol of death and rebirth. The loggia archway leading to the Enamel Room may have been symbolic of the Royal Arch Degree — a degree conferred on the candidate after he has become a Master Mason and before he "enters" the Temple.

*Left:* THE LIBRARY

Henry Clay Frick used this oak-paneled room almost as much as the Living Hall, his office, and his second-floor sitting room. When in the 1916 Morgan estate sale Frick bought the many bronzes and porcelains "to acquire warmth" for the house, the waist-high bookshelves permitted their effortless display – and provided Frick with the easy access he needed. When his grandchildren visited, Frick allowed them to play with the smaller bronzes on the library floor. A voracious but slow reader, Frick kept his most important books in this room, and Allom designed special tooled-leather pads to protect them from dust. The Allom-designed library table contains *The Book of Wealth* – a history of riches commencing with the pharaohs and including Henry Clay Frick. The preface reads: "Wealth in its nobler aspect is not an unworthy theme. If, as it is written, it is hard for a rich man to enter the kingdom of heaven, it may be a still more difficult task for the poor man."

The paintings are, from left to right, *Mortlake Terrace* by Joseph Mallord William Turner, *Mrs. Charles Hatchett* and *Sarah, Lady Innes* by Thomas Gainsborough, and *Julia, Lady Peel* by Sir Thomas Lawrence.

*Following pages:* Sir Charles Allom designed most of the library furniture, and Frick often took naps on the sofa beneath *Miss Mary Edwards* by William Hogarth – particularly during his final days. In 1943, Helen Frick gave the Frick Collection the Danish-born John C. Johansen's *Henry Clay Frick,* now on view above the library mantel and framed by exquisite wood carving by Abraham Miller. The Hogarth was moved to the dining room where it now is displayed. To the left of the mantel can be seen Turner's *Antwerp: Van Goyen Looking Out for a Subject. Salisbury Cathedral* by John Constable is flanked by two portraits by Sir Joshua Reynolds: *Selina, Lady Skipwith* on the left and *Elizabeth, Lady Taylor* on the right.

*Left:* THE WEST GALLERY

This room — one and a half stories high, thirty-five by one hundred feet — has forest-green velvet on the walls, a heavy entablature, a coffered ceiling, and an extensive amount of marble, all meant to evoke the Italian Renaissance and antiquity. A classical chamber, it contains paintings, bronzes, and with the exception of the modern sofas and chairs seen in this photograph, a fine collection of primarily sixteenth-century Italian furniture: three large tables; four pairs of walnut chests, called cassoni, that evoke classical sarcophagi and were used as "hope chests" for brides' trousseaux, as well as for storage or seating; and numerous "Savonarola" chairs, named after the Florentine reformer-monk.

In Frick's day the West Gallery was the largest private art gallery in New York. And it was high-tech. Duveen and Allom fitted the room with a special electrical system that illuminated each painting by an individual spotlight concealed in the glass ceiling, directed so the light fell only on the canvas. With the frame and surrounding wall lost in shadow, the portraits took on what Frick's secretary, James Howard Bridge, described as "a weird semblance of life." William Rieder, curator of European sculpture and decorative arts at the Metropolitan Museum of Art, also notes, in *A Charmed Couple: The Art and Life of Walter and Matilda Gay,* that Matilda commented on the effects of this lighting in her diary. In 1926–28 Helen Frick commissioned Walter Gay to paint an interior scene of both the Living Hall and the Fragonard Room. The couple visited Helen Frick at One East Seventieth Street during this time, and Matilda wrote of their after-dinner visit to the West Gallery: "All the light was extinguished, with the exception of the special lights over the pictures; so that the pictures stared out of the gloom at us. This gave the effect of projections on the screen; the masterpieces therefore lost the quality of painting and looked like ghosts."

Frick had experienced the apparition of his deceased daughter Martha when Alexander Berkman tried to assassinate him during the 1892 Homestead Steel Strike. He never resolved the child's death, nor did he recover from the experience of Martha's life-saving reappearance from the dead. Frick is known to have had a mystical relationship to his paintings and often would sit alone at night, in the dark of the West Gallery, gazing at these paintings with their mysterious glow, perhaps remembering the people from his past that the portrait subjects may have recalled. Many visitors to the gallery claimed that the special lighting effects did cause changes in the portrait subjects' expressions, making them seem alive. Helen Frick remembered in "Grandfather," a memoir she wrote for Henry Clay Frick's grandchildren: "[He] took so much joy in his paintings and loved changing them around . . . I love to think of him in that beautiful room [the West Gallery] — of his wonderful appreciation and understanding of everything there, and the accuracy of his memory when he recounted little incidents connected with the different pictures and how he came to acquire them."

*Right:* THE WEST GALLERY

In Frick's day, the paintings were "skied," or double-hung – a practice no longer employed in the West Gallery. Three Spanish paintings hang on the east wall of the West Gallery: *The Forge* by Francisco de Goya y Lucientes, *King Philip IV of Spain* by Diego Rodríguez de Silva y Velázquez, and *Vincenzo Anastagi* by El Greco. The photograph of Henry Clay Frick on the table is a reminder of his habit, during his fatal decline, of sleeping on the sofa beneath *Philip IV.* During the 1931 renovation, the fireplace was removed – as was Frick's office on the other side of the wall – and archways to the new Oval Room and East Gallery installed.

To the far right in this photograph, on the north wall, are exhibited *Mr. James Cruikshank* by Sir Henry Raeburn; *Mistress and Maid* and *Girl Interrupted at Her Music* by Johannes Vermeer; *Margareta Snyders* and *James, Seventh Earl of Derby, His Lady and Child* by Sir Anthony Van Dyck; *Officer and Laughing Girl* by Vermeer; *River Scene* by Aelbert Cuyp; *Portrait of a Young Artist,* then considered to be by Rembrandt van Rijn, as well as his *Polish Rider* and *Self-Portrait; River Scene: Men Dragging a Net* by Salomon van Ruysdael; and *Portrait of a Painter* by Frans Hals.

The west wall of the gallery exhibits a pair of majestic works by Paolo Veronese. To the left of the door is *Allegory of Virtue and Vice,* and to the right is *Allegory of Wisdom and Strength.* In the 1931 renovation an archway replaced the door into "Mr. Frick's Room." It matches the new archways connecting the Oval Room and the East Gallery.

194

*Left:* "Mr. Frick's Room" (The Enamel Room)

The original purpose of this room is unknown. Frick apparently used it often because Helen Frick recorded in her memoir, "Grandfather," that he loved to sit in front of the Enamel Room windows. There he could watch the way people walked down the street, look out for a "beauty," or marvel at the way the traffic came in bunches. The Limoges enamels – purchased by Frick in 1916 from the estate of J. P. Morgan – were executed between the early sixteenth century and mid-seventeenth century and are among the finest in the United States. The furniture, largely sixteenth-century French, also was acquired in 1916.

The paintings shown in this c. 1931 photograph are largely posthumous additions made by the Frick Collection trustees. *The Annunciation* by Fra Filippo Lippi hangs in the northwest corner, a 1924 purchase by the trustees. On the same wall, in the northeast corner, two paintings known as "the twins" are exhibited one above the other. In 1907 Henry Clay Frick acquired the top painting – a fifteenth-century Burgundian Pietà. Helen Frick purchased the lower painting, a Pietà from the School of Konrad Witz, in or around 1926 and took pleasure from the fact that hers was deemed the original and the finer of the two paintings. In 1960, when the artworks bequeathed by John D. Rockefeller Jr. were accepted by the Frick Collection and Helen resigned as trustee, she loaned the collection her Pietà, providing that Rockefeller's works never be placed on exhibition at the Frick Collection. The trustees agreed and the objects were sent to the Princeton University Art Gallery. But on Helen's death, the trustees reclaimed the Rockefeller bequest, and now the three items are on display: two marble busts in the North Hall and *The Crucifixion* by Piero della Francesca in the Enamel Room. "The twins" now reside in the anteroom of the Frick Collection, formerly One East Seventieth Street's butler's pantry.

Exhibited in this room today is *The Temptation of Christ on the Mountain* by Duccio di Buoninsegna, a 1927 addition by the trustees. The oldest work of art in the collection – and one of the finest – it was painted between 1308 and 1311. The trustees agreed to its acquisition when Helen Frick offered them a quid pro quo: she would give the collection a companion piece – her $35,000 *Christ Bearing the Cross* by Barna da Siena (now exhibited in the anteroom) – if they purchased the Duccio.

197

*Facing page and right:* HENRY CLAY FRICK'S OFFICE

Originally this room was located behind the east wall of the West Gallery. Access to the office was gained through a small passageway leading to the North Hall. Often Frick would leave his office, stand in the North Hall, and peek at guests touring the West Gallery. The office was demolished in the 1931 renovation, as was the building to its east where Helen housed the Frick Art Reference Library. In the reconstruction, the library, office, and carriageway were reworked into the present East Gallery, Oval Room, Music Room, and Garden Court. During this remodeling, the fireplace on the east wall of the West Gallery was removed and an archway installed in its place.

The furniture and cabinets in this room were not period pieces. The paintings, however, are among the finest in Henry Clay Frick's collection. Frick chose *George Washington* by Gilbert Stuart for the overmantel. *Lady Meux* by James Abbott McNeill Whistler was displayed to the left of this mantel, and his *Mrs. Frederick R. Leyland* to the right.

Behind Frick's desk was another Whistler, *Miss Rosa Corder,* and most probably his *Robert, Comte de Montesquiou-Fezensac* was exhibited beside her. On either side of the doorway can be seen portraits by Francisco de Goya y Lucientes, *An Officer* and *Doña María Martínez de Puga.*

*Above:* THE SECOND-FLOOR LANDING

Henry Clay Frick moved into One East Seventieth Street in 1914; among the many acquisitions he made that year was *Mother and Children* by Pierre-Auguste Renoir. He placed the painting at the entrance to the family's private quarters. The two strawberry-haired girls who seem to walk toward the viewer only could have served as a sad reminder of what life would have been like if his daughter Martha had lived. Frick exhibited *The Ocean* by James Abbott McNeill Whistler over the mantel and placed a Louis XV–style canapé with a Gobelins tapestry cover against the stair railing.

The canapé is part of a ten-piece suite purchased in 1914 for what is now the Fragonard Room. The suite cost Frick approximately $250,000, one of his most expensive furniture acquisitions to date. The tapestry covers originally were mounted onto eighteenth-century English chair frames of gilded wood. Although these were among the most important frames of their period, Frick had new chairs made in the Louis XV style for the tapestry covers. When he acquired the Fragonard panels in 1915, however, the style and scale of the remounted suite were no longer appropriate for

the redesigned room. So in 1918, he replaced the suite with one acquired from Duveen: three canapés and four fauteuils with Beauvais tapestry covers by Nicolas Heurtaut, one of the most important French chairmakers of the eighteenth century. Although Frick offered the remounted suite to Edward T. Stotesbury of Philadelphia for $250,000, the collector declined and it remains in the Frick Collection, though not in the Fragonard Room.

*Right:* THE SECOND-FLOOR HALL

Elsie de Wolfe decorated this hall and all the bedrooms it served in the Fricks' family quarters. The cove lighting was one of her many accents. The ceiling, commissioned by de Wolfe, was painted by Robert Twachtman. The chairs are *en suite* with the canapé on the second-floor landing, and the rare Louis XV wrought-iron console (now on display in the anteroom) is an Elsie de Wolfe purchase from the Paris collection formed by the fourth marquess of Hertford. The only identifiable work of art in this photograph is *Perseus Rescuing Andromeda* by Giovanni Battista Tiepolo. Records at M. Knoedler & Company document this as Helen Frick's purchase in 1916. At the time of the acquisition Helen was doing provenance work on her father's collection. In the photograph, the painting is displayed outside her bedroom door.

*Above:* THE BREAKFAST ROOM

This room — now an office, as are all the rooms on the second and third floors of the Frick Collection — has a southern exposure. Friendly and warm, it was decorated by Sir Charles Allom. The marble mantel is George III. The chairs are in the Queen Anne style; the table is an invention; the consoles are Edwardian; and the side tables with gilt-bronze ormolu are in the Louis XVI style.

The damask-covered walls held many paintings recalling Frick's Mennonite farming heritage. Over the mantel is *The Village of Becquigny* by Pierre-

Etienne-Théodore Rousseau. On the south wall, Frick displayed *Woman Sewing by Lamplight* by Jean-François Millet. It was purchased in 1906, a year after his mother's death. To the right of the mantel is *A Pasture in Normandy* by Constant Troyon, and on the north wall are two of Frick's early purchases, *The Washerwoman* by Charles-François Daubigny and *The Pond* by Jean-Baptiste-Camille Corot. The east wall also exhibited a Corot, *The Boatman of Mortefontaine.* Quite probably Frick's other Corots — *The Lake* and *Ville-d'Avray* — also were in this room.

*Above:* ADELAIDE HOWARD CHILDS FRICK'S
BEDROOM

Adelaide Frick's bedroom was on the west side of the house overlooking Fifth Avenue. For the wife of her wealthy client, Elsie de Wolfe created a simple but luxurious room in the Louis XVI style. The curtains of blue and cream silk were dramatically sculpted by de Wolfe to enhance the design. The curtain material also was used to upholster the bed and the carved, gilt-wood bed canopy purchased by de Wolfe. According to the c. 1931 inventory the bed and canopy came from the court of Marie Louise, second wife of Napoleon Bonaparte – not from the court of Marie Antoinette as previously thought. The headboards and footboards were further enhanced by silk swags, trim, and tassels; the canopy with silk trim and an outer fringe of lace. The three-fold screen was covered in

blue and cream petit point. The large armchair and the miniature chair next to the bed were covered in gray-blue damask; the chaise longue in a gray-blue, narrow striped velvet; and the two gilt-wood carved side chairs in blue-striped, flowered silk. The long, carved wood bench before the fireplace was painted gray and covered in blue and yellow petit point. The ceiling was painted in the Louis XVI style, and a blue, beige, and off-white Chinese rug covered the floor.

Elsie de Wolfe's purchases for this room included an important Louis XVI gilt-wood mirror and a marquetry commode with a marble top, as well as a Louis XVI secrétaire documented in the 1931 inventory as "by Schmidt." Duveen bought a Louis XV tapestry banquette that stood in front of the secrétaire, and in

1914 de Wolfe acquired, from the Paris collection formed by the fourth marquess of Hertford, the bedside table simulating a set of books, probably by Jean-Henri Riesener. After Adelaide Frick's death and the conversion of One East Seventieth Street to a public facility, Helen Frick sent the commode, mirror, and bedside table to Clayton in Pittsburgh. She gave other pieces to family members, but reserved the bed (without its canopy) for her New York apartment at the Westbury Hotel.

For the most part, engravings, prints, and family photographs decorated Adelaide's bedroom. A posthumous portrait of her husband, Henry Clay Frick, and *Portrait of Martha Frick* by Théobald Chartran were the only paintings.

*Left:* ADELAIDE HOWARD CHILDS FRICK'S
BOUDOIR

Adelaide's boudoir, like her bedroom, was strictly in
the French taste. Largely decorated by de Wolfe, and
later Duveen, it was an all-blue room in the Louis XV
style with a south-southwest exposure. It boasted eight
canvas panels by François Boucher entitled *The Arts
and Sciences.* Thought to have been commissioned
by Madame de Pompadour, mistress of Louis XV,
for an octagonal room in the Château de Crécy near
Chartres, they depict children humorously occupied
with architecture, painting, sculpture, hydraulics,
chemistry, astronomy, poetry, music, fowling, horticulture, fishing, hunting, singing, and dancing, as well as
children expressing comedy and tragedy. In addition,
the room contained various Louis XV–style chairs
covered in blue silk brocade, blue velvet, or yellow
silk brocade; a blue velvet rug graced the floor. The
Riesener bureau plat was purchased by Elsie de Wolfe
from Sir John Murray Scott's estate and is one of the
finest examples of this cabinetmaker's work. Upon
it rests a pair of ormolu candlesticks attributed to
Etienne Martincourt. The commode against the
north wall is attributed to André-Louis Gilbert. Helen
inherited from her mother the Vincennes and Sèvres
porcelain seen throughout the room, including the
water jug and basin on the commode. Feeling that the
porcelains always had been part of this room, she gave
them to the Frick Collection. Also on the commode is
*Bust of a Young Girl,* a nineteenth-century work after
François-Jacques-Joseph Saly purchased in 1914 for
the Fricks by Duveen. The bust is repeated in the
Boucher panel entitled *Painting and Sculpture* to
the left of the door. The built-in glass cabinet on the
west wall contains Sèvres and Vincennes porcelain
purchased by Duveen. A dressing and writing table by
Louis-Nöel Malle stands to the left of the cabinet.

Pictures of Henry Clay Frick appear twice in this
photograph: on the Gilbert commode, beneath the
panel *Fowling and Horticulture;* and on the dressing
and writing table on the west wall. The room also
contained a c. 1919 picture of a little girl, on a bench
probably designed by Elsie de Wolfe. The picture was
of the Fricks' eldest grandchild and Adelaide Frick's
namesake, Adelaide Frick (Blanchard).

During the 1931–35 reconstruction, the Boucher
panels were taken downstairs and reassembled in the
area formerly used as the ladies' reception room.
Today many of the furnishings in these photographs
can be seen in the reconstructed Boucher Room, but
period furniture now replaces those pieces formerly in
the Louis XV style. A posthumous portrait of Adelaide
Frick by the famous American watercolorist Elizabeth
Shoumatoff is a 1959 gift to the collection from Helen
Frick and today is in the Boucher Room.

205

*Above:* ADELAIDE HOWARD CHILDS FRICK'S
BATHROOM

Elsie de Wolfe also created an all-blue bathroom for
Adelaide. It contained a glass-topped dressing table in
the Louis XVI style. On it can be seen Adelaide's
fifteen-piece set of crystal toilet articles. A three-fold
mirror, clothes stand, stool, wastebasket, and clothes
hamper — all lacquered in blue and gold to match the
dressing table — completed the decor. For the window
treatment de Wolfe employed cream silk shades
trimmed in ribbon and fringe that were sheer enough
for sunlight to shine through.

*Above:* HELEN CLAY FRICK'S BEDROOM

Helen Frick's bedroom was between her mother's and her father's rooms, in the center of the building's western facade. Although the photographs show an austere room with few precious furnishings, it probably was more cheerful and luxurious than it appears. Entirely a creation of Elsie de Wolfe, the predominately green and pink room, with a bathroom to match, was decorated with curtains and valances of green-and-rose-figured silk taffeta. A dressing table with an Edwardian mirror, probably made for the room, boasted skirting of green silk with an appliquéd band of roses. The chair to the left of the fireplace was covered in gray-green velvet while a sofa, the armchair to the right of the mantel, and two fauteuils that seem to match those

purchased by Elsie de Wolfe for Adelaide's bedroom were covered in a gray-and-rose-figured velvet stripe. Of interest are the eighteenth-century satinwood table to the left of the fireplace, the Louis XVI–style commode to the left of the bed that may have been made for the room, a Louis XV kingwood and tulipwood three-drawer table to the right of the bed, and a carved and gilded Louis XVI bed. The c. 1931 inventory reveals that after Henry Clay Frick's death in 1919 Helen moved her father's bed into her own room and placed hers in his room. Pictures of her father are ever-present, as are family photographs and engravings of eighteenth-century ladies after portraits by Sir Joshua Reynolds, George Romney, and Sir Thomas Lawrence.

*Left:* HENRY CLAY FRICK'S BEDROOM

Although French eighteenth-century classicism largely prevailed at One East Seventieth Street, Henry Clay Frick's bedroom was decidedly eighteenth-century English. The warm, masculine room had mauve brocade curtains and English walnut paneling. Among its treasures were a majestic George III tester bed; an elaborate Chinese Chippendale-style, late eighteenth-century carved mirror with ho-ho birds, later taken to Eagle Rock by Helen Frick and now in the Frick Art Museum at Clayton, Pittsburgh; a George I stool at the end of the bed; and a double-domed, George I japanned secretary with mirrored doors, also taken to Eagle Rock by Helen. She later gave the secretary to the Frick Art Museum, Pittsburgh; it is now on display in the English Gallery at the Metropolitan Museum of Art in New York. The two paintings Frick reserved for his bedroom were *Lady Hamilton as Nature* by George Romney and a studio copy of *Miss Louisa Murray* by Sir Thomas Lawrence. A diary kept by Helen recalling her father's fatal decline reveals that Frick would stare first at *Lady Hamilton* and then roll to his right side and stare at *Miss Louisa Murray.* These portraits may well have reminded Frick of his deceased daughter, Martha, whose death he never was able to resolve. The bathroom had a white rug with green border designed by de Wolfe and a black-and-gold lacquer dressing table.

209

*Left:* HENRY CLAY FRICK'S PRIVATE SITTING ROOM

The c. 1931 photograph of this room, decorated by
Sir Charles Allom, indicates that it was similar in func-
tion to a contemporary family room. Here Helen
played the piano for her father or she and her parents
either read or played cards. The original curtains –
made in April 1914 of Allom's signature red velvet
and lined, interlined, and finished with a fringe – cost
$273. Three pairs of cream silk undercurtains costing
$326 accompanied them. The c. 1931 inventory states
that these curtains were found in wooden boxes in
the attic, thus the curtains seen in this photograph
probably are replacements. Most of the furniture –
a Louis XV bureau plat, the George III chairs at the
desk and card table, and an Edwardian wing chair –
had been used by the Fricks in the art gallery at 640
Fifth Avenue. Allom designed a special panel above
the mantel for El Greco's *Purification of the Temple*.
To the left of the mantel is *Motherhood* by Eugène
Carrière. On the west wall hung *The Rehearsal* by
Edgar Degas (left) and *Fishing Boats Entering Calais
Harbor* by Turner. This room also held many posthu-
mous additions: a framed photograph of Henry Clay
Frick II; a rendering of the Fragonard Room by Walter
Gay, commissioned by Helen Frick in 1928 and now
in the Frick Art Museum in Pittsburgh; *Madonna and
Child* by Andrea di Bartolo, purchased by Helen in
1925 and now in the Frick Art Reference Library; and
golfing photographs on either side of *The Bullfight* by
Edouard Manet.

Although no photograph exists of Helen Frick's
personal library, it was located across the hall from
her father's sitting room. The room provided space for
Helen to work on the provenance of her father's art
collection. It was, therefore, the precursor to the Frick
Art Reference Library, founded by Helen in 1920
shortly after her father's death. Decorated by Elsie
de Wolfe, this library had green silk taffeta curtains, a
sofa upholstered in cream-and-gray-striped velvet with
green silk cushions, two easy chairs in dark green velvet, and a leather armchair. The room also contained
a pair of painted and gilded iron torchères; a Louis XV
tulipwood bureau plat with a Sèvres porcelain inkstand; a Louis XVI bergère signed "Jacob"; and a
portrait bust of Claudine Houdon.

*Facing page and above:* THE GUEST ROOMS

The second- and third-floor guest bedrooms (a total of seven) were decorated entirely by Elsie de Wolfe. The two pictured here demonstrate her restrained simplicity, as well as her use of mirrors, painted furniture, and antique or reproduction eighteenth-century French and English furniture. The guest room (above) shows a George III commode in the French taste and a George III pier mirror. The Green Guest Room to the left contains a nineteenth-century green lacquer writing table and bench with chinoiserie decoration. This bedroom also boasted a secrétaire à abattant with a brèche marble top and green lacquered Edwardian bamboo furniture in the Regency style. Two departures from the heretofore English or French decor are the Venetian glass mirror above the mantel and a pair of Venetian wall brackets to either side. On Henry

Clay Frick's death in 1919, Childs Frick inherited most of the furniture in these rooms. He placed the pieces in Leftover — the guest cottage at the Clayton Estate on Long Island.

Although no pictures of the guest bathrooms seem to have survived, the c. 1931 inventory reveals that of the four on the second floor all were decorated in typical de Wolfe fashion: two in green and white stripes, one in ivory and blue stripes, and one in blue and white stripes. Of the three guest baths on the third floor, one was fitted in blue and white stripes, another in red and white stripes. The third is not described in the inventory.

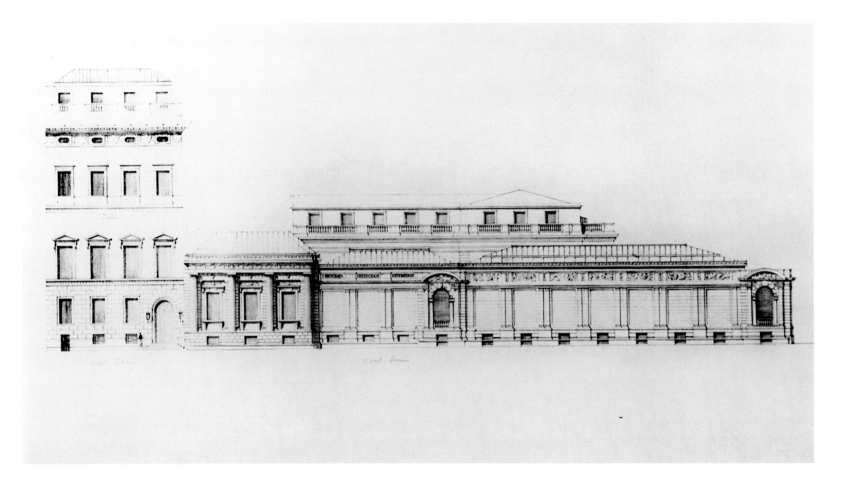

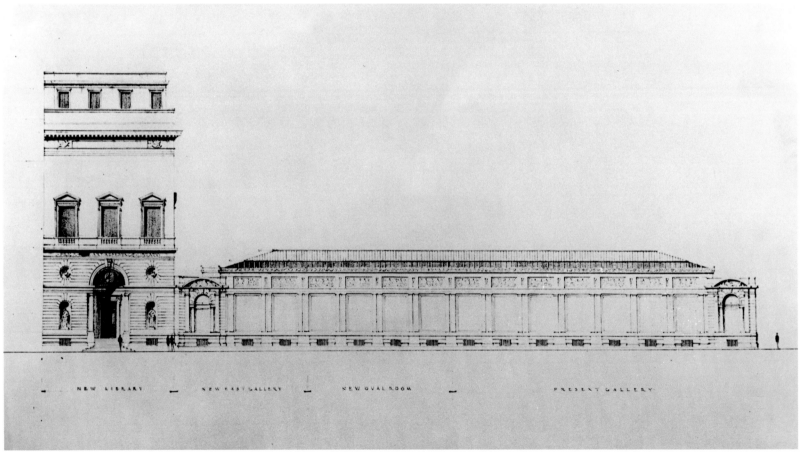

*Facing page, right, and below:* ARCHITECTURAL
RENDERINGS FOR THE FRICK COLLECTION, C. 1931

All these drawings by John Russell Pope date from the
conversion of One East Seventieth Street from family
home to public facility. The rear elevation of Scheme A
shows the Carrère & Hastings design for the Frick Art
Reference Library in the left center. The rear elevation
of Scheme B indicates the eastward extension and the
new Frick Art Reference Library (left in drawing), also
designed by Pope.

The rendering of the new entrance to the Frick
Collection shows the original Fry pediment in its new
location.

The one of the Garden Court evokes a Roman
atrium, a design Pope repeated in the National Gallery
of Art in Washington, D.C. Today the Frick Collection
Garden Court is used for exhibitions and parties and is
a place where visitors can relax, listen to concerts or to
the organ music that is played daily.

*Following pages:* THE CLAYTON ESTATE, NOW THE
NASSAU COUNTY MUSEUM OF ART, ROSLYN,
LONG ISLAND

# CHAPTER IV

# THE CLAYTON ESTATE

### THE HOME OF MR. AND MRS. CHILDS FRICK
### LONG ISLAND, NEW YORK

*Right:* Childs Frick leaning on the entrance balustrade.

*Facing page:* The entrance portico of Clayton, designed by White, Allom & Company.

IN 1918, HENRY CLAY FRICK PURCHASED a house in Roslyn, Long Island, as a gift to his son, Childs, and his daughter-in-law, Frances Dixon Frick. Originally, the two-hundred-acre hillside property on the north shore of Long Island, with sweeping views of Hempstead Harbor to the west and Westchester County and Long Island Sound to the north, belonged to William Cullen Bryant (1794–1878). Editor of the *New York Evening Post* and at one time America's most famous poet, Bryant was also a nature lover and a passionate gardener. In 1844, at age fifty, he moved from New York City to Springbank, as the property was called then, located in what was still a remote Quaker community. He soon planted an orchard in the upper pastures – where Clayton would stand one day – and also engaged his friend, the prominent architect Calvert Vaux, to build his house, Cedarmere, on the edge of the harbor. He asked another friend, Frederick Law Olmsted, to design the formal garden next to the house. When completed, the estate, the first home Bryant had owned, had an aura of enchantment. These sylvan surroundings may well have inspired some of Bryant's best poetry: "The Voice in Autumn," "The Snow Shower," "The Wind and Stream," "The Planting of the Apple Tree," all completed during Bryant's Cedarmere years.

The estate remained in the Bryant family until 1900 when General Lloyd Bryce (1851–1917) bought the upper pasture land and orchard from Harold Godwin, a Bryant heir. Bryce belonged to one of America's first families. Educated at Oxford with a law degree from Columbia University, in 1879 he married Edith Cooper, daughter of the mayor of New York City and granddaughter of Peter Cooper, inventor of the open hearth furnace and the first person to make steel in America. At the time of his marriage, Bryce was postmaster general for the state of New York, and within seven years he became a Democratic member of the U.S. Congress. Three years later, he inherited the *North American Review,* a forum for international opinions on social, political, and cultural issues, bequeathed to him by his good friend Allen Thorndyke Rice. Coincidentally, the *Review* had published Bryant's poem "Thanatopsis."

Without streams or rivers to power mill turbines, Long Island was an idyllic retreat. It had escaped the factory invasion of the industrial revolution and was fast becoming a highly desirable place to live. A seasonal resort since the seventeenth century, and now accessible by rail, road, and water, it provided welcome relief from the noise and grit of New York City.

Bryce engaged forty-year-old Ogden Codman Jr. to design his house. Codman, who was a good friend of Arthur Little's and Herbert Browne's, the architects for Eagle Rock, and known as one of their "Colonial Trinity," just had completed decorating the bedroom floors of Eagle Rock's prototype, the Breakers, for Cornelius Vanderbilt. Codman, however, was also at the time estranged from his *Decoration of Houses* co-author, Edith Wharton, who had as her

*Above left:* An early view of Hempstead Harbor and the estate of William Cullen Bryant, as seen from the eventual site of the Lloyd Stephens Bryce residence, later the Clayton Estate.

*Above right:* William Cullen Bryant.

Newport neighbor Bryce's friend Thorndyke Rice. Although Codman traditionally collaborated with Wharton on interior design projects that included her own homes, and despite the fact that he had won many of his commissions through her recommendations, at the time of the Bryce project the two had fallen out. Wharton was building the Mount, a new house in the Berkshire Mountains and, offended by Codman's high fees, hired another architect-decorator. In the meantime, Codman proceeded with the Bryce commission — and also took delight in the many problems Wharton encountered with her new architect.

This estrangement meant that everything from architecture to interior design in the Bryce house would be entirely the work of Ogden Codman. An expert at adapting the eighteenth-century English and French styles to the needs of wealthy Americans, Codman believed a home should be a "mechanism for living." The harmony of all elements — suitability to its owners' lifestyle, simplicity of design, and proportion — was his creed. He relied solely on what he loved and knew — classical design. As his friend and fellow architect Welles Bosworth noted of Codman's strict interpretation of classical motifs, his motto was: "Order for the sake of harmony and in the hope of beauty." For Codman the classical period was the simplest, the most functional, and the most beautiful.

The Bryce commission represented one of Codman's most important to date. He met the challenge by designing a Georgian-style country house not unlike the eighteenth-century prototype the young Lloyd Bryce very likely had seen when studying in England. Although the neo-Georgian style was relatively new to Long Island — the preferred style was Tudor or Elizabethan — a Georgian house with large, open rooms was just what Bryce and his wife required for entertaining their literary and political friends. It evoked a world of wealth, privilege, and aristocratic ways. At the same time, it succeeded in being a comfortable and romantic home. A graceful example of Codman's understanding of classical architecture in general, and of the Georgian style in particular, the Bryce house is surrounded by sweeping lawns and ancient forests and ponds as it overlooks distant water. Made of rose-colored brick laid in Flemish bond, the structure is spacious and well proportioned and gives the impression that it always has been part of the landscape. Two of its more charming features are the identical, one-story, Palladian-style pavilions on the north and south sides connected to the central block by curved, arcaded galleries. A low-hipped roof with a wooden balustrade running along the top gives way to generously spaced large windows. Devoid of ornamental devices, the building is decorated only by the broad, white, cement quoins at the corners of the house and the white trim on the headers and sills of the windows.

In Bryce's day, the interior of the house was equally gracious. After passing through an entrance portico with broken pediment on the west facade, guests entered a circular vestibule with a polished marble colonnade, marble floor, and semicircular, apse-like alcoves. Because Codman believed in the sanctity of each room, rectangular antechambers stood between the circular vestibule and the adjoining rooms — a pearl gray, paneled drawing room with white trim on the north side, a green and gold dining room on the east, and a walnut-paneled library on the south. As was Codman's custom, most of the furnishings — if not all of them — probably

*Above:* General Lloyd Stephens Bryce.

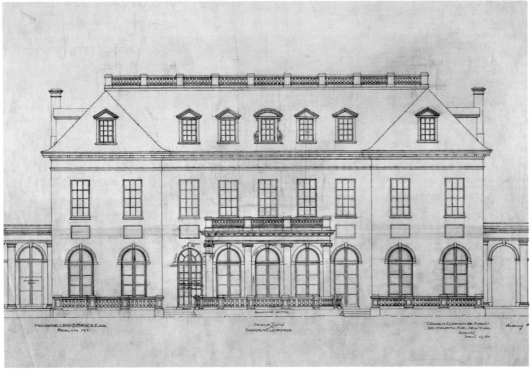

*Above:* Front elevation (west facade), Lloyd Stephens Bryce residence. Ogden Codman Jr., March 28, 1901.

*Below:* Garden elevation (east facade), Lloyd Stephens Bryce residence, Ogden Codman Jr., March 28, 1901.

were made in France and shipped to America. His foreman would have traveled with them and stayed at a local hotel for a number of weeks to supervise the installation of rugs and curtains, as well as the placing of furniture.

When Bryce died seventeen years after building the house, Ogden Codman was about to close his New York office and move to France. But the classical architecture he had helped popularize was now one of the most fashionable styles in America. As such it offered the Fricks just what they desired. When the Bryce heirs decided to sell the estate in 1918, Childs Frick,

*Above:* The garden facade, Lloyd Stephens Bryce residence.

Henry Clay Frick's only surviving son, was thirty-five years old, married, and the father of three young daughters — Adelaide (1915–56), Frances (1916–71), and Martha (1917–96). More important, by this time his childhood fascination with trapping and tagging animals and practicing taxidermy had evolved into a passion for big-game hunting, as well as an interest in fossil mammals, botany, and horticulture. He needed a grand house and he needed land.

In 1908 — five years before he married Frances — Childs traveled to Wyoming where he shot wapiti and bear. The following year he hunted moose in New Brunswick, and then, inspired by Theodore Roosevelt, who was conducting an African shooting expedition for the Smithsonian Institute, Childs in 1909–10 organized a similar trip to British East Africa. In these years big-game specimens were not adequately represented in the collections of most American museums, so Childs was intent on securing them, as well as a few small animals and birds for the American Museum of Natural History in New York and the natural history galleries at the Carnegie Museum in Pittsburgh.

After this trip Childs hunted caribou in British Columbia and in 1911 led another expedition, to Abyssinia, this time a traverse south from Addis Ababa through part of southern Ethiopia, into unexplored country east of Lake Rudolf, and south through Northern Guaso, the Nyiro River country, and territories east of Mount Kenya, before finally ending at Nairobi.

This was a first-of-its-kind expedition, born of Childs's belief that there was a scientific necessity to expand the current knowledge of paleontology. In this way, humanity could have a fuller understanding of the origin and history of the diverse groups of mammals making up the fauna of an area. As mammalian paleontology and fossil collecting increasingly captivated Childs's imagination, his interest in big-game hunting began to wane.

On his return to America in 1911, apart from bringing home the trophies and scientific data he had assembled, Childs returned with something still more unusual – Ku Zitti, an African chieftain. He had supplied Childs with guns, beaters, and camp servants; but when Childs saved his life by bringing down a charging lion, the African became devoted and refused to leave Childs's side. Childs brought him back to America as his manservant, but a few months after Childs's wedding the odd story came to a bizarre end. Despondent when the Fricks left their Bryn Mawr, Philadelphia, home for a short stay in Pittsburgh and New York, Ku Zitti tied a leather trunk strap around his neck and hung himself from a rafter in his room.

Although this death must certainly have upset Childs and Frances, Childs's scientific career proceeded undaunted. By 1915 his focus had expanded to include the preservation of wilderness areas and of mammals threatened with extinction, such as the desert bighorn sheep and grizzly bear. But fossil mammals still remained his primary fascination. During World War I, Childs, Frances, and their daughters moved to California where he served as a first lieutenant in the Signal Corps and studied the geology and faunal history of the Pacific Coast under a University of California program. When the war ended in 1918 and the family returned to the East Coast, Childs continued his chosen scientific career. Although he and his father had been estranged during the war years – largely because the elder Frick was disappointed that his only son wrote poetry, was passionate about fossils, and was more interested in natural history and wildlife conservation than banking and business – Henry Clay Frick was delighted by their return. He asked his daughter-in-law if she would like an important jewel he had seen at Tiffany, but Frances demurred. Pregnant with her fourth child and hoping for a son to name after her father-in-law, she instead asked for a house where she could raise her children.

The Bryce house, therefore, came on the market at just the right moment for Childs and Frances. Much appealed to them about the $550,000 estate besides the connection of its architect to their beloved Eagle Rock. It befitted their station in life, offering an isolated, independent, and completely private lifestyle. It also boasted a distinguished list of previous owners with similar interests in politics, poetry, and nature – not to mention a connection to the steel industry. Equally important, the estate was regarded as one of the largest and finest properties on Long Island's north shore, itself an exclusive enclave of mile-long driveways leading to grand estates. The rural pursuits offered by over seventy private clubs serving New York's wealthiest sons and daughters were many: fishing, shooting, car and horse racing, horse shows, yachting, golf, tennis, fox hunting, and polo. Since the 1880s, for instance, the Meadow Brook Club had maintained eight polo fields, each one larger than seven football fields. With Childs Frick's interest in polo, and with the couple's love of fox hunting, Long Island was more than ideal.

Still more important, however, the estate offered Childs enough space to pursue his research in paleontology, as well as botany and horticulture. As easily as he could display his many trophies on the walls of Bryce's house, commute to the American Museum of Natural History to work on his fossil mammals, and organize paleontological exhibitions, so too he could plant a pinetum, a collection of rare hardy conifers ranging from dwarf size to twenty feet high. They would enable him to compare species of a genus and make comparisons within a species, as well as between related species of foliage types, shades of color, and plant forms. Moreover, he could study their reaction to the Long Island climate and determine their suitability for a coastal environment.

Since most of the best sites on the north shore had been purchased by 1918 (over four hundred houses had been built since 1900, spread among two hundred different architectural firms), when the Bryce heirs decided to sell the property Henry Clay Frick immediately bought it. He gave it to Frances, just as he had given Clayton in Pittsburgh to his wife in 1882, and in the family tradition, the Childs Fricks renamed their house Clayton — undoubtedly a gesture of thanks to Henry Clay Frick for the gift, as well as acknowledgment that his grandchildren would be raised in a home bearing his name.

Although the firm of Little & Browne then was designing a house in nearby Oyster Bay and asked Frick for the Roslyn house commission, Frick instead engaged Sir Charles Allom. For all the upbraiding Frick had given Allom, he obviously had been satisfied with Allom's work at One East Seventieth Street, and with Elsie de Wolfe now retired to France, he charged Allom with the interior decoration as well as the architectural changes. Codman had designed a beautiful house, yet a great many exterior and interior alterations were needed to satisfy the new owners' aesthetics, lifestyle, and the needs of their growing family. So, while an Austrian arborist began planting trees in the pinetum, Allom grassed over Codman's formal Italian parterre garden on the east side, with its fountain and reflecting pool, and replaced it with an intimate lawn terrace where the Fricks could hold receptions and outdoor dinner parties. Then Allom began reorganizing the interior and ordering the furnishings. On January 24, 1919, Frick issued an edict regarding the structural changes and his son's desire to decorate the house with African trophies:

> If I am to pay for the changes in the house I am going to give to my daughter-in-law . . . the library must remain where it is and the dining room also; neither would I approve of cutting off part of the drawing room for a study . . . If my son desires a place for his heads and other trophies of his expeditions to Africa, I am willing to assist in building on some location on the place to be agreed to, a room for that purpose. [B]ut if my daughter-in-law's house is to be made a refuge for all kinds of animals [sic] heads, I would take no pleasure in it. At the most I do not think it should contain more than three well selected heads properly located.

On March 17, he warned Allom to follow the established procedure regarding the purchase of rugs, antiques, porcelains, and other furnishings: "You must have my authority in writing

*Above and below:* THE GARDEN FACADE

An Italian parterre garden was designed by Ogden Codman Jr. for Lloyd Stephens Bryce, c. 1901. Sir Charles Allom later redesigned this area and created an extended lawn for entertaining. It is shown here as it looked September 8, 1939, as prepared for the wedding reception for the second of Childs Frick's daughters.

before I become responsible." Ever watchful of his money — and with the constant leitmotif accompanying every house Frick built or renovated — Frick complained: "The specifications above referred to contain many extravagant items, for which I presume you are responsible, among others, quantities of marble. I told you repeatedly I wanted what work we did [at Clayton], and what material was furnished to be of good quality, but not expensive, and that the house should be kept simple and homelike." But Frick was not able to see his orders enforced. His death on December 2, 1919, came less than one year after the Clayton renovations began and only ten days after a hurried, spur-of-the-moment drive to Clayton, against doctors' orders, to view his infant namesake.

The Childs Fricks, however, now were wealthy enough to complete the house on their own, and suddenly, they were free to do as they wished. Most of the furnishings already had been ordered, and the structural changes were completed. Codman's entrance portico was replaced with an open loggia connecting the projections on either side of the central block. The vestibule and antechambers were removed to create a large, rectangular entrance hall, and a giant fireplace and fluted Ionic oak columns added. A substantial wing was built on the south end of the house, behind the enclosed pavilion and its connecting arcade, to create a new dining room, breakfast room, and large pantry.

Now, with the architectural work accomplished, up went Childs's trophies — caribou, water buffalo, gazelle, and antelope. A neoclassic frieze in the library featuring bighorn sheep and lions in relief also was installed. And in Childs's study, a large glass case built into the east wall displayed two of his most splendid trophies — a lion and lioness stalking through tall African grass.

In October 1920, Allom still was working on the house, and the pine paneling for the North Room would not be installed until 1924. By the mid-1920s, however, the estate largely had reached a high standard. Guy Lowell — a prominent Boston architect with a predilection for colonial architecture who also was helping with plans for Frick Park in Pittsburgh — designed a charming gatehouse. Childs acquired a motorboat, the *Claytonia,* and was commuting between his Hempstead Harbor dock and his Frick Laboratory in the American Museum of Natural History. Five miles of bridle paths, a polo field, a ski slope, a shooting range, two tennis courts, two ponds for skating and canoeing, a zoo for large mammals (bear) and reptiles (alligators and six-foot-long gouffer snakes), and an enlarged swimming pool completed the estate.

In the 1930s, Clayton took on a still grander air. The Fricks engaged the prominent pioneer landscape architect Marian Cruger Coffin to create a formal French parterre garden. And in 1937, after Childs was involved in a serious car accident, Frances insisted he no longer commute to New York and instead build a research laboratory in the pinetum at Clayton. Childs acquiesced, but in actual fact Millstone, as the laboratory was called, was a necessity for reasons other than Childs's safety. By 1937, his collection of fossils from California, Arizona, Texas, Florida, Nebraska, Wyoming, New Mexico, Montana, and the Dakotas, as well as Alaska, Ecuador, and China (where he negotiated with drug dealers to prevent the bones he wanted for his collection from being ground up as aphrodisiacs), had outgrown the Frick Laboratory. Extra space was needed to house and conduct his ongoing, serious research, research that now placed him in contact with the most important paleontologists of the day. Neither a bon vivant nor a hobbyist, Childs performed his own dissections, and when on a dig he took meticulous samples of the sediments encasing the fossils — samples that today remain available for pollen analysis. He now had become convinced that there was no sharp line dividing the living and the fossil past, and on the completion of Millstone he kept there a series of skulls and other bones of recent mammals to compare with their fossil predecessors. Millstone, therefore, became a valued addition to the Clayton Estate — and to the success of fifty-four-year-old Childs Frick's scientific pursuits.

During World War II, Childs continued his research, but as the new garden flourished and the Fricks' first grandchildren were being born, the family decided to downsize. With their children grown and living on their own, Childs and Frances closed the main house and moved into a small, Gothic Revival, board-and-batten cottage on the grounds. It had been designed by Fred S. Copley of Roslyn and Staten Island for Jerusha Dewey, the sister of William Cullen Bryant's good friend and minister, Orville Dewey. When Lloyd Bryce owned the cottage, it was put on stilts so a first floor could be inserted beneath. But the Fricks wanted to further improve the site by adding two small gardens. In 1941 they asked Umberto Innocenti and Richard Webel of Innocenti & Webel, a prominent Long Island landscaping firm, for a design. The firm previously had worked for the Frick family, assisting Childs in placing Millstone in the pinetum, altering the driveway and entrance court, and designing *Claytonia*'s dock, the Captain's Cottage, and the ski trails. In 1937 Helen Frick commissioned the firm to design "The Little Garden" at Eagle Rock, and she and Childs used these landscape architects for the layout of Frick Park in Pittsburgh.

Now Childs asked Innocenti & Webel to create a walled terrace garden on the south side of the cottage and a parterre garden to the north. Dorothy Nicolas, another landscape designer, planted the flower beds. The Fricks renamed the cottage Leftover and made it so attractive that they did not return to the main house until 1951.

Thanks to the opportunities the Clayton Estate offered, Frances Frick became an expert gardener, and Childs Frick — head of the American Committee for International Wildlife Protection covering the entire broad field of living mammals, fauna, flora, and ecology — left an indelible mark in his chosen fields. He wrote many books and specialized treatises, and among the many honors bestowed upon him were honorary curator of late tertiary and quaternary mammals at the American Museum of Natural History in 1930 and an honorary doctorate in science from Princeton University in 1942.

Just as Henry Clay Frick had intended, his grandchildren grew up in a veritable paradise. He may well have been surprised, however, by Childs's achievements, as well as his grandchildren's. Although Frick never supported his son in his scientific pursuits, Childs became preeminent in his chosen profession. One of Frick's granddaughters became a pediatrician, and

*Above:* Garden gate on the south lawn of the main house, designed by White, Allom & Company.

his grandson became a cancer surgeon, as well as chairman of the Frick Collection (Childs had been its president) and a proponent of horticulture, botany, and wildlife preservation.

Childs spent $6 million in his forty-five years of scientific research, and on his death he gave his unprecedented fossil collection to the American Museum of Natural History and endowed it with $7.5 million. The museum then built a wing known as the Frick Building to house the unique assemblage of paleontological treasures, among which is the only specimen of a three-toed horse and a 21,000-year-old mummified baby mammoth. The collection's other statistics were equally impressive: its 7,400 crates, containing approximately 500,000 individual specimens meticulously catalogued, classified, and preserved, weighed approximately 600 tons.

But just as important, this remarkable achievement was nurtured in a home that resembled an English country house, long regarded as the ideal setting for studying and enjoying nature. Although greatly altered from Ogden Codman's design, the Clayton Estate still embodied the principles of suitability, simplicity and proportion he and Edith Wharton had professed. A highly structured attempt at informal formality and rustic charm, Clayton remained a house filled with treasures that reflected the personality and interests of its owners and the elegance of the Golden Era from whence it was born.

Unlike most of the maintenance-intensive Long Island houses built between 1900 and World War I, Clayton did not fall to the wrecker's ball after World War II. Although Frances Frick died in 1953, Childs continued to live in and maintain the estate until his death in 1965. Today, although no longer a family home, the estate remains a living entity. Now home to the Nassau County Museum of Art, it hosts a full program of lectures, concerts, exhibitions, and seminars. Additionally, the pinetum survives for study and enjoyment, as does the recently restored Marian Cruger Coffin formal garden. Clayton, therefore, continues to enchant two hundred thousand visitors annually and remains a fine example of neo-Georgian architecture. Most important, the graceful landscape still echoes its former owners' love of beauty and nature — a love the Clayton Estate has inspired since the days of William Cullen Bryant.

The enlarged, rectangular entrance hall, designed by
Sir Charles Allom, was gracious and inviting. The
black and white marble floor, rich oak paneling, and
large fireplace all provided a warm background for
the Fricks' various paintings, bronzes, and sixteenth-
century French Renaissance furniture of carved
walnut: a cabinet to the left of the mantel, a carved
high-backed chair to the right, another cabinet to the
right of the door leading into the North Room, and a
draw-top table to the right of the powder-room door.
Duveen purchased these pieces (as well as another
cabinet and an upholstered chair) for Henry Clay Frick
in 1916, possibly for the Enamel Room at One East
Seventieth Street or more probably for the bowling
alley. Childs Frick bequeathed them to the Frick
Collection, and on his death in 1965, they reentered
the collection. Today the draw-top table stands in the
center of the East Gallery.

In addition, the entrance hall contained six
William and Mary walnut side chairs and two walnut
upholstered armchairs in the Charles II style. The
decor was completed by five crayon and chalk drawings of court ladies attributed to François Clouet;
a Qianlong ancestral portrait of a lady; a large painting
of the eighteenth-century French School after
Fragonard (to the right); a nineteenth-century Spanish
velvet hanging embroidered in gold thread entitled
*Corrida de Toros;* and a Louis XIV carved, gilt-wood
console mirror.

At 6:30 every morning, Childs Frick practiced golf
in the front hall. He would string a large sheet across
the south end of the hall and create a "tee" out of a
hemp doormat. A basket held his cotton golf balls,
and as he began his backswing, his dachshunds
watched from beside a convex mirror that Childs
placed on the marble floor so he could adjust his grip
before driving the cotton ball.

The powder room (entered through the small door
to the left of the mirror) provides an indication of
the luxurious interior decoration Sir Charles Allom
created for Clayton. A symphony of red and black
lacquer with gold decoration, it boasted a Chinese rug,
a Louis XV chinoiserie dressing table, a nineteenth-
century Regency settee in black lacquer with gold
decoration, and a red lacquer jewel box from the same
period. Willy the otter, a favorite Frick family pet, was
allowed to splash and play in the toilet — something he
did regularly and with great delight.

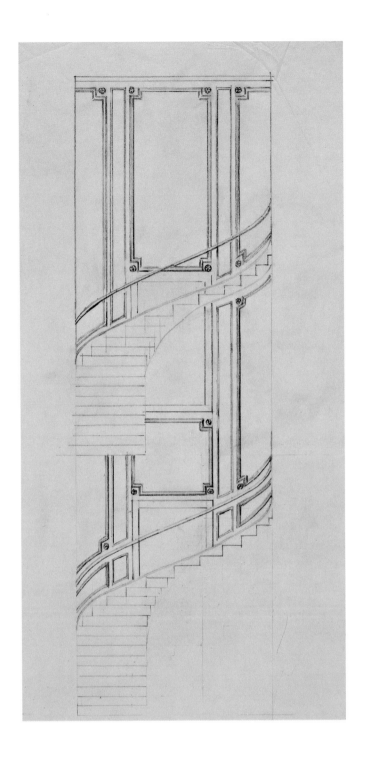
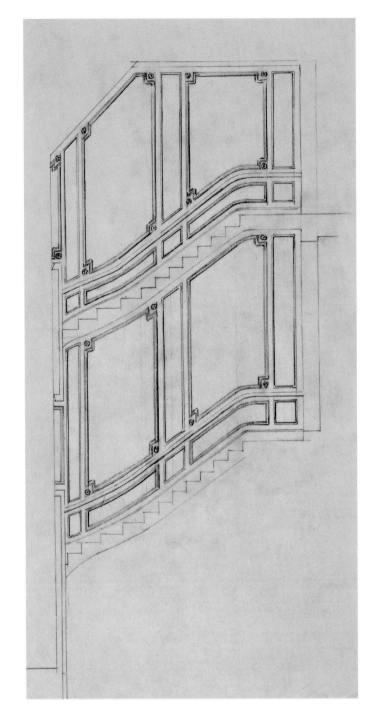

*Above:* THE STAIR HALL

Sections of the stairwell by Ogden Codman Jr.,
c. 1901.

*Facing page:* The continuous, molded oval staircase
with turned balusters wound without interruption
from the entrance hall to the third floor. It was
untouched by Sir Charles Allom during his renovation.
Along the walls were displayed eight 1883 aquatints
of the Beaufort Hunt engraved by Henry Alken, four
1838 lithographs by J. W. Jules, and set number fourteen of a limited edition of four hunting prints — *The
Meet, First Flight, Full Cry,* and *Run to Earth* — by
William J. Hays.

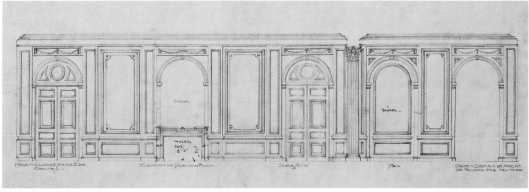

*Left:* THE NORTH ROOM

The North Room at Clayton, as decorated and designed by Sir Charles Allom for the Childs Fricks, was an elegant but welcoming room. Only the parquet floor and Chinese Chippendale hardware on the doors were original to the 1901 Codman design. Evident in the pre-Allom (top) and post-Allom (left) views are the modifications made by the British designer: he removed the awkward screen and the Corinthian columns that divided the room into two unequal parts, bricked in the west windows, and designed the elaborately paneled plaster ceiling with a motif of acanthus leaves and pinecones. In 1924 he installed pine paneling from a sixteenth-century English manor house located in Stanwick Park, Yorkshire, formerly the seat of the dukes of

Northumberland. In 1920 the manor house was demolished, and of the four salvaged rooms, the Fricks installed one and the Minnesota Art Institute, the Royal Ontario Museum, and a private office in New York City installed the other three. Allom also removed the carved Italian marble mantel and replaced it with one of finely carved wood.

*Above:* The Lloyd Stephens Bryce drawing room and den (later the North Room in Clayton) as decorated and designed by Ogden Codman Jr., c. 1901.

*Below:* Elevation of the Lloyd Stephens Bryce drawing room and den by Ogden Codman Jr., c. 1901 (later the North Room in Clayton).

*Right:* THE NORTH ROOM

One of a pair of Brussels tapestries from the *Don Quixote* series (the other was in the dining room), signed by F. van den Hecke, and with a double B monogram, stretched across the bricked-in west wall. Purchased by Henry Clay Frick in 1909 when he was living at 640 Fifth Avenue, these tapestries – the only two that have surfaced from a series of eight since the French Revolution – were given to Childs for his new house. Part of Childs's bequest to the Frick Collection in 1965, the tapestries are now on view in the Music Room. The recent discovery of ink stamps in their inner linings proves a proud provenance: the tapestries arrived at Versailles in 1755 and were listed in the royal inventory as number 222. Throughout the room are many pieces from the Fricks' large collection of Kangxi porcelain.

The Frick family used this room at Christmas and for all formal entertaining. Wedding receptions for two of their daughters were held here, as was a debut for one of their granddaughters. One memorable year a trained chimpanzee joined the family Christmas celebration. After Frances Frick's sudden death in 1953 from pancreatic cancer, the North Room still was used for family reunions, but rarely for large receptions.

*Right:* THE NORTH ROOM

Six gracefully arched windows look out over the estate to the north and east, making the North Room spacious yet warm and inviting. Four oil portraits of the Frick children by Clarence R. Mattei and three oils of the Frick daughters by Bernard de Mouvel, as well as two mezzotints — *The Honorable Miss Moncton* after Sir Joshua Reynolds and *Lady Mildmay* after John Hoppner — hung on the walls. The furniture was a combination of English and French antiques and reproductions. The most important pieces included a George I carved mahogany card table; a Louis XV petite commode-chiffonier in red lacquer; a late eighteenth-century Hepplewhite carved desk armchair; a seventeenth-century Jacobean carved oak child's armchair; a William and Mary upholstered stool; a nineteenth-century Hepplewhite carved mahogany bench; a gold-decorated, red lacquer Queen Anne chinoiserie ladies' secrétaire; four George I walnut spoon-back side chairs; and a Sheraton-style mahogany mantel clock. A pair of Charles X cut-crystal wall sconces with bead pendants added to the glitter.

*Above and right:* THE LIBRARY

The Bryce family used the Clayton Estate library as a dining room. A c. 1904 photograph (above) shows their dining room as decorated by Ogden Codman Jr.

Sir Charles Allom converted the Bryce dining room into the Frick family library and sitting room (right). With its eastern exposure and Venetian arched windows overlooking the lawn and ponds, the library is a sunny, cheerful room. Here the Frick family played cards, read, and gathered before having lunch or dinner in the main dining room. The neoclassical frieze, specially designed by Sir Charles Allom for Childs Frick, depicts lions and bighorn sheep in relief. The caribou trophies, a zebra cushion before the mantel, a bronze Asiatic ibex by James L. Clark, and a twenty-one-inch ivory elephant tusk served as reminders of Childs's youthful interest in trapping and taxidermy as well as his subsequent big game hunting. The c. 1899 portrait of Childs Frick by Pascal-Adolphe-Jean

Dagnan-Bouveret on the south wall originally was in the library at Clayton, Pittsburgh; it has been returned to the Clayton house-museum. *Frances Dixon Frick* by Clarence Mattei is over the mantel; other portraits in this room included the three Frick daughters (1923) and young Henry Clay Frick II (1923), both by Harrington Mann, and Henry Clay Frick II (1953) by Elizabeth Shoumatoff. Also in this room were a seventeenth-century Italian refectory table of carved walnut; a pair of William and Mary turned walnut side chairs (c. 1700); a pair of Queen Anne spoon-back side chairs (c. 1720), also in walnut; a late eighteenth-century Chippendale carved mahogany candle stand; a mahogany Sheraton chess table with ivory inlay (c. 1800); Chippendale wall sconces of carved gilt-wood; and an early nineteenth-century gallery-top table.

*Above and facing page:* THE STUDY

The wood-paneled library (above) in the Lloyd Stephens Bryce house, as decorated and designed by Ogden Codman Jr., later became Childs Frick's study.

The study (right) as designed by Sir Charles Allom, was entirely Childs Frick's room. Bookcases were added by Allom, and casket-like structures were inserted in the west window embrasures — one a radiator cover and the other a concealed opening to a circular iron stairway to a workroom and laboratory. Structurally, however, the room was largely unchanged from Codman's design. Here Childs attended to his business and scientific correspondence and did much of his reading. A favorite teatime gathering place for the Frick children and grandchildren, the oak-paneled

study was dominated by a large glass case containing a stalking lion and lioness. Sixteen of Childs's trophies were kept in this room — heads of a water buffalo, rhinoceros, bighorn sheep — as well as a wastebasket made from an elephant's leg and two sets of elephant tusks, one measuring sixty-two inches, the other fifty-four inches. To the left of the arched window is an impala; an oryx is to the right; photographs of Childs's expeditions and an entire, full mounted dik-dik are below. Bronzes of a moose, an antelope, an elephant helping a wounded comrade, and a giraffe also recalled Childs Frick's big game hunting days. An 1896 carved oak terrestrial globe by W. A. K. Johnson of Edinburgh stood beside Childs's Queen Anne–style

walnut desk. An electrified raffia and brass oil lamp — an African water bottle fitted with an oil font and a green glass shade, suspended from an adjustable fixture — hung above this desk. A nineteenth-century English writing table and library step bench of turned mahogany completed the list of important furniture, together with a novelty stand: a stationery rack with a glass inkwell mounted on antelope horns. Pictures in the room included two very small watercolors by Henry Alken alluding to the Fricks' passion for fox hunting; a 1935 portrait of Frances Frick with her long-haired dachshund by Elizabeth Shoumatoff; and three others dated 1953, the year of Frances's death.

*Left:* THE PORCELAIN ROOM

The porcelain room was actually a curved hallway with glass display cases that connected the library and dining room. The architectural breakfront on the right contained many pieces of the Imperial blue-and-white Kangxi porcelain Childs and Frances Frick collected over the years. They celebrated birthdays and anniversaries by giving pieces to each other, and soon their collection grew to include unique bowls, vases, scent bottles, plates, teapots, and tea caddies. Childs Frick bequeathed most of the pieces to the Frick Collection where they remain as beautifully displayed as they once were at his Clayton home.

*Facing page:* CORRIDOR TO THE BREAKFAST LOGGIA

This corridor, created by Sir Charles Allom by removing servants' rooms and reducing the size of Childs Frick's study, is a light and airy passage. It contained a pair of Carrara marble pietra dure tables and a sculptured fountain also of Carrara marble. The breakfast loggia featured a pair of nineteenth-century, Adam-style, carved gilt-wood girandoles. Most of the time the Fricks' four children and, later, their fifteen grandchildren took their meals here.

*Right:* THE DINING ROOM

Sir Charles Allom fashioned the dining room out of the Bryces' former kitchen wing. He moved the kitchen to the basement, installed a dumbwaiter, and placed a butler's pantry at the service entrance to the new dining room. The mate to the famous van den Hecke *Don Quixote* tapestry in the North Room covered the dining room's south wall. A 1923 portrait of Henry Clay Frick II by Harrington Mann hung over a marble mantel carved with fruits, masks, and figures of Pan and putti pouring wine down the throat of a goat. The carved and painted dining suite in the Georgian style was copied from Henry Clay Frick's Allom-designed dining set at One East Seventieth Street. The four-fold screen, from the late eighteenth century, is leather, painted in a floral and bird design. A pair of Anglo-French, nineteenth-century Sèvres porcelain and crystal candelabra once graced the mantel, as did a pair of *famille verte* porcelain rice bowls; statuettes of Kyln (Kangxi); and a pair of blue-and-white temple jars. On the sideboard can be seen a ginger jar and a pair of beaker vases. Between the windows on the east facade were watercolors of Frances Frick and Childs Frick (1954) by Elizabeth Shoumatoff. Once decorated in yellow and white, the room has graceful, Venetian arched windows that look over the east lawn and two ponds.

*Right:* THE MASTER BEDROOM

The master bedroom, decorated in the Adam style, was a comfortable, sunny room with southern and western exposures. The delicately painted chinoiserie designs in the wallpaper depicted floral sprays and exotic birds and butterflies. The room contained a pair of triangular Louis XV tulipwood and marquetry encoignures (corner cabinets) with *brèche rouge* marble tops. The late eighteenth-century Adam mantel was made of Carrara and Siena marble. Decorated with flowers and urns, it displayed a pair of *famille rose* plates. The beds, made in the Georgian style, were covered in a cream ribbed fabric. The dressing room contained a late eighteenth-century Sheraton jewel chest of inlaid satinwood, and mounted heads of antelope and elk lined the walls.

248

*Above and facing page:* The Master Bedroom

Situated at the southwest corner of the house, the master bedroom, with its corner cabinets, small portrait of Henry Clay Frick, and breakfast tray beside the chaise longue, was warm and elegant.

*Right:* THE MORNING ROOM

Frances Frick used her morning room to write letters, organize the household staff, read, or entertain friends. It faced west and had a view of the front drive, the ski slope, Hempstead Harbor, and Leftover Cottage. Among the many objects in this room were a collection of blue-and-white Kangxi porcelain and pieces from the more colorful Qianlong period; four eighteenth-century, Queen Anne walnut spoon-back side chairs; and a pair of nineteenth-century, Queen Anne walnut girandole wall mirrors. The five-light, bronze doré, early Georgian-style chandelier with three cherub heads matches the wall sconces on either side of the mantel. A copy of the Gilbert Stuart *George Washington* that Henry Clay Frick acquired in 1918 hung above the mantel.

252

*Above and facing page:* THE WALNUT BEDROOM

One of the most handsome bedrooms in Clayton, the Walnut Room with its decidedly English air was reserved for guests. When the Childs Fricks' youngest daughter, Martha, married and later visited Clayton, she and her husband stayed in this room, fondly remembered by her family. It was where they opened their much-anticipated Christmas stockings.

All the furniture was of walnut: the eighteenth-century Georgian slope-front desk; the Queen Anne parcel-gilt console mirror; the shaving mirror; the three eighteenth-century Queen Anne spoon-back side chairs (matching those in the morning room); and the nineteenth-century Queen Anne dressing table. A Kirmanahah rug with a field of blue, red, green, and yellow covered the floor.

*Facing page and above:* THE BLUE BEDROOM

The Blue Bedroom – as splendid as the Walnut Room, but largely eighteenth-century French in character – was used primarily by the Frick's fourth child, Henry Clay Frick II, when he returned to Clayton with his family. The room contained an important Louis XV marquetry acajou and tulipwood slant-front desk signed by Carel, a pair of Louis XV carved and painted upholstered fauteuils, a Louis XVI marquetry tulip-wood and palisander commode with a gray St. Anne marble top, and a Louis XVI acajou semanier (narrow chest of drawers) by C. M. Leclerc, also with gray St. Anne marble. An Adam marquetry satinwood chest of drawers, a pair of early nineteenth-century English Regency black lacquer girandole pole screens (electrified), and a suite of painted bedroom furniture

also filled the room. Of the many decorative objects, a French nineteenth-century bronze doré and white marble clock sat on the mantel. The desk held an early nineteenth-century French Empire Vieux Paris gold-decorated china inkwell. A pair of Sèvres rose-and-leaf-decorated porcelain cachepots and a pair of electrified nineteenth-century Limoges enamel candlesticks also were in this room. An antique tan, blue, and red Chiordes prayer rug and an antique green and red Persian prayer rug were on the floor. The bathroom boasted a painting entitled *A Quiet Pond* by R. W. van Boskerck, an artist friend whose work Henry Clay Frick had collected in his early years at Clayton, Pittsburgh.

*Facing page:* THE GUEST SITTING ROOM

Decorated with red and ivory curtains, the guest sitting room was comfortable and inviting. Largely English in feeling, it contained such eighteenth-century pieces as a leather fire bucket; a carved and gilt-wood console mirror; an Adam-style painted and decorated console table; and a Sheraton gilt-wood mirror. Decorative objects included a bronze, ship's bell mantel clock from Tiffany & Company and fourteen silver trophy cups. Four paintings on glass (*eglomisé*) of ladies in a landscape with Qianlong lacquer frames, as well as an 1896 portrait of Henry Clay Frick by his artist friend Théobald Chartran, were displayed on the walls. The latter portrait now is owned by a trust for a family member and is on loan to the Frick Art and Historical Center in Pittsburgh.

*Right above and below:* THE PINK BEDROOM

The pink bedroom was located on Clayton's northeast corner. The floral chintz curtains coordinated with a boudoir easy chair, upholstered and fringed in red faille, and a plaid sofa. A skirted dressing table, needle-point cushions, and decorative objects such as a pair of bronze Foo dogs from the Ming period, a pair of French nineteenth-century Chinese gold-decorated tole cachepots, a Russian blue-and-white bowl and saucer, and a *blanc de chine* ribbed vase enhanced the room's feminine quality.

*Above and left:* THE ZOO

Childs Frick's interest in wildlife was given full expression in his large animal zoo. The top photograph shows Prinny, his youngest daughter's pet bear, in the bear pit. In the lower photograph Martha is giving Prinny a bottle. The bear was quite tame, but she did have a habit of running away across Northern Parkway to a beekeeper's farm in Roslyn.

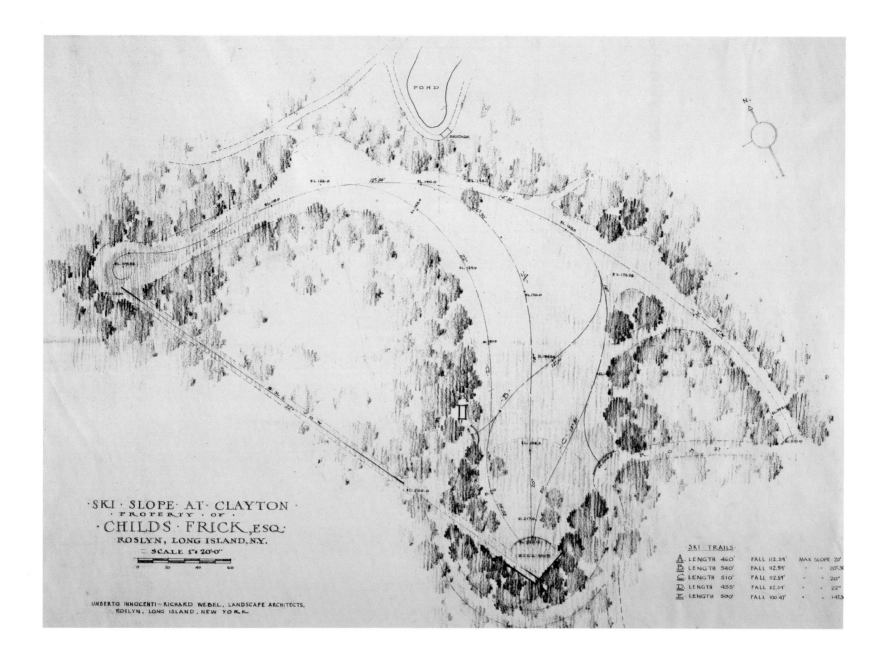

*Above:* THE SKI SLOPE

The Ski Slope was designed by Innocenti & Webel. To keep the run skiable, new-fallen snow on the lawn and polo field was bulldozed into neat, rectangular piles. When the run began to melt, the snow piles were transferred to the runs and dumped into a snow-spreading machine called "the Hurricane" that spewed the snow out onto the slope. Although the Frick family used the ski slope into the 1940s, Childs Frick broke his leg on it and took up golf instead. He practiced his drive and iron shots on the lawn where the snow was gathered.

*Above and facing page:* MILLSTONE LABORATORY

In 1937 Childs Frick built a research laboratory in the pinetum to accommodate the overflow from his laboratory in the American Museum of Natural History. Millstone, as the new laboratory was called, received its name after a pair of giant millstones mysteriously appeared one day at the laboratory's front door. A friend of the Fricks, Archibald B. Roosevelt, put them there because he enjoyed playing tricks on Childs. The stones, originally from Belgium, had been discovered during the excavation of an early colonial mill near Wall Street. Roosevelt heard of the discovery, and in making the connection between the stones, Childs's own excavations, and his Mennonite farming heritage, he must have delighted in the ensuing days of speculation caused by the appearance of these stones at Clayton.

*Following pages:* THE SWIMMING POOL

Three generations of the Frick family — and some of their pets — enjoyed this pool. Childs Frick's daughter, Martha, swam her alligator here and once rescued him from the bottom, fearing he had drowned.

*Left:* THE GARDEN

In 1931 the Fricks commissioned Marian Cruger Coffin to create a formal French garden out of the Bryces' neglected 450-foot rectangular garden beyond the house, in the southwest corner of the estate. Then at the height of her profession, Coffin was sociable, tactful, discreet, and a good business-woman. More important, she was well known to those who influenced, directly or indirectly, the evolution of the Clayton Estate. Coffin knew Edith Wharton, who was a close friend of Ogden Codman Jr., Clayton Estate's original architect; she was a cousin of Walter Berry, a devoted friend and mentor of Edith Wharton's; and as a student at MIT, she studied under Guy Lowell — the architect for the Clayton Estate gatehouse.

Born to an old but impoverished New York family, Coffin was forced to support herself and her mother. In 1901 she began training as a landscape gardener, an uncommon profession for women at the time. She attended a first-of-its-kind undergraduate program in architecture at MIT where she became a "special" student in landscape architecture. After her graduation in 1904, she opened a New York office and soon became one of the first and foremost women in her field. Henry Francis du Pont, who also attended MIT and whose gardens she later designed at Winterthur, Delaware, was the mainstay of her personal and professional life. Her social connections and her talent guaranteed a successful career in what became known as the "golden era" for American gardens.

At Clayton the formal parterre garden — influenced by seventeenth-century French royal gardens — survives as a magnificent example of Coffin's work. She liked her plants arranged artistically with "the right plant for the right place," and she created "living pictures" using line, form, and texture, as well as daring but harmonious colors. Coffin designed a long central walk with a perennial border. The two quartiles to the west of the walk featured scrolled boxwood designs in diamond or circular patterns. The two to the east were planned as rose gardens requiring 650 rose bushes and 150 box bushes for edging.

The decorative, wrought-iron gate was designed by Carrère & Hastings and fabricated by John Williams, Inc. of New York for One East Seventieth Street. One of two, in the early 1930s it was installed in the Fricks' Marian Cruger Coffin garden. In the 1970s both gates returned to the Frick Collection.

267

*Right:* THE GARDEN

These July 3, 1931, photographs — by one of Coffin's favorite photographers, Samuel Gottscho — show how Coffin used axial symmetry, geometric organization, a strong spatial design (rather than a display of bloom), the sculptural effect of trees, and classical ornamentation for the "architecture" of her garden design. Clipped boxwood laid in gravel and yew hedging separated the parterres.

The east axis of the garden terminates at a large rectangular bower of pleached privet with a central arch. The north axis leads from the iron gate to a monumental garden pavilion designed in the 1930s by the architects Henry O. Milliken and Newton P. Bevin. One of very few in America, it incorporates elements of classical architecture and provides the main focal point for the garden. The dome rises more than thirty feet and has decorative trellis wings on either side and four Ionic columns supported by brass pipes.

The north end of the Clayton garden connects to the main house by a winding walkway lined with several varieties of flowering trees and shrubs. A circular area known as the Astrological Garden once contained a flagstone zodiac.

On her death in 1953, Frances Dixon Frick was buried among the roses in the Clayton garden. The headstone for her grave was a small lunette depicting two putti sculpted by Attilio Piccirilli for One East Seventieth Street. Every day until his own death in 1965, Childs brought fresh carnations to Frances's grave. He also was buried in the rose garden, but when Nassau County purchased Clayton from the Frick heirs in 1969, Childs's and Frances's remains, and the lunette, were taken to Pittsburgh. Today the lunette serves as a dual headstone for Childs and Frances, who are buried in the Frick plot at the Homewood Cemetery beside Henry Clay Frick, his wife, their daughter Helen Clay Frick, and their two small children, Martha and Henry Clay Frick Jr., who died in 1891 and 1892, respectively.

*Above and right:* THE GARDEN

The Henry O. Milliken and Newton P. Bevin pavilion and
view looking west from the bower of pleached privet.

*Above and facing page:* THE GARDEN

The rose garden where Childs and Frances Frick were
buried and the Astrological Garden looking south.

*Above and left:* THE GARAGE

The garage housed the Frick family's fleet of Cadillacs. From left to right are a 1936 model, a 1930 V16, a 1933 model, and a 1935 model.

*Above:* THE STABLES

The Frick family enjoyed fox hunting and polo. They
often stabled their horses in Maryland and hunted
with the Elkridge Harford Hounds. Their daughters
were expert horsewomen, winning prizes both in local
horse shows and at Foxcroft, the Virginia boarding
school they attended.

*Facing page and above:* THE JERUSHA DEWEY
HOUSE/LEFTOVER COTTAGE

The Jerusha Dewey House, now called Leftover, is a
Gothic Revival cottage. It was built by William Cullen
Bryant in 1860 for Jerusha Dewey, sister of the noted
theologian Dr. Orville Dewey. Shortly after General
Bryce purchased the upper portion of the former
Bryant estate, he became minister to the Netherlands
and Luxembourg under President William Howard
Taft, a post he held until 1913. In need of a larger
guest house, Bryce had the Dewey cottage placed on
stilts so a large first floor could be inserted beneath it
and added an east wing.

During Bryce's time, Theodore Roosevelt and
Woodrow Wilson are known to have stayed in the
Dewey House. After his father's death in 1919, Childs

Frick furnished the house – renamed Leftover – with
much of the furniture from the guest rooms at One
East Seventieth Street. In 1941, prior to moving into
Leftover for World War II, the Fricks asked Innocenti
& Webel, the firm that already had completed many
projects for the family, to design a walled garden to the
south of the cottage as well as a parterre garden to the
north. In 1942 H. O. Milliken and Newton P. Bevin,
the New York architects who had designed the massive
pavilion for the Coffin garden, made minor structural
changes to the cottage. Although the war ended in
1945, the Fricks enjoyed the house so much they did
not return to the main house until 1951, sadly just two
years before Frances's sudden death.

# ENDINGS: WESTMORELAND FARM

## THE COUNTRY HOME OF HELEN CLAY FRICK
## WESTCHESTER COUNTY, NEW YORK

IN 1919, ONE YEAR AFTER HENRY CLAY FRICK PURCHASED the Clayton Estate for his son and daughter-in-law, Childs and Frances Frick, the wealthy industrialist died. Helen Frick, who never had owned her own home, inherited the lion's share of the one-sixth of his fortune left to family and friends and instantly purchased a tract of meadow and woodland in Westchester County, New York. She named the property Westmoreland Farm, and both by its purchase and her choice of name, Helen brought the story of the Henry Clay Frick houses full circle. When she bought the property in 1920, over a century had passed since her paternal Mennonite great-great-grandfathers, Henry Overholt and Johann Nicholas Frick, crossed the Allegheny Mountains and ventured through the Pennsylvania wilderness from Bucks County to Westmoreland County. They had not considered their new homes to be symbols of wealth and social position, or even places of rest as Helen's farm came to be for her; owning a farm in Westmoreland County had meant new economic opportunity and a hoped-for increase in fortune. In 1920, however, Helen Frick, who was called "America's richest bachelor girl," disdained the pretenses associated with wealth and social position. For her, the farm represented not a contained economic system, a source of income, or a status symbol, but rather an

*Above:* Helen Clay Frick by the lake at Westmoreland Farm, c. 1930.

*Facing page:* Westmoreland Farm, c. 1930.

emotional and spiritual sanctuary — a place where she could replenish herself. In the natural beauty of Westchester County, Helen could forget her Frick legacy and the burdens she carried as principal heir to Henry Clay Frick's fortune. With rustic informality she could entertain friends and relatives or relax with the staff of her library.

Over the years, the simple, ramshackle, but quaint white-clapboard main house became ever more important to Helen Frick. On her mother's death in 1931, she inherited her father's former residences, Eagle Rock and Clayton. Although Helen maintained Eagle Rock until she demolished it in 1969 — reserving many of its treasures and architectural elements for her new Frick Art Museum at Clayton — and cared for Clayton until it became a museum on her death, Westmoreland Farm remained her place of renewal. Spring saw the naturalized daffodils and bluebells Helen had planted poke through the frozen earth. Dogwoods bloomed in profusion, as did apple trees Helen named after her great-nieces and great-nephews. Nature trails wound through the pastures and woodland. Often Helen took her guests for a walk or a ride and stopped deep in the forest for a picnic casually spread upon a blanket, but always served by her. In the summer, fresh fruits and vegetables filled the menu when Helen and her guests ate lunch comfortably seated in wicker chairs clustered beneath a pair of tall evergreen trees. In the winter, a fire blazed in the large open hearth in the almost doll-size living room and in her equally small dining room. Loveliest of all, the sound of the distant waterfall lulled the household to sleep; all would awaken to the smell of home-baked bread — knowing fresh milk, butter, and cream from her cows Buttercup and Honeybunch also awaited.

No one who visited Helen at Westmoreland Farm, however, would have guessed her sizable fortune or her importance in the world of art and historic preservation. In fact, so modest was the farm complex that first-time visitors invariably drove past, looking for a mansion, never suspecting a "Frick" could live so simply. Although the house contained some early American antiques and hooked rugs, it offered only a cozy, unpretentious lifestyle.

But for all the outer simplicity, Helen Frick's life was complicated. The responsibility for the future and the integrity of the former Frick residences had fallen to her. As Matilda Gay, wife of the artist Walter Gay, noted in her 1928 diary, Helen was "an excellent, intelligent girl, doing a good educational work in her art library, shouldering the responsibility of her great wealth with courage and good will." And rather than embracing modernism, therefore, her mission became preserving the past. This was not mere sentimentality. She had a passionate desire to expose the younger generations of Fricks — and eventually the public — to the beauty and historic importance of her father's houses and their contents. Thus was born her fierce determination to maintain them as prime examples of the cultural sensibilities of their time.

In 1981 the story of the Frick family houses came to a close. Throughout her six decades at Westmoreland Farm, Helen Frick concentrated on her historic preservation efforts, always having kept Pennsylvania as her legal residence. To avoid having her estate probated in New York, and fearing for her health, her trustees insisted that ninety-three-year-old Helen return to Clayton where her medical needs could be more properly met. But before Helen left, she transferred the title to Westmoreland Farm to another great-niece so the property would remain in the family.

When Helen Frick died at Clayton three years later, the Golden Era with its varied architectural and interior styles long since had given way to a style Helen loathed — modernist abstraction. Her parents and siblings were gone, the era of luxurious American domestic architecture and interior design they had enjoyed was over, but the legacy of the Frick family houses could live on primarily because of Helen's efforts during her lifetime. Although Eagle Rock was demolished in 1969 and a few years after Helen's death both Westmoreland Farm and her brother's estate on Long Island were sold, all remain in the memory of the Frick family: Westmoreland Farm, the place Helen organized her campaign to preserve her father's houses as examples of a bygone era; Eagle Rock, the house Helen had to sacrifice, yet preserved in the Frick Art Museum as carefully as she could; One East Seventieth Street, a museum that still feels like home; and the Clayton Estate (now the Nassau County Museum of Art), where Frances and Childs Frick pursued their scientific interests in botany, horticulture, wildlife, and paleontology.

From the Federal farmhouse in Westmoreland County to Clayton's high Victorianism to the neoclassicism of Eagle Rock and the Beaux Arts style of One East Seventieth Street and then to the Long Island English country house also called Clayton — the story of the Frick houses had a more than fitting ending in 1981 when Helen left her agrarian retreat, Westmoreland Farm, for Clayton, Pittsburgh, the first home that Henry Clay Frick owned — the house where Helen Frick was born and the house where she died.

*Right:* In a photograph by Helen Frick, two of her great-nieces garden at Westmoreland Farm, 1947.

# NOTES

*Unless identified in the text, the location of paintings no longer in Henry Clay Frick's collections is unknown to the author. With the exception of the Childs Frick bequest to the Frick Collection, the majority of the Clayton Estate's contents passed to Frick family members. Their names have been withheld to preserve their privacy.*

### ABBREVIATIONS

*Individuals*

| | |
|---|---|
| Sir Charles Allom | SCA |
| Elsie de Wolfe | EdW |
| Helen Clay Frick | HF |
| Henry Clay Frick | HCF |
| Thomas Hastings | TH |
| D. B. Kinch | DBK |
| Roland F. Knoedler | RFK |
| H. C. McEldowney | McE |

*Institutions*

| | |
|---|---|
| Frick Archives, Pittsburgh, Pa. | FA |
| Frick Art & Historical Center | FA&HC |
| The Frick Collection, New York, N.Y. | FC |
| Rockefeller Archive Center, Sleepy Hollow, N.Y. | RAC |
| Rockefeller Family Archives, Sleepy Hollow, N.Y. | RFA |

### PREFACE

**page xiv** "The story of houses": de Wolfe, *After All*, 83.

### INTRODUCTION: WESTMORELAND COUNTY, PENNSYLVANIA

**page 4** "gold and silver money": Fretz, *Descendants of Martin Oberholtzer*, 63.

**6** "fancy one": Rodney Sturtz, director of West Overton Museums, to author, August 9, 2000.

**9** "not enough to hurt": *New York Times*, June 2, 1907.

### CHAPTER ONE: CLAYTON, PITTSBURGH, PENNSYLVANIA

**page 15** "Forge of the Universe"; "Hell with the lid"; "A smoky dismal city": quoted in Toker, *Pittsburgh: An Urban Portrait*, 10, 11.

**16** the then astonishing sum: According to Holly, *Modern Dwellings in Town and Country*, 1878 estimates for the construction of houses similar to Homewood (renamed Clayton) were $6,500 to $17,000.

**17–18** "I would like your Mr. Hess": HCF to D. S. Hess & Company, January 1883, FA.

**19** "At no other time": Rosenthal in Hellerstedt et al., *Clayton, the Pittsburgh Home of Henry Clay Frick*, 26.

**21** "I think it simply": HCF to Frederick J. Osterling, June 25, 1891, FA.

**22** "You could to very good": George Megrew to A. J. Kimbel Jr., March 11, 1892, FA.

**23** "The decorated [window] shades": HCF to A. J. Kimbel Jr., May 6, 1892, FA.

**23** "rapidly being hung": HF, "Clayton Memoir," 5.

**23** "[The work] is rough": HCF to Alden & Harlow, July 1897, FA.

**24** "Have asked Mr. Hiss": HCF to Roland Knoedler, October 25, 1898, FA.

**26** "Mrs. Frick and I are going over": HCF to Daniel H. Burnham, January 11, 1900, FA.

**26** Patek Philippe watch: Antiquorum Auctioneers, *Important Watches, Wristwatches and Clocks,* Geneva, October 15–16, 1994.

**27** "Mrs. Frick is inclined": HCF to Mr. Inglis, October 17, 1903, FA.

**27–28** "[Mrs. Frick] also objects": HCF to Cottier & Company, October 26, 1903, FA.

**28** "the superb art of Clayton": Pittsburgh *Bulletin*, January 24, 1903.

**28** "The few hours spent": Frederick Taylor Gates to HCF, May 1904, RFA, RG 1, vol. 357, RAC.

**29** "East to West": HF, 1914 Friendship Calendar, FA.

**29** "dear old home": HF, "Clayton Memoir," 1.

**29** "Very often in the summer": HF, "Clayton Memoir"; also in Rosenthal, "Furnishings Plan: Clayton," 312.

**29** "neither condone nor forget": HF to John D. Rockefeller Jr., July 24, 1947, FA. For more information on the fight between Helen Clay Frick and John D. Rockefeller Jr., see Sanger, *Henry Clay Frick: An Intimate Portrait.*

**29** "as the most intensive": Toker, *Pittsburgh: An Urban Portrait*, 16.

**30** "to be preserved": quoted in Rosenthal, "Furnishings Plan: Clayton," 309, 310, 311.

**31** expanded her Pittsburgh philanthropy: see HF to Edward Litchfield, University of Pittsburgh Archive Service Center.

**34** "as if [the Fricks]"; "It feels like a home": "Frick's Homey Mansion," *Wall Street Journal*, September 24, 1990.

**34** "We are trying to": "A Triumph of Restoration," *Architectural Digest*, December 1990.

**34** "Frozen in time": "Restoring Baronial Splendor in Pittsburgh," *New York Times*, November 5, 1987.

**35** "the finest fence": Annie Stephany, "Memoir," FA.

**36** "something that will give great": Andrew Carnegie to HCF, June 3, 1892, FA.

**41** "[all was] gold and white with tapestries": "Mrs. Henry Clay Frick Introduces Her Young Daughter at Clayton," *Pittsburgh Press*, November 1908; also in Rosenthal, "Furnishings Plan: Clayton," 19.

**49** "pictures are brought out": Rosenthal, "Furnishings Plan: Clayton," 86.

**55** "Mrs. Frick's room is in": George Megrew to HCF, January 27, 1892, FA.

**59** "Considering that [Helen] used": Rosenthal, "Furnishings Plan: Clayton," 200.

**59** "My bedroom has three beds": Helen Frick, "Description of My Bedroom," March 18, 1898, FA.

**65** "having the fidgets": HF, "Clayton Memoir," 3.

**72** "[they] were delightful": HF, "Clayton Memoir," 9.

**73** "serves . . . as the equivalent": *New York Times*, March 21, 1993.

**77** "tiny [and] *homely*": HF to Miss Duff, Oct. 8, 1905, FA.

**79** "real hobby was speed": Harvey, *Henry Clay Frick*, 359.

### CHAPTER TWO: EAGLE ROCK (RAZED 1969), BOSTON'S NORTH SHORE

**page 87** "the supreme excellence": Metcalf, *Ogden Codman and the Decoration of Houses,* 156.

87 "outside men": HCF to Little & Browne, April 22, 1905, FA.

87 "I want nothing but": HCF to Little & Browne, January 21, 1905, FA.

87 "I want everything": HCF to Little & Browne, May 22, 1905, FA.

87 "We will have all in grass": HCF to Little & Browne, November 3, 1905, FA.

87 "After looking at the two photographs": HCF to Little & Browne, November 27, 1905, FA.

88 "It seems impossible": HCF to Little & Browne, December 13, 1905, FA.

88 "It is all I shall ever want": Harvey, *Henry Clay Frick*, 270; see also Mellon, *Judge Mellon's Sons*, 516.

89 "the grandest mansion": *Beverly Times*, May 14, 1985.

90 "Enclosed you will find": Lester Couch to HCF, August 2, 1905, FA.

90 "I have several andirons": Joseph Duveen to HCF, August 26, 1906, Bill Book, FC.

91 "Physicians have recommended": "No Salt Water for Mr. Frick," *New York Times*, December 18, 1911.

91 "The reason is that [Graham's]": HF to James B. Stevenson, July 1, 1964, author's collection.

92 "Goodness! What in the world": quoted in Garland, *The North Shore*, 237.

93 "These we have placed"; "not insured": RFK to HCF, May 1911, Bill Book, FC.

93 "I have given instructions": HCF to RFK, November 8, 1904, FA.

93 "The President is anxious": HCF to Andrew Carnegie II, October 10, 1910, FA.

93 "Taft's Summer Capital": *New York Times*, December 18, 1911.

93–94 "enjoyed special privileges": Harvey, *Henry Clay Frick*, 360.

94 "intended to build an art gallery": *New York Times*, December 1911.

94–95 "It was necessary for me"; "As the [Eagle Rock gallery]"; "would no more think"; "I do not know what effect": Daniel H. Burnham to HCF, January 2, 1912, FA.

95 "I know Mr. Widener": HCF to Daniel H. Burnham, January 8, 1912, FA.

96 For Adelaide Frick's inheritance: see Sanger, *Henry Clay Frick*, second printing, 561, note to p. 413.

99 "with the care given"; "It is Miss Frick's wish": *Beverly Times*, December 17, 1968.

107 Henry Clay Frick's habits: HF, "Grandfather," FA.

122 "the broom of the stomach": HF, "Grandfather," 9, FA.

125 "new toy": HF "Grandfather," 6, FA.

125 "Well, well, look": HF, "Grandfather," 3, FA.


Chapter Three: One East Seventieth Street, The Frick Collection, New York

**page 137** "look like a miner's shack": John McCarten, "Daughter of Her Father," *The New Yorker*, July 15, 1939, 24. This quote has been used extensively by scholars. Though amusing, no primary source has been identified.

137 "high appreciation": RG 5, Board of Trustees Executive Committee Minutes, December 4, 1908, New York Public Library Archives.

139 "loudly denounced the work": Metcalf, *Ogden Codman and the Decoration of Houses*, 67.

139 house to be his monument: Harvey, *Henry Clay Frick*, 336.

140 "I spent a delightful": James Howard Bridge to HCF, July 13, 1912, FA.

140 "seems quite anxious": HCF to TH, June 6, 1912, FA.

140 "I go to see him": Bridge, *Millionaires and Grubb Street*, 71.

142 "We sure are going fast": DBK to McElroy, July 17, 1913, FA.

142 "Sometimes I wonder why"; " was just as nice": DBK to McElroy, August 15, 1913, FA.

142 "One of the men": DBK to HCF, July 21, 1913, FA.

142 "[It] sure is a darling": DBK to McElroy, July 17, 1913, FA.

142 "so busy with [his] big baby": DBK to McElroy, August 15, 1913, FA.

143 "I think Allom is": Charles S. Carstairs to HCF, July 11, 1913, FA.

143 "Please see that ceilings": HCF to SCA, June 24, 1913, FA.

143 "so far ahead of"; "Why start plastering": DBK to McElroy, September 20, 1913, FA.

143 "Gee, if Hastings": DBK to McElroy, August 22, 1913, FA.

143 "We desire a comfortable": HCF to SCA, December 12, 1913, FA.

143 "I think the various percentages": HCF to SCA, March 24, 1914, FA.

143 "modern women": de Wolfe, *The House in Good Taste*, 237.

144 "Mr. Frick, when I": quoted in Smith, *Elsie de Wolfe*, 158.

145 "Our understanding": HCF to EdW, March 1914?, FA.

145 "admitted he lost his temper"; "agreed to see that": HCF to EdW, June 4, 1914, FA.

145 de Wolfe pleads for more rooms: EdW to HCF, March 20, 1914, FA.

147 "all . . . shall be done": DBK to McElroy, undated, c. 1914, FA.

147 "I do hope we will not": HCF to SCA, March 24, 1914, FA.

147 "Went almost immediately": HCF to RFK, June 3, 1914, FA.

147 Frick's compliments: HCF to EdW, May 27, June 4, 1914, FA.

149 "You are very much behind"; "There are a number of things": HCF to White, Allom & Company, September 29, 1914, FA.

149 "only able to move": HCF to Jacques Seligmann, September 26, 1914, FA.

149, 151 "I am glad to say"; "Rather surprised": HCF to White, Allom & Company, September 29, 1914, FA.

151 "Your failure to make good": HCF to White, Allom & Company, October 21, 1914, FA.

151 "Simply outrageous": HCF to White, Allom & Company, October 29, 1914, FA.

151 "Certain doors"; "I can tell you" : SCA to HCF, October 30, 1914, FA.

152 "Your Mr. Allom's letter": HCF to White, Allom & Company, November 17, 1914, FA.

152–53 "don't you think it rather": HCF to White, Allom & Company, November 18, 1914, FA.

153 "it is true there are": HCF to EdW, December 24, 1914, FA.

153 "I am willing to pay"; "undertake not to accept": HCF to EdW, February 8, 1915, FA.

153–54 "That we desire to check"; "Your taste is unquestionable": HCF to EdW, March 15, 1915, FA.

154 "without charge": HCF to Duveen Brothers, February 22, 1915, FA.

154 "Much as I wish": HCF to SCA?, June 19, 1915, FA.

154 "Please arrange to have": HCF to EdW, September 29, 1915, FA.

154 "I think the house cost": HCF to TH, June 2, 1915, FA.

154–55 "I am in receipt of your absurd": HCF to TH, March 18, 1916, FA.

155 "do very little talking": Miller, *The Architecture of Benno Janssen*, 49.

155  "not only abreast of": quoted in Lee, "A Grand Dame Named William Penn," *Pennsylvania Heritage Magazine,* Spring 1991, 31.

158  "a legacy of beauty"; "unsurpassed anywhere": quoted in Frick Collection, "Legacy of Beauty," 5.

158  fabricated by John Williams: for more information see the 1911 trade catalogue for Jno. Williams, Inc., New York, Winterthur, fiche no. 1224 at the New York Historical Society. See also *Jno. S. Williams: Cast and Wrought Brass and Bronze Work, Wrought Iron.* New York: Sackett & Wilhelms Lithography and Painting Company, c. 1899 at the New York Public Library, New York.

162  For more information on the division of scrap items from the 1931–35 renovation see "Re: The Frick Collection," RFA, RG 2, series H, box 63, folder 472, RAC.

165  For the wrought-iron grillework see: "Contracts for New York Residence of H. C. Frick, March 30, 1914," located in the Frick Family Archives. It documents what Yellin charged for his work at One East Seventieth Street: $25 dollars per day, $7600 for two entrance doors and grilles in the vestibule opening from the porte cochère, and $250 for the samples of iron work. Yellin also made a panel for the fence at the entrance door. According to Jack Andrews, author of *Samuel Yellin: Metalworker,"* the Yellin job cards for this panel and for the entrance doors read: no. 1308, panel for fence at entrance, grilles, doors; no. 1322, Glazed doors.

165  "It is necessary, that a metal worker": quoted in Gerakaris, ed., "Samuel Yellin: Metalworker," 1.

165  "A smith cannot busy himself": quoted in Davis, *Sketches in Iron,* 7–8.

167  "What I make must be real": quoted in Davis, *Sketches in Iron,* 11–2.

169  "born with a hammer": quoted in Andrews, *Samuel Yellin: Metalworker,* 1.

169  "a dead metal": quoted in Gerakaris, ed., "Samuel Yellin: Metalworker."

169  "It is the stuff of which": quoted in Andrews, *Samuel Yellin: Metalworker,* 13.

169  "a hammer for a pencil": quoted in Davis, *Sketches in Iron,* 8.

169  "Iron cannot be molded in clay": quoted in Gerakaris, ed., "Samuel Yellin: Metalworker," 8.

169  "The effect of a piece of work": quoted in the Southern Highland Craft Guild, *Samuel Yellin Metalworkers: Three Generations,* 6.

169  "When I go to rest": quoted in Davis, *Sketches in Iron,* 12.

171  "this work . . . to be artistically": TH to HCF, September 16, 1915, FA.

179  "beyond the criticism": HCF to TH, September 16, 1915, FA.

187  "one of the costliest": quoted in Munhall, *The Frick Collection: A Tour,* 67.

187  "absolutely wonderful": Cochrane, "The Mystery of the Mino Tomb," 140.

187  "for study purposes": Mortimer Clapp to University of Pittsburgh Art Department, February 8, 1933, University of Pittsburgh Archive Service Center.

189  "to acquire warmth": HF, "Henry Clay Frick and His Collection," Frick Collection, *An Illustrated Catalogue,* vol. 1.

189  "Wealth in its nobler": quoted in Munhall, *The Frick Collection: A Tour,* 55.

193  "a weird semblance of life": Bridge, *Millionaires and Grubb Street,* 86–87.

193  "All the light was": Rieder, *A Charmed Couple,* 188.

193  "[He] took so much": HF, "Grandfather," 17.

197  look out for a "beauty": HF, Diary, 1919.

CHAPTER FOUR: THE CLAYTON ESTATE, LONG ISLAND, NEW YORK

page 221  "mechanism for living": Platt, *America's Gilded Age,* 68.

221  "Order for the sake": quoted in Metcalf, *Ogden Codman and the Decoration of Houses,* x.

225  "If I am to pay": HCF to SCA, January 24, 1919, FA.

225, 227  "You must have"; "The specifications above": HCF to SCA, March 17, 1919, FA.

267  "the right plant"; "living pictures": "The Lady and the Architect," *The House and Garden,* Nassau County Museum of Art.

EPILOGUE: WESTMORELAND FARM, WESTCHESTER COUNTY, NEW YORK

page 278  "America's richest": *New York Evening World,* December 3, 1919.

280  "an excellent, intelligent girl": Rieder, *A Charmed Couple,* 189.

| | |
|---|---|
| à abattant | With a flap, or drop-front, which opens to make a writing surface. |
| Adamesque | Referring to the neoclassic style of Robert and James Adam. |
| Aesthetic Movement | An English artistic reform movement advocating "art for art's sake." |
| allegory | A work of art representing an abstract quality or idea from scripture, as well as Greek and Roman legends and literature. |
| appliqué | A method of decorating in which a motif is cut from one piece of material and applied to another. |
| apse | A semicircular, vaulted space. |
| arcade | A series of arches supported by columns or piers. |
| architrave | The molding around a mirror, door, or window frame. Also the bottom third of the entablature, the part resting on the column or pilaster and supporting a frieze. |
| Aubusson | Referring to the style of carpets and tapestries produce at the Aubusson factory in France beginning in the mid-eighteenth century and characterized by smooth-faced weaving, soft feminine colors, symmetrical designs, and pastoral themes. |
| banquette | A small bench. |
| baroque | A type of classicism characterized by elaborate ornamentation of sculptural, curving forms. |
| Beauvais | Tapestry made at the Beauvais factory founded by Louis XIV in 1664. |
| Beaux Arts | An academic and eclectic style of the nineteenth and twentieth centuries associated with the Ecole des Beaux Arts in Paris, founded in 1671. |
| bergère | An enclosed armchair. |
| bisque | Unglazed ceramic, particularly porcelain. |
| boiserie | Richly carved and painted wooden paneling used in French interiors of the seventeenth and eighteenth centuries. |
| breccia | A type of Italian marble formed from a composite of stones that do not melt in a lava form as other marbles do. Breccia reveals the angular stones. |
| brèche rouge | A pink breccia marble. |
| brocade | A rich fabric with a raised pattern created during the weaving process, often with gold and silver thread. |
| broken pediment | A pediment with the upper angle left open or with the upper segmental curve missing the central section. |
| bronze doré | Gilded bronze. |
| bureau plat | A large, ornamented, French writing table. |
| Caen stone | A fine-grained French limestone cream in color and easily carved. |
| caisson | A sunken panel in a coffered ceiling. |
| canapé | A settee or sofa. |
| cassoni | An Italian marriage chest. |
| chinoiserie | A playful, decorative style based on oriental motifs popularized in the eighteenth century. |

| | |
|---|---|
| clapboard | A long, narrow board with one edge thicker than the other and overlapped. |
| classical | Pertaining to the architecture of ancient Greece and Rome. |
| coffer | A sunken panel in a ceiling. |
| colonnade | A row of columns. |
| commode | A chest of drawers more decorative than utilitarian. |
| console table | A table supported against a wall on "console" or scrolled legs. |
| cornice | The internal ornamental molding around the walls of a room, linking the wall to the ceiling. |
| cove | A concave surface connecting a ceiling and a wall. |
| dado | The lower part of an interior wall consisting of a baseboard, a die, and an upper rail or cap molding. |
| damask | Cloth of velvet, silk, or cotton woven or printed with large-scale, stylized, and raised floral patterns. Also used on wallpaper. |
| dentil | A small projecting block used in rows forming part of a cornice and resembling teeth. |
| dome | A convex roof or ceiling, hemispherical, semi-ovoidal, or saucer-shaped, built over a square, octagonal, or circular space. |
| Edwardian | A style, characterized by light colors and an airy atmosphere, that came into fashion in 1901 when Edward VII assumed the throne and, in a reaction against the Victorian style, embraced the Louis XVI style. |
| entablature | The upper part of an order, supported by columns. Made up of three major horizontal members: architrave, frieze, and cornice. |
| *famille rose* | Chinese enameled porcelain with a predominant rose color. |
| fauteuil | An armchair. |
| Federal | The name given to England's Adamesque style of neo-classical decoration popular in America from the establishment of the Federal government in 1730 to about 1830. |
| festoon | A garland of fruits, flowers, leaves, husks, or ribbon hanging in a curve. Also called a swag. |
| Flemish bond | Brickwork with each course made up of alternate headers and stretchers. |
| frieze | The interior space between the top of wall paneling, or picture rail, and the ceiling. |
| gadrooning | A series of convex curves usually found on a curved surface, often with embossed metalwork. |
| Georgian | Referring to a style of architecture, interior design, and decorative arts in Britain and Ireland that spread to the United States during the reigns from George I to George IV, between 1714 and 1830, or sometimes considered without the reign of George IV (see Regency). Encompasses Renaissance and rococo forms and a range of neoclassical styles such as Pompeiian Revival and Etruscan style, as well as the dominant classical forms and motifs. |

| | |
|---|---|
| Georgian Revival | Referring to the late nineteenth- and early twentieth-century English style of architecture, furniture, and decorative arts that revived the forms and decorative motifs of the Georgian period from 1714 to 1830. Features symmetrical brick facades, pitched roofs, sashes, and fanlights, with furniture styles drawn from the Adam brothers, Hepplewhite, Sheraton, and Chippendale. Also known as neo-Georgian. |
| girandole | An ornate wall sconce with one or more candle branches mounted on a wall or attached to the sides of a mirror. |
| Gobelins | Tapestry made at the Gobelins factory, which excelled during the reign of Louis XIV and through the eighteenth century. |
| Gothic | An ornamental style dating from the twelfth century characterized by pointed arches and vaulting. |
| Greek Revival | Referring to a style popular in America from 1820 to 1860 and based on the Greek temple motif. Also known as Grecian. |
| guéridon | A tripod table. |
| half-timbering | Wall construction in which the spaces between the members of a timber frame are filled with brick, stone, or other material. |
| ho-ho bird | A cranelike bird used decoratively in Chinese art and chinoiserie decoration. |
| Italianate | A style derived from Italian Renaissance architecture and decoration. |
| Jacobean | Referring to the English style of architecture and fine decorative arts during the reign of James I, 1603–25. |
| japanned | European imitations of oriental lacquer. |
| lacquer | A hard, waterproof varnish originally from the Far East. |
| lambrequin | Stiff, flat valances with decoratively shaped lower edges, often descending at either side. |
| lattice | Narrow bars arranged to make a crossed pattern. |
| loggia | A gallery open to the air on one or more sides. |
| marquetry | Wooden inlay used on furniture. |
| measured drawing | An exact scale drawing based on measurements taken from an existing building. |
| Modernism | Abstract styles in art and architecture, devoid of ornament, that dominated twentieth-century Western culture. |
| modillion | A small bracket used in rows under the corona of a cornice and extending from the bed mold. |
| mosaic | A design made by cementing small pieces of hard, colored material such as marble, glass, ceramic, or semiprecious stones to a base. |
| neoclassicism | The mid-eighteenth-century return to Greek and Roman classicism showing a preference for the linear, the symmetrical, and the flat rather than the three-dimensional. |
| niche | A recess in a wall, usually with semidome, designed as a place for a statue. |
| order | A column with a base (except in the Greek Doric), shaft, and capital and its entablature, in the Tuscan, Doric, Ionic, Corinthian, or Composite style. |
| ormolu | Gilded bronze used for furniture mounts and ornamental objects. |

| | |
|---|---|
| parcel gilt | Partially gilded silver or wood. |
| parquet | Made of wooden blocks and laid in a geometric design. |
| pavilion | A part of a building projecting from the rest. |
| pediment | Crowning element used over doors, windows, and niches. |
| petit point | Tapestry with small stitches. |
| pietra dure | A type of mosaic made of semiprecious stones in relief and representing such motifs as birds and fruit. |
| pilaster | A vertical rectangular projection from a wall, treated like a column with base, shaft, and capital. |
| porte cochère | A large covered entrance porch that vehicles can drive through. |
| portico | A roof supported by columns and usually attached to the front or sides of a building. |
| portiere | A heavy curtain suspended on rods used in place of doors to separate rooms. |
| provenance | The record of all known owners and locations of a work of art. |
| quoin | Stone or brick used to accentuate the corner of a building. |
| Regency | A classical style drawing on French Empire in the period from 1811 to 1820 when the prince regent, later George IV, ruled in place of his father, George III. |
| rococo | A late baroque style in the early part of eighteenth-century France involving scrollwork, shell motifs, and highly decorative, florid patterns. |
| secrétaire | A writing desk with a place to keep papers and valuables, usually with a flap that opens to make a writing surface. |
| semanier | A narrow chest of drawers. |
| shakes | A seventeenth- and eighteenth-century term for wooden shingles, made by splitting sections from a log. |
| strapwork | A form of ornamentation consisting of folding and interlacing bands that resembles leather straps. |
| terra-cotta | Unglazed, fired clay. |
| tole | Tin plate objects painted with late eighteenth- and early nineteenth-century designs. |
| tooled leather | Leather with a decorative design impressed by heated tools. |
| torchère | A tall candle stand. |
| tripartite wall | A wall that is divided into three parts: the dado, the field or filling, and the frieze. |
| trompe l'oeil | A painted surface that creates the impression of a three-dimensional object or scene. Derives from the French "deceives the eye." |
| tyg | A muglike drinking vessel usually having two or four handles but sometimes as many as twelve. |
| Venetian window | A triple window consisting of a round-headed light flanked by two slightly lower flat-headed ones. |
| vernacular architecture | Architecture built of local materials to suit local needs. |
| vestibule | An anteroom, entrance, hall, or foyer. |
| wainscoting | Woodwork, often paneled, covering the lower portion of the walls of a room. |

Andrews, Jack. *Samuel Yellin: Metalworker.* Ocean Pines, Md.: SkipJack Press, 2000.

Aslet, Clive. *The American Country House.* New Haven, Conn.: Yale University Press, 1990.

Aurand, Martin. "Frederick John Osterling and a Tale of Two Buildings." *Pennsylvania Heritage,* spring 1989, 16–21.

Avery, Charles. *Renaissance and Baroque Bronzes in the Frick Art Museum.* Pittsburgh, Pa.: Frick Art and Historical Center, 1993.

Bates, Elizabeth Bidwell, and Jonathan L. Fairbanks. *American Furniture 1620 to the Present.* New York: Richard Marek Publishers, 1981.

Bedford, Steven McLeod. *John Russell Pope: Architect of an Empire.* New York: Rizzoli, 1998.

Benstock, Shari. *No Gifts from Chance: A Biography of Edith Wharton.* New York: Charles Scribner's Sons, 1994.

Brady, Henry. "Appraisal of Personal Property: Estate of Childs Frick." New York, 1965. Author's collection.

Bridge, James Howard. *Millionaires and Grubb Street: Comrades and Contacts in the Last Half Century.* New York: Brentano's, 1921.

Brignano, Mary. *The Frick Art and Historical Center: The Art and Life of a Pittsburgh Family.* Pittsburgh, Pa.: Frick Art and Historical Center, 1993.

Cahill, Bill. "60-Room Frick House Will Be Dismantled." *Beverly Times,* December 17, 1968.

Campbell, Nina, and Caroline Seebohm. *Elsie de Wolfe: A Decorative Life.* New York: Clarkson N. Potter, 1992.

Church, Ella Rodman. *How to Furnish a Home.* New York: Appleton and Company, 1882.

Churchill, Lady Henrietta Spencer. *Classic Georgian Style.* New York: Rizzoli, 1997.

Cochrane, Albert Franz. "The Mystery of the Mino Tomb." *Harpers Monthly Magazine,* July 1938, 137–47.

Collier, Bernard. "Frick Fossils Given to Museum." *New York Times,* December 15, 1967.

Cook, Clarence. *The House Beautiful: Essays on Beds and Tables, Stools and Candlesticks.* New York: Charles Scribner's Sons, 1881.

Davis, Myra Tolmach. *Sketches in Iron: Samuel Yellin, American Master of Wrought Iron, 1885–1940.* Published in conjunction with the exhibition "Sketches in Iron: Samuel Yellin," George Washington University, Washington, D.C., March 5–26, 1971.

Dell, Theodore. *Furniture in the Frick Collection: French Eighteenth- and Nineteenth-Century Furniture (part 1).* New York: Frick Collection, 1992.

_____. *Furniture in the Frick Collection: French Eighteenth- and Nineteenth-Century Furniture (part 2) and Gilt Bronzes.* New York: Frick Collection, 1992.

Despont, Thierry W. *The Helen Clay Frick Foundation Restoration of Clayton, Phase One, Final Report.* New York: privately printed, July 16, 1978.

de Wolfe, Elsie. *After All.* New York: Harper Brothers, 1935.

_____. *The House in Good Taste.* New York: Century Co., 1914.

Donnelly, Max Kolbe. "Cottier and Company (1864–1915): Establishing a Context for the Second Glasgow School." Master's thesis, Sotheby's Institute, London, 1998.

Dubrow, Eileen, and Richard Dubrow. *American Furniture of the Nineteenth Century.* Atglen, Pa.: Schiffer Publishing, 1983.

Dwight, Eleanor. *Edith Wharton: An Extraordinary Life.* New York: Abrams, 1994.

Eastlake, Charles L. *Hints on Household Taste.* Boston: J. R. Osgood & Co., 1872.

Edgell, G. H. "Boston Exhumes Its Mino Tomb: A Re-Investigation of the Monument Purchased in 1924." *Art News* 36, no. 11 (December 11, 1937): 12, 22–23.

_____. "A Modified Tomb Monument of the Italian Renaissance." *Bulletin of the Museum of Fine Arts* (Boston) 35, no. 207 (February 1937): 83–90.

Fitzgerald, Oscar P. *Three Centuries of American Furniture.* Englewood Cliffs, N.J.: Prentice-Hall, 1982.

Fleming, Nancy. *Money, Manure, and Maintenance: Ingredients for Successful Gardens of Marion Cruger Coffin, Pioneer Landscape Architect, 1876–1957.* Weston, Ma.: Country Place Books, 1998.

Flemming, George Thornton. *The History of Pittsburgh and Environs, from Prehistoric Days to the Beginning of the American Revolution.* Vol. 4. New York: American Historical Society, 1922.

Fretz, A. J. *A Genealogical Record of the Descendants of Martin Oberholtzer.* Milton, N.J.: Evergreen News, 1903.

Frick, Childs. Diary, 1883–1965. Author's collection.

Frick, Helen C. "Clayton Memoir," c. 1950. Frick Archives.

_____. Diary entitled "Grandfather." Frick Archives.

Frick Collection, The. *A Guide to Works of Art on Exhibition.* New York: Frick Collection, 1996.

_____. *Handbook of Paintings.* New York: Frick Collection, 1985.

_____. *An Illustrated Catalogue of the Works of Art in the Collection of Henry Clay Frick.* Vol. 1, *Paintings and Text.* Pittsburgh, Pa.: University of Pittsburgh Press, 1949.

_____. *An Illustrated Catalogue of the Works of Art in the Collection of Henry Clay Frick.* Vol. 4, *Drawings and Prints.* New York: Frick Art Reference Library, 1951.

_____. *An Illustrated Catalogue of the Works of Art in the Frick Collection.* Vols. 5–6, *Sculpture.* New York: Frick Art Reference Library, 1954.

_____. "Legacy of Beauty." New York: Frick Collection, 1995.

_____. "The Red Book" (paintings and furnishings owned by Henry Clay Frick). Curatorial files, Frick Collection.

Fullam, Anne C. "Bizarre 30's Trellis Is Being Rescued." *New York Times,* June 1988.

Galusha, Theodore. "Childs Frick and the Frick Collection of Fossil Mammals." 1975. Possibly a publication of the American Museum of Natural History.

Garland, Joseph E. *The North Shore: A Social History of Summers among the Noteworthy, Fashionable, Rich, Eccentric and Ordinary on Boston's Gold Coast, 1823–1929.* Beverly, Ma.: Commonwealth Editions, 1998.

Garrett, Wendell. *Classic America: The Federal Style and Beyond.* New York: Universe, 1995.

_____. *Victorian America: Classical Romanticism to Gilded Opulence.* New York: Rizzoli, 1993.

Gerakaris, Dimitri, ed. "Samuel Yellin Metalworker." Reprinted from *Anvil's Ring,* summer 1982.

Gere, Charlotte. *The House Beautiful: Oscar Wilde and the Aesthetic Interior.* London: Lund Humphries, 2000.

Goddard, Conrad Godwin. *The Early History of Roslyn, Long Island.* Privately printed, 1972.

Goldstein, Malcolm. *Landscape with Figures: A History of Art Dealing in the United States.* New York: Oxford University Press, 2000.

Gore, Alan, and Ann Gore. *The History of English Interiors.* London: Phaidon, 1991.

Hampton, Mark. *Legendary Decorators of the Twentieth Century.* New York: Doubleday, 1992.

Handler, Frederick John. "Moments of Kings, Moguls, and Millionaires: The Clayton Legacy." *GN News Magazine,* November 1986. Bryant Library, Roslyn, Long Island.

Handlin, David P. *The American Home: Architecture and Society, 1815–1915.* Boston, Mass.: Little, Brown, 1979.

Hannegan, Barry. "Historical Summary: Frick Park." Pittsburgh, Pa.: Pittsburgh History and Landmarks Foundation, June 1999.

Harvey, George. *Henry Clay Frick: The Man.* New York: Charles Scribner's Sons, 1928.

"The H. C. Frick Mansion: Most Pretentious Estate on the North Shore, Now Nearing Completion." *North Shore Breeze,* 1906, 12–13.

Healey, Edna. *The Queen's House: A Social History of Buckingham Palace.* New York: Carroll & Graf, 1997.

Hellerstedt, Kahren Jones, et al. *Clayton, the Pittsburgh Home of Henry Clay Frick: Art and Furnishings.* Pittsburgh, Pa.: Helen Clay Frick Foundation, 1988.

Hilderbrand, Gary R., ed. *Making a Landscape of Continuity: The Practice of Innocenti & Webel.* Cambridge, Mass.: Harvard University Graduate School of Design, 1997.

*A History of the Company and of the Overholt Family.* A. Overholt & Co., Inc., August 1940.

"History of the Westmoreland-Fayette Historical Society 1928–1987." N.d. Author's collection.

Hobart College. *Gardens Designed by Marian Cruger Coffin, Landscape Architect, 1876–1957: Memorial Exhibition of Photographs of 17 Gardens.* Geneva, N.Y.: Hobart College, 1958.

Holly, H. Hudson. *Modern Dwellings in Town and Country: Adapted to American Wants and Climate.* New York: Harper & Brothers, 1878.

*The House and Garden: Tenth Anniversary Exhibition.* Roslyn, N.Y.: Nassau County Museum of Art, 1986.

"How Fake Angels Failed to Guard a Fake Renaissance Tomb." *Art Digest* 5 (May 15, 1931): 8.

Hughes, Peter. *The Wallace Collection Catalogue of Furniture.* Vol. 3. London: Trustees of the Wallace Collection, 1996.

*In Pursuit of Beauty: Americans and the Aesthetic Movement.* New York: Metropolitan Museum of Art/Rizzoli, 1986.

Jones, Chester. *Colfax and Fowler: The Best in English Interior Decoration.* Boston: Little, Brown, 2000.

Kaldor, Andras. *New York: Masterpieces of Architecture.* Woodbridge, England: Antique Collector's Club, 1999.

Lambourne, Lionel. *The Aesthetic Movement.* London: Phaidon, 1996.

Lee, Marianne. "A Grande Dame Named William Penn." *Pennsylvania Heritage Magazine,* spring 1991, 31–37.

Leopold, Allison Kyle. *Victorian Splendor: Re-Creating America's Nineteenth-Century Interiors.* New York: Stewart, Tabori and Chang, 1986.

Lewis, Arnold, James Turner, and Steven McQuillin. *The Opulent Interiors of the Gilded Age: All 203 Photographs from "Artistic Houses."* New York: Dover, 1987.

Lockard, Ray Anne. "Helen Clay Frick: Pittsburgh's Altruist and Gentlewoman Avenger." *Art Documentation* 16, no. 2 (1997): 9–113.

Lowe, David Garrard. *Beaux-Arts New York.* New York: Watson-Guptill, 1998.

MacKay, Robert B., et al., eds. *Long Island Country Houses and Their Architects: 1860–1940.* New York: Society for the Preservation of Long Island Antiquities/W. W. Norton, 1997.

MacKenna, John. "The Jewel of Boston's Gold Coast." *Beverly Times,* May 15, 1985.

"Mantle of Authenticity Draped Over Boston's 'Dossena Tomb.'" *Art Digest* 12, no. 6 (December 15, 1937): 5, 14.

Maxwell, Marianne. "Pittsburgh's Frick Park: A Unique Addition to the City's Park System." *Western Pennsylvania Historical Magazine* 68, no. 3 (July 1985): 243–64.

Mayhew, Edgar deN., and Minor Myers Jr. *A Documentary History of American Interiors from the Colonial Era to 1915.* New York: Charles Scribner's Sons, 1980.

McCarten, John. "Daughter of Her Father." *The New Yorker,* July 1939.

Mellon, William Larimer. *Judge Mellon's Sons.* [Pittsburgh?]: privately printed, 1949.

Metcalf, Pauline C., ed. *Ogden Codman and the Decoration of Houses.* Boston: David R. Godine, 1988.

Miller, Donald. *The Architecture of Benno Janssen.* Pittsburgh, Pa.: Carnegie Mellon University, 1997.

"Milliken-Bevin Trellis Dedicated in Roslyn." *Friends for Long Island's Heritage Newsletter* 23 (1991).

Milner, John. "An Architectural Analysis of Clayton: The Henry Clay Frick Mansion." Submitted to the Helen Clay Frick Foundation by John Milner Associates, Inc., 1986.

Moss, Roger W., and Gail Caskey Winkler. *Victorian Interior Decoration: American Interiors, 1830–1900.* New York: Henry Holt, 1986.

Munhall, Edgar. *The Frick Collection: A Tour.* New York: Frick Collection/London: Scala Publishers, 1998.

Nelson, J. Franklin. *Works of Frederick J. Osterling, Architect.* Pittsburgh, Pa.: Murdoch-Kerr Press, 1904.

Newton, Charles. *Victorian Designs for the Home.* London: V&A Publications, 1999.

*Old Westbury Gardens.* Old Westbury, N.Y.: Old Westbury Gardens, Inc., 1985.

Overholt, Karl. Diary, c. 1919. West Overton Museums, Pa.

Peterson, Harold L. *Americans at Home: From the Colonists to the Late Victorians.* New York: Charles Scribner's Sons, 1971.

Pinkham, Harold A., Jr. *A Reference Guide to the Residential Development of the Eastern Shore of Beverly, Massachusetts, 1844–1919.* Privately printed, 1997.

"Plant Distribution List for Childs Frick." Jamaica Plain, Mass.: Arnold Arboretum, 1924.

Platt, Frederick. *America's Gilded Age: Its Architecture and Decoration.* New York: A. S. Barnes, 1976.

Poppeliers, John C., et al. *What Style Is It? A Guide to American Architecture.* New York: John Wiley & Sons, 1983.

Reed, Henry Hope. *Beaux-Arts Architecture in New York: A Photographic Guide.* New York: Dover, 1988.

Rieder, William. *A Charmed Couple: The Art and Life of Walter and Matilda Gay.* New York: Abrams, 2000.

Robinson, John Martin. *The Royal Palaces: Buckingham Palace.* London: Michael Joseph Limited/Royal Collection Enterprises Limited, 1995.

Roper, Matthew, and Leesa Rittelmann, Diane Poole, et al. *Planning the Pitt Campus: Dreams and Schemes Never Realized.* Pittsburgh, Pa.: University of Pittsburgh, Henry Clay Frick Fine Arts Department, 1993.

Rosenthal, Ellen M. "The Furnishings Plan: Clayton." April 12, 1988. Helen Clay Frick Foundation.

*Samuel Yellin Metalworkers: Three Generations.* Exhibition catalogue, May 16–August 5, 1998. Ashville, N.C.: Southern Highland Craft Guild, 1998.

Sanger, Martha Frick Symington. *Henry Clay Frick: An Intimate Portrait.* New York: Abbeville, 1998.

Schumacher, Caroline. *Preliminary Inventory of Clayton.* Pittsburgh, Pa.: Helen Clay Frick Foundation, 1985.

Seebohm, Caroline, and Christopher Simon Sykes. *English Country: Living in England's Private Houses.* New York: Clarkson N. Potter, 1987.

Simpson, Colin. *The Partnership: The Secret Association of Bernard Berenson and Joseph Duveen.* London: Bodley Head, 1987.

Smith, Jane. *Elsie de Wolfe: A Life in the High Style.* New York: Atheneum, 1982.

Stewart, Howard. *Historical Data: Pittsburgh's Public Parks.* Pittsburgh, Pa.: Greater Pittsburgh Parks Association, 1943.

"The Story of Pittsburgh and Vicinity." *Pittsburgh Gazette Times,* 1908.

Summerson, John. *The Classical Language of Architecture.* London: Thames and Hudson, 1963.

Tauranac, John, and Christopher Little. *Elegant New York: The Builders and the Buildings, 1885–1915.* New York: Abbeville, 1985.

Thornton, Peter. *Authentic Decor: The Domestic Interior 1620–1920.* New York: Crescent Books, 1984.

Toker, Franklin. *Pittsburgh: An Urban Portrait.* University Park, Pa.: Pennsylvania State University Press, 1986.

Toman, Rolfe, ed. *Neoclassicism and Romanticism: Architecture, Sculpture, Painting, Drawings, 1750–1848.* Cologne: Könemann, 2000.

Trocme, Susan. *Influential Interiors: Shaping Twentieth-Century Style through Key Interior Designers.* New York: Clarkson N. Potter, 1999.

van Trump, James D. *Legend in Modern Gothic: The Union Trust Building, Pittsburgh.* Pittsburgh, Pa.: Pittsburgh History and Landmarks Foundation, 1966.

Watkin, David. *English Architecture.* London: Thames and Hudson, 1979.

Wharton, Edith, and Ogden Codman Jr. *The Decoration of Houses.* 1902. New York: W. W. Norton, 1978.

Williams, Jno. "American Art in Bronze and Iron: Ornamental Wrought Iron Work." *Forge and Furnace* 4 (1911).

_____. *Cast and Wrought Brass and Bronze Work, Wrought Iron Work.* New York: Sackett and Wilhelms Lithography & Painting Company, c. 1899.

Winkler, Gail Caskey, and Roger W. Moss. *Victorian Interior Decoration: American Interiors, 1830–1900.* New York: Henry Holt, 1986.

Yale University School of Architecture. *Samuel Yellin: Metalwork at Yale.* Exhibition catalogue, October 29–November 16, 1990. New Haven, Conn.: Yale University, 1990.

Zingman-Leith, Elan, and Susan Zingman-Leith. *The Secret Life of Victorian Houses.* Washington, D.C.: Elliott & Clark, 1993.

# ARCHIVAL RESOURCES

THE OVERHOLT HOMESTEAD (Henry Clay Frick Birthplace), Scottdale, Pa.
Frick Archives. Helen Clay Frick Foundation, Pittsburgh, Pa.
West Overton Museums. Scottdale, Pa.

CLAYTON (Frick Art and Historical Center), Pittsburgh, Pa.
Frick Archives. Helen Clay Frick Foundation, Pittsburgh, Pa.
Frick Art and Historical Center. Pittsburgh, Pa.
Frick Collection. New York, N.Y.
Frick Woods Nature Reserve. Frick Environmental Center, Pittsburgh, Pa.
Innocenti & Webel. Locust Valley, Long Island, N.Y.
Rockefeller Archive Center. Sleepy Hollow, N.Y.

EAGLE ROCK, razed 1969, Pride's Crossing, Mass.
Beverly Historical Society. Beverly, Mass.
Frick Archives. Helen Clay Frick Foundation, Pittsburgh, Pa.
Frick Collection. New York, N.Y.
Innocenti & Webel. Locust Valley, Long Island, N.Y.
Peabody and Essex Museum. Salem, Mass.
Rockefeller Archive Center. Sleepy Hollow, N.Y.
Society for the Preservation of New England Antiquities. Boston, Mass.

ONE EAST SEVENTIETH STREET (The Frick Collection), New York, N.Y.
Frick Archives. Helen Clay Frick Foundation, Pittsburgh, Pa.

Frick Art Reference Library Archives. New York, N.Y.
Frick Collection Archives. New York, N.Y.
New York Public Library Archives. New York, N.Y.
Rockefeller Archive Center. Sleepy Hollow, N.Y.
The Royal Archives. London.
Samuel Yellin Museum. Chadds Ford, Pa.
Smithsonian Institution. Washington, D.C., Peter A. Juley and Son Collection.
Wallace Collection Archives. London.

THE CLAYTON ESTATE (Nassau County Museum of Art), Roslyn, Long Island, N.Y.
American Museum of Natural History. New York, N.Y.
Arnold Arboretum. Jamaica Plain, Mass.
Avery Architectural Library. Columbia University, New York, N.Y.
The Bryant Library, Local History Department. Roslyn, Long Island, N.Y.
Innocenti & Webel. Locust Valley, Long Island, N.Y.
Metropolitan Museum of Art Print and Drawing Archive. New York, N.Y.
Nassau County Museum of Art. Roslyn, Long Island, N.Y.

WESTMORELAND FARM, Westchester County, N.Y.
Bedford Village Garden Club. Bedford Village, N.Y.
Frick Archives. Helen Clay Frick Foundation, Pittsburgh, Pa.
Smithsonian Institution. Archives of American Gardens, Washington, D.C.
Westmoreland Sanctuary. Bedford Village, N.Y.

# ACKNOWLEDGMENTS

BEFORE I THANK MY GRANDFATHER for the wonderful years visiting him at the Clayton Estate and thank my great-aunt for maintaining Henry Clay Frick's former residences and opening her heart to her Frick family within them, I would like to thank my mother for keeping the photograph collection safe until this book was ready to be born. Now, five years after her death in 1996, her collection has given me the great privilege of being able to share the stories behind the Henry Clay Frick houses with others.

Equally important to me are those extraordinary individuals who have given me professional advice and have helped me bring this book to publication. I would like to thank my consultant, Judith Joseph of Joseph Publishing Services, for managing this project. Her wisdom and advice brought *The Henry Clay Frick Houses* to a level of perfection. Her enthusiasm for the project and her guidance benefitted the writing, design, and publishing process. I also would like to thank Catherine Marshall for her brilliant editing. Her demand for accuracy and her ability to smooth out the manuscript for this book enhanced and enriched the project at all levels. Thanks also to Susan Leon for her editorial suggestions that again made me dig deeper and think harder. Alex Castro, award-winning artist and architect, has brought his innate genius and unique sense of design to my second Frick book. Once again he has created a book far more beautiful than I ever could have dreamed possible, a book whose design program reflects the elegant taste and times of the Golden Era. For believing in *The Henry Clay Frick Houses,* for lending their expertise and advice to the project, and for bringing the book to publication, heartfelt thanks go to all at The Monacelli Press, particularly Gianfranco Monacelli, my publisher; Andrea Monfried, editor; Steven Sears, production director; and Susan Enochs, marketing and sales.

In addition, many other people made this book possible. First and foremost, I must thank my sister, Arabella Symington Dane, for generously sharing her historical understanding of Clayton in Pittsburgh, Eagle Rock, and the Marian Cruger Coffin garden on the Clayton Estate. The Frick Family Archives were not made available to me, so without my sister's help, and her permission to reproduce her collection of historic interior photographs of Clayton, Pittsburgh (now the Frick Art and Historical Center), given to her by our great-aunt, the Clayton chapter — and probably this book — would not have been viable. I also am indebted to Arabella for giving me permission to reproduce other photographs critical to this book, her willingness to permit my study of important material in her extensive archival collection, and her valued advice and constant encouragement of this project.

I also would like to thank Rod Sturtz, director of the West Overton Museums, for his assistance with research on the Henry Clay Frick birthplace. My heartfelt thanks go to him for his enthusiasm and generosity — a spirit that sustained me throughout the research and writing process.

I am indebted to Ellen M. Rosenthal, former curator at Clayton, Pittsburgh, for her work on Clayton's "Furnishings Plan." I used this detailed inventory extensively when writing the Clayton chapter. I also am indebted to Charles R. Altman — a Clayton docent since 1991 and the godson of Ralph Lynch, son of the H. C. Frick Coke Company's last president, Thomas Lynch — for giving me a fine arts tour of Clayton. Charles identified many of the decorative objects described in the "Furnishings Plan" and illustrated in the historic Clayton photographs reproduced in this book. He gave me insights about the house and its collection that were of great value to my general understanding and appreciation of the house. Additionally, Charles shared valuable research material from his personal collection that enriched the scholarship of the Clayton chapter. My thanks also to John Axtell for sharing his knowledge of his great-uncle, Frederick J. Osterling, the 1892 architect for Clayton and the Union Arcade building in Pittsburgh. In addition, Brent Glass, Pennsylvania state historian, as well as Lewis Waddell, Jonathan Stayer, and John Slovaker of the Division of Archives and Manuscripts of the Pennsylvania Historical and Museum Commission, provided me with records from the Pennsylvania Supreme Court concerning the Osterling versus Henry Clay Frick Estate lawsuit. My gratitude to them for their hard work and to Martin Aurand, architecture librarian at Carnegie Mellon University, for providing me with still more important information on Frederick J. Osterling. At the University of Pittsburgh Archives Service Center, Dennis East, head archivist, and Marianne Kasica, university archivist, gave me valuable assistance regarding the development of the Henry Clay Frick Fine Arts Building at the University of Pittsburgh and the Frick Art Museum at Clayton, Pittsburgh. To Franklin Toker, professor of the history of art and architecture at the University of Pittsburgh, go my thanks for bringing this material to my attention, and I thank Christine M. Torie for sharing her research on Andrew W. Peebles, the 1882 architect for Clayton in Pittsburgh. In addition, I would like to thank Max Donnelly, registrar of the Fine Art Society, London, for sharing his master's thesis on Daniel Cottier and for giving me many insights about Cottier & Company, and Steve Gross for lending his original photographs to this work.

I would like to thank Lorna Condon, director of library and archives at the Society for the Preservation of New England Antiquities (SPNEA), and Rebecca J. Aaronson, librarian and archivist, for their interest, encouragement, and assistance with the Eagle Rock research and for granting me permission to reproduce the many beautiful and previously unpublished architectural drawings of the Eagle Rock house from SPNEA's collection. Stuart A. Drake also gave me much valuable material pertinent to the relationship between Henry Clay Frick and his Eagle Rock architects, Arthur Little and Herbert W. C. Browne, and offered helpful comments on the Eagle Rock chapter. David Goss, director of the Beverly Historical Society, and Steve Hall, archivist, also provided me with important material relating to Eagle Rock. In addition, I am deeply grateful to Lydia Dufour, public services librarian of the Frick Art Reference Library at the Frick Collection, for identifying paintings in the Eagle Rock Collection.

Samuel Sachs II, director of the Frick Collection, and Robert Goldsmith, deputy director of administration, granted me permission to reproduce the archival photographs that make the chapter on the historical development of the Frick Collection complete. I also would like to thank, at the Frick Collection, Susan Grace Galassi, curator, and William Stout, director of research, for their warm greetings and ever-present generosity in answering my many queries. Galen Lee, horticultural designer, and Sally Brazil, archivist, also answered many questions. I am deeply grateful to Peter Hughes, head curator of the Wallace Collection, London, for his assistance in identifying the furniture in the Frick Collection purchased from the Wallace Collection (2, rue Laffitte) by Elsie de Wolfe in 1914. I am equally grateful to Phillips Hathaway, senior vice-president of European and French furniture at Sotheby's, New York, for identifying the furniture in the archival photographs of the second and third floors of One East Seventieth Street and of Eagle Rock. I also am grateful to Pamela Clark, deputy registrar of the Royal Archives, St. James Palace, London, for providing me with information about Sir Charles Allom and his work at Buckingham Palace. My thanks also to Robert Sink, archivist and record manager at the New York Public Library Archives, for providing me with documents and correspondence related to Henry Clay Frick's purchase of One East Seventieth Street, as well as to Stephen Van Dyk, chief librarian at the Cooper-Hewitt Museum of Design. And warmest thanks also to Clare Yellin of the Samuel Yellin Museum, Chadds Ford, Pennsylvania, for generously making her records of the wrought-iron entrance doors from One East Seventieth Street available to me for publication in this work.

Constance Schwartz, director of the Nassau County Museum of Art, also embraced and encouraged this project from its inception. My thanks to her for her interest and enthusiasm, to her assistant, Rita Mack, and to Jean Henning, head of education, for help with my research and with the architectural drawings of the Clayton Estate and the Marian Cruger Coffin garden. Harrison deF. Hunt of the Museum Division of the Nassau County Department of Recreation and Parks, as well as Linda Fischer, librarian, and Myrna Sloam, archivist, of the Local History Department of the Bryant Library in Roslyn, New York, also offered invaluable help regarding the Clayton Estate and provided many images for this book. I am deeply grateful for their efforts on my behalf. James Epstein and Janet Parks at the Avery Architectural Library also were generous with their help regarding the architectural drawings by Ogden Codman Jr. for the Bryce House/Clayton Estate in Long Island. Heather Lemonedes at the Metropolitan Museum Prints and Drawing Archives was equally helpful regarding photographs of the former Bryce House. At the American Museum of Natural History in New York the following members of the Division of Vertebrate Zoology, Department of Mammalogy, helped identify the mounted heads in the photographs of the Clayton Estate, Long Island, and of Childs Frick's room in Clayton, Pittsburgh: Nancy B. Simmons, curator-in-charge; Darrin Lunde, collections manager; Robert C. Randall, scientific assistant — loans; and Christopher A. Norris, curatorial associate. My deepest gratitude to them for their time, effort, and expertise.

Dr. David Jett and Barbara Balbot at the Frick Woods Nature Reserve contributed greatly to my understanding of Frick Park, as did Barry Hannegan, director of Pittsburgh History and Landscape Preservation, and Albert M. Tannler of the same organization. Hermann F. Schultz and Roose Badde at Innocenti & Webel provided me with beautiful architectural land-scape drawings for Clayton, Pittsburgh; Frick Park; Eagle Rock; and the Clayton Estate, Long Island. In addition, I would like to thank James Strong for making sensitive reproductions of the many architectural drawings of Clayton, Long Island. To photographer David Prencipe of the Maryland Historical Society, Baltimore, my thanks for an equally sensitive reproduction of my sister's archival photograph collection of Clayton in Pittsburgh, the many architectural landscape drawings from Innocenti & Webel, and those from the Samuel Yellin Museum. Dana Salvo of SPNEA also has my deep gratitude for making transparencies of the many architectural drawings of Eagle Rock for use in this book, as does Gregory Heins of the Boston Museum of Fine Arts for his reproduction of the Eagle Rock trellis garden. Deepest gratitude also to Joyce Connolly, museum specialist, Smithsonian Institution, Archives of American Gardens, for providing me with images of Westmoreland Farm and to Marianne Lee for the architectural rendering of the Omni William Penn Hotel.

I also must thank Wendell Garrett, senior vice-president, American decorative arts, Sotheby's, New York, for reading the manuscript and honoring this book by writing the foreword. I am equally grateful to William R. Johnston, associate director and curator of eighteenth- and nineteenth-century art at the Walters Art Museum, Baltimore, for reading the manuscript and for writing jacket commentary. William Rieder, curator of European furniture and decorative arts at the Metropolitan Museum of Art, and Keith Irvine, president, Irvine & Fleming, Inc., New York, and former president of the Soane Foundation, made important contributions. They read the manuscript and took time from their busy schedules to provide commentary. Many others read the manuscript and offered invaluable advice. P. Raab Christhilf, art historian and fine arts appraiser at Alex Cooper Auctioneers, read the manuscript meticulously, corrected descriptions and definitions, gave me invaluable insights about Victorian eclecticism and the Aesthetic Movement, lent me books for further study, and brought the Karl Marx quote to my attention. Frederick A. Hetzel, former director of the University of Pittsburgh Press, gave advice and encouragement always when most needed. Cindy Colemane of Frankel & Colemane helped with interior design terms, as did Stiles T. Colwill, interior decorator and former chief curator and museum director of the Maryland Historical Society. My cousin Barbara Janney Trimble and my dear friends Isabel and Laurance Roberts gave me much appreciated advice and encouragement, while Kurt Rosenthal, Robert Talbert, and Sandy Storck deserve warm thanks for their love, support, and constant enthusiasm. My daughters — particularly Annie — and their husbands were ever supportive. While I was on tour for *Henry Clay Frick: An Intimate Portrait* (New York: Abbeville Press, 1998), I was also in the process of writing this book. Unable to print a hard copy of the manuscript for my editor, Catherine Marshall, who then was vacationing in a cabin in the wilds of Wisconsin, I e-mailed chapters to Annie in California. She mailed the hard copy to Catherine, saving me much time and energy. I am grateful to her for being my courier and to all my children for cheering me on. Now another Frick book is theirs to read and I hope they — and all those who read this book — will enjoy *The Henry Clay Frick Houses*.

M.F.S.S.

*All illustrations were furnished by the author except those listed below:*

Adaptation of original drawing by the office of Thierry Despont, New York, N.Y.: 33

Avery Architectural Library. Columbia University, New York, N.Y.: 222, 232, 235 (below)

Bryant Library, Local History Department. Roslyn, Long Island, N.Y.: 220 (above right), 221

Carnegie Library. Pittsburgh, Pa.: 10, 25

Carnegie Mellon University, School of Architecture. Pittsburgh, Pa.: 150

Cedarmere, Nassau County Division of Museum Services. Roslyn, Long Island, N.Y.: 220 (above left)

Arabella S. Dane Collection. Boston, Mass.: 14, 24, 35, 36, 39, 40–41, 42, 43, 44, 46–47, 48, 50–51, 53, 54–55, 56–57 (left), 58, 60–61, 62, 63, 64, 65, 66–67, 68–69, 70, 71 (below), 72–73, 73, 74, 75, 76, 77, 78 (above), 79, 81, 82–83, 100–101 (above), 102–3, 108 (above), 130–31 (above), 132, 266–67

Frick Art & Historical Center. Pittsburgh, Pa.: 20, 21

Frick Collection. New York, N.Y.: 137, 138, 141, 144, 146, 152, 157, 171, 214

Gross & Daley. New York, N.Y.: 12–13, 37, 52, 57 (below)

Helen Clay Frick Foundation. Frick Family Archives, Pittsburgh, Pa.: 18, 19, 22, 41 (above), 47 (above), 49, 61 (above), 71 (right), 78 (below), 85, 91, 92, 97, 120–21, 160, 161

Innocenti & Webel. Locust Valley, Long Island, N.Y., 80, 261

Metropolitan Museum of Art Print and Drawing Archives. New York, N.Y.: 223, 226 (above), 235 (above), 240 (above), 242

Omni William Penn Hotel. Pittsburgh, Pa.: 149

*Pittsburgh Post-Gazette:* 31, 32

Smithsonian Institution. Archives of American Gardens, Washington, D.C.: 279

Smithsonian Institution. National Museum of American Art, Peter A. Juley and Son Collection, Washington, D.C.: 215

Society for the Preservation of New England Antiquities, Collection of Arthur Little and Herbert W. C. Browne. Boston, Mass.: 88, 90, 100 (left), 101 (right), 102 (below), 105, 108 (below), 111, 116, 117, 120 (above), 122, 123, 125, 126–27, 128, 129, 130, 131

West Overton Museums. Scottdale, Pa.: 2, 5

Clare Yellin, Samuel Yellin Collection/Archives. Chadds Ford, Pa.: 165, 166, 167, 168, 169

Adam, Louis-Emile, 51

Adamesque style, 6, 244, 257, 259

Aesthetic Movement, xi, 22, 27

Alden & Harlow, 23, 24, 52, 78

Alken, Henry, 232, 242

Allegheny Building (Pittsburgh), 27, 89

Allom, Sir Charles Carrick: xii; and Buckingham Palace, 142, 143; and Clayton Estate, 225, 227, 231, 232, 235, 240, 242, 244, 246; and One East Seventieth Street, 142–43, 144–47, 149, 151–53, 189, 193, 202, 211, 225, 227, 231, 232, 235, 240, 242, 244, 246; and Union Arcade, 155

American Museum of Natural History, 227, 228, 229, 262

Andreoni, Orazio, 15

Anne, Princess Royal, 129

Archer, James, 65

Barbizon School, 39

Barna da Siena, 197

Beaux Arts architecture, 139

Bellini, Giovanni, 185

Berenson, Bernard, 31, 187

Berkman, Alexander, 23, 51, 193

Berthoud, Ferdinand, 175

Bevin, Newton P., 162, 268, 270, 277

Bogert, G. M., 63

Boskerck, R. W. van, 69, 257

Boucher, François, 155, 179, 205

Bouguereau, Adolphe-William, 59, 73

Boulle, André-Charles, 182, 185

Bradley, Robert S., 85

Breton, Jules-Adolphe, 44

Bridge, James Howard, 139–40, 193

Browne, Herbert W.C., xi, 86, 139, 220

Bryant, William Cullen, 219–20, 229, 277

Bryce, Gen. Lloyd, 220–22

Buckingham Palace, London, 87, 142, 143

Burnham, Daniel H., xi, 24–25, 26–27, 94–95, 138, 139

Carlin, Martin, 33, 116, 144, 152, 179

Carnegie, Andrew, 9, 15, 16, 18–19, 24, 26, 27, 28, 36, 65, 86, 89, 137

Carrère & Hastings, 95, 139, 158, 162, 215

Carrière, Eugène, 211

Carstairs, Charles S., 142–43

Cazin, Jean-Charles, 65, 67

Charles II style, 231

Charles X style, 238

Chartran, Théobald, 65, 77, 203, 259

Childs, Martha Howard, 149

Clay, Henry, 8

Clayton (Pittsburgh), 15–83; Adelaide's bedroom, 24, 34, 55, 57; art gallery, 24, 26; author's memories of, xi; bathrooms, 23, 52, 57; breakfast room, 49; Child Frick's bedroom, 71; decorative elements, 21–23, 27, 28, 33, 39, 116; dining room, 22, 44, 45, 47; entrance hall, 38, 39; exterior views, 12–13, 18, 19, 80; family archives in, 34; family events in, 23, 28, 41, 43; fence, 35; guest rooms, 62, 63, 75; gymnasium, 77; Helen Clay Frick's bedroom, 59, 61; Henry Clay Frick's bedroom, 51; library, 22, 65; Mlle. Ogiz's room, 77; orchestrion, 36, 37, 39, 42; parlor, 24, 42, 43; playhouse, 78; playroom, 72; porch, 36, 37; purchase of, 11, 16, 18; reception room, 15, 34, 39, 41; renovations of, 16–22, 27–28, 30, 34, 42, 43, 49, 59; restored as museum, 29, 30, 32–34, 99, 280; sewing room, 77; sitting room, 67, 69; stable, 79; stairway, 49; telephone room, 52

Clayton Cadets, 78

Clayton Estate (Long Island), 216–77; author's memories of, xi, xii, xiii; Blue Bedroom, 257; as Bryant property, 220, 277; as Bryce property, 220–22, 223, 224, 225, 226, 228, 235, 240, 242, 246, 277; Childs's collections in, 227–28, 240, 242; corridor to breakfast loggia, 244; decorative elements, 162, 213, 225; dining room, 246; entrance hall, 231; exterior views, 216–18, 219; gardens, 226, 227, 228, 267, 268, 270, 272; guest sitting room, 259; Leftover Cottage, 213, 228, 277; library, 240; master bedroom, 248, 250; Millstone Laboratory, 227–28, 262; morning room, 252; as Nassau County Museum of Art, 215, 229, 268, 281; north room, 235, 236, 238; outbuildings, 224, 225, 228; Pink Bedroom, 259; por-celain room, 244; purchase of, 219, 222–23, 224–25, 278; renovation of, 225, 227; ski slope, 261; stairways, 232; study, 242; swimming pool, 262; Walnut Bedroom, 254; zoo, 260

Clouet, François, 231

Codman, Ogden Jr., xi, 27, 75, 86, 87, 139, 143, 220–22, 226, 229, 232, 235, 240, 242, 267

Coffin, Marian Cruger, xii, xiii, 227, 267

Coleman, William, 15

Constable, John, 189

Coolidge, T. Jefferson, 86

Copley, Fred S., 228

Corot, Jean-Baptiste-Camille, 39, 202

Cotes, Francis, 120

Cottier & Company, xi, 27, 28, 41, 43, 49, 75, 88, 90

Cuillion, L. R. de, 69

Curran, Charles Courtney, 75

Cuyp, Aelbert, 194

Dagnan-Bouveret, Pascal-Adolphe-Jean, 47, 57, 65, 240

Daubigny, Charles-François, 39, 202

David, School of, 30, 120

Degas, Edgar, 211

della Francesca, Piero, 197

Despont, Thierry, 34

Devis, Arthur, 116

Dewer & Clinton, 55

Dewey, Jerusha, 228, 277

de Wolfe, Elsie, xi, xiv; and One East Seventieth Street, 96, 143–47, 149, 152, 153–54, 155, 201, 203, 205, 206, 207, 209, 211, 213, 225

Diaz de la Peña, Narcisse-Virgile, 39, 41

Domingo y Marques, Francisco, 69

Duccio di Buoninsegna, 197

Dupré, Jules, 41, 179

Duveen, Joseph: xi; and Buckingham Palace, 87; and Clayton Estate, 231; and Eagle Rock, 86–87, 90, 116; and One East Seventieth Street, 87, 142, 146, 154, 156, 179, 193, 200, 203, 205, 231; and 640 Fifth Avenue, 88; and Union Arcade, 155

Eagle Rock (Prides Crossing), 28, 84–133, 139, 220; art collection in, 94–96, 138; Atlantic beach access, 92; author's memories of, xi, xii, xiv; breakfast room, 125; decorative elements, 87–88, 89–91; demolition of, 32, 96, 98–99, 116, 120, 122, 280, 281; dining room, 118, 120, 122; drawing room, 116, 118; driveway, 101; entrance hall, 107, 108, 111; exterior views, 81–84, 88, 105, 126–27; fence, 89, 101, 102; gardens, 98, 105, 133; items relocated from, 30, 31–33, 99, 116; library, 115; outbuildings, 91, 125, 129, 131; refugees in, 97–98; social life in, 92–94; stairways, 111

Eastlake, Charles L., 11, 18, 21, 22–23

Elmore, James, 79

Federal style, 6

Fragonard, Jean-Honoré, 154, 179

Freemasons, 24, 187

French Renaissance style, 62, 231

Friant, Emile, 45

Frick, Adelaide (granddaughter), 97, 223

Frick, Adelaide Howard Childs, 55; children of, 17, 19; and Clayton, 16, 23, 24, 26, 28, 49; death of, 28, 96, 125, 156, 280; and Eagle Rock, 87, 89,

90, 91, 93, 96, 108; horses of, 79; houses of, xi;
ill health of, 23, 77, 91, 92; marriage of, 11, 16;
and One East Seventieth Street, 142, 147, 203–6;
and railway car, 91

Frick, Childs, 17, 19, 97; big-game trophies of,
223–24, 225, 227–28, 240, 242; and Clayton
Estate, xi, xiii, 97, 162, 213, 219, 222–25,
227–29, 231, 235, 236, 242, 246, 260, 261, 262,
277, 278; death of, 229, 231, 268, 272; and
Eagle Rock, 96; family of, 96, 97, 98, 223, 225,
228–29, 238, 240, 244; and Frick Collection,
156, 182, 229, 231, 236, 244; and Frick
Laboratory, 227–28; and Millstone Laboratory,
227–28, 262; as paleontologist, 224, 225, 228,
229; and polo, 79, 85, 93, 224, 275

Frick, Frances (granddaughter), 97, 125, 223

Frick, Frances Dixon, 97; and Clayton Estate, xi, 219,
224, 225, 227, 228, 252, 278; death of, 229,
236, 268, 272, 277; and porcelain collection,
244; portraits of, 240, 242

Frick, Helen Clay, 17, 19, 22, 41; author's memories
of, xii, xiii; and Clayton, 23, 28–30, 32–34, 49,
59, 61, 72, 77, 280; death of, 34, 36, 47, 268,
281; and Eagle Rock, 28, 32, 85, 96–99, 108,
116, 120, 122, 280; and father's collections, 96,
145, 201, 211; and father's image, xi, 29, 182;
and Frick Collection, xiii, 29, 156–57, 182; and
Frick Park, 80, 97; and historic preservation,
xiii–xiv, 6, 29–30, 34, 80, 182, 280–81; and
horses, 93; and Iron Rail, 93, 96, 98, 144–45;
and One East Seventieth Street, 207, 211; and
Red Cross, 73, 96, 144; and war refugees, 97–98;
and Westmoreland Farm, xi, xiii, 28, 278–81

Frick, Henry Clay, 97; art collection of, 10, 22, 26, 28,
29, 85, 87, 90, 93, 193, see also specific houses;
assassination attempt on, 23, 51, 193; author's
memories of, xi; birth and early years of, 3, 5,
8–9; business affairs of, 9–11, 16, 18–19, 24, 26,
27, 34, 51, 86; and card games, 49, 107, 108;
and Clayton, 16–19, 21–29, 51; and Clayton
Estate, 219, 224, 225, 227, 278; death of, 28, 91,
96, 156, 175, 179, 213, 227, 268, 278; and Eagle
Rock, 85, 87–96, 133, 137; eating habits of, 122,
125, 175; European tour of, 10–11, 16; forebears
of, 3–8, 278; ill health of, 26, 95, 96, 149, 151,
209; marriage of, 11, 16; and One East
Seventieth Street, 137–40, 142–47, 149, 151–58,
211; portraits of, ii, 31, 51, 137, 182, 185, 187,
203, 205, 250, 259; will and estate of, 156–57,
182, 280

Frick, Henry Clay II (grandson), 246, 257

Frick, Henry Clay Jr. (son), 23, 57, 59, 61, 167, 268

Frick, Martha (daughter), xii, 19, 59; death of, 23, 72,
209, 268; images of, 15, 17, 55, 57, 65, 167,
193, 203

Frick, Martha (granddaughter), 97, 223, 254, 260, 262

Frick Art Museum (Pittsburgh), 32–34, 91, 99, 116,
122, 280, 281

Frick Art Reference Library (New York), xiii, 30, 73,
158, 187, 199, 211, 215

Frick Building (Pittsburgh), 24–25, 26, 156

Frick Collection (New York): xii–xiii, 87, 116, 267;
Acquisitions Committee of, 29, 156, 182; architectural renderings for, 215; board of trustees,
156, 182, 197, 229; home converted to museum,
138–40, 157–58; location of, see One East
Seventieth Street; public opening of, 158;
in wartime, 158

Frick Park (Pittsburgh), 30, 80, 97, 227

Fry, Sherry Edmundson, 157, 158

Gainsborough, Thomas, 30, 120, 189

Gardner, Isabella Stewart (Mrs. John L.), 94, 138

Gay, Walter, 193

George I style, 238

George III style, 213

Georgian Revival style, 99

Ghieny, Eugene S., 63

Gibson, Archer, 171

Gilbert, André-Louis, 205

Gilbert, Cass, 149

Godwin, A. & Company, 19, 22, 49

Golden Era, xii, 11, 34, 80, 281

Gothic Revival style, 149, 228, 277

Gottscho, Samuel, 268

Goya y Lucientes, Francisco de, 30, 194, 199

Graham, Charles, 91

Greco, El, 147, 182, 194, 211

Greek Revival style, 6

Greenough, John, 86

Guardi, Francesco, 107

Hals, Dirk, 122

Hals, Frans, 194

Harnett, William Michael, 69

Hastings, Thomas, xi, 139–40, 143, 145, 146–47,
149, 154, 158, 171, 187

Hays, William J., 232

Hecke, F. van den, 236, 246

Heinz, Henry John, 15–16

Helen Clay Frick Foundation, 29, 30, 33

Henry Clay Frick Fine Arts Building (Pittsburgh), 29,
31–32, 73, 99, 158, 187

Hepplewhite furniture, 238

Hess, D. S. & Company, 17–18, 21, 42, 49, 57

Heurtaut, Nicolas, 180, 200

Hiss, P. Hansen, 22, 42, 51

Hoffman, Malvina, 31, 187

Hogarth, William, 30, 189

Holbein, Hans the Younger, 182

Hoppner, John, 43, 120, 175, 176, 238

Houdon, Jean-Antoine, 29, 179

Hunt, Richard Morris, 20

Huntington, Henry E., 44

Innocenti, Umberto, xii, 228

Innocenti & Webel, 30, 80, 97, 98, 228, 261, 277

Italian Renaissance style, 20, 99, 187, 193

Jacquet, Gustave-Jean, 69

Janssen & Abbott, 149

Johansen, John Christen, 137, 189

Johnson, John A., 94

Johnson, W. A. K., 242

Johnstone, B. Kenneth, 31

Joubert, Gilles, 179

Jules, J. W., 232

Kangxi porcelain, 244, 246

Kimbel, A. & Sons, 15, 22–23, 39, 44, 62, 67

Knoedler, Roland, 24, 93, 142, 146, 147, 172

Knox, Philander K., 16, 49, 65, 79, 93

Koch, G. W. & Sons, 22

Ku Zitti (African chieftain), 224

Lacroix, Roger, 179

Lapini, Cesare, 65, 67

Lawrence, Sir Thomas, 30, 120, 189, 209

Leclerc, C. M., 257

Lemoyne, Jean-Louis, 162

Lhermitte, Leon Augustin, 45

Lippi, Fra Filippo, 197

Little, Arthur, xi, 86, 87–88, 139, 220

Little & Browne, 87, 88, 90, 101, 102, 105, 108, 111,
115, 116, 118, 125, 129, 131, 225

Lochoff, Nicholas, 31, 187

Lorenzi, Stoldo, 182

Loring, Catherine Peabody, 92

Louis XIV style, 22, 231

Louis XV style, 15, 180, 203, 207, 238, 248, 257

Louis XVI style, 10, 31, 33, 39, 116, 153, 175, 179,
203, 206, 207, 257

Lowell, Guy, xii, 80, 227

McMillan, James, 86

Malle, Louis-Noël, 205

Manet, Edouard, 211

Mann, Harrington, 240, 246

Marcott, L. & Company, 158

Maris, Jacobus Hendrikus, 107

Mathews Brothers, 22

Mattei, Clarence R., 238, 240

Mauve, Anton, 62

Megrew, George, 22, 23

Mellon, Andrew W., 10–11, 47, 49, 88, 179

Mellon, Paul, 179

Mellon, Richard Beatty, 16

Mellon, Thomas, 9, 16

Miller, Abraham, 189

Millet, Jean-François, 15, 33, 39, 41, 202

Milliken, Henry O., 162, 268, 270, 277

Millstone Laboratory, 227–28, 262

Monongahela House (Pittsburgh), 10, 15, 16, 17, 39

Moore, William H., 86

Morgan, J. P., 26, 86, 116, 165, 179, 197

Mouvel, Bernard de, 238

Nassau County Museum of Art (Long Island), 215, 229, 268, 281; see also Clayton Estate

Nattier, Jean-Marc, 42

neoclassicism, xii, 89

New York: 640 Fifth Avenue, 28, 41, 77, 88, 93, 147, 158; Woolworth Building, 149; see also One East Seventieth Street

Ogiz, Mademoiselle, 77

Olmsted, Frederick Law, 219

Olmsted Brothers, xii, 91

One East Seventieth Street (New York), 134–215, 225, 281; Adelaide Frick's bedroom, boudoir, and bathroom, 147, 152, 154, 155, 203, 205, 206; art collection in, see Frick Collection; author's memories of, xii–xiii; breakfast room, 202; construction of, 95, 140, 142, 143, 147; converted to museum, 139–40, 157–58; decorative elements in, 96, 142–47, 152–54, 168, 169; dining room, 175, 176; Enamel Room, 147, 197; entrance hall, 137, 165, 167, 168; exterior views of, 134–35, 138, 158; Fragonard Room, 143, 154, 156, 179, 180, 200; Frick's bedroom, 209; Frick's bequest of, 138–39, 156–57; Frick's office, 199; Frick's sitting room, 211; garden, 187; garden court, 215; guest rooms, 213; Helen Clay Frick's bedroom, 147, 207; inner courtyard, 140, 162; library, 189; living hall, xi, 182, 185; north hall, 187; organ console, 171; purchase of, 92, 137; second-floor hall, 201; second-floor landing, 200; south hall, xi, 172; stairways, 171; and war, 149, 151, 154, 156, 158; west gallery, 140, 157, 193, 194

Osterling, Frederick J., xi, 15, 18, 19–22, 30, 33, 39, 41, 42, 43, 44, 49, 59, 65, 149, 155

Overholt, Abraham, 5–8, 9

Overholt, Henry, 3–4, 5, 278

Overholt Homestead, 6–8

Page, Russell, 158

Peebles, Andrew W., 16, 21, 25, 26

Piccirilli, Attilio, 147, 268

Pitcairn, Robert, 16

Pittsburgh: Allegheny Building, 27, 89; Clayton in, see Clayton; Frick Art Museum, 32–34, 91, 99, 116, 122, 280, 281; Frick Building, 24–25, 26, 156; Frick cenotaph, 26; Frick Park, 30, 80, 97, 227; Frick's business affairs in, 10–11; Henry Clay Frick Fine Arts Building, 29, 31–32, 73, 99, 158, 187; Homewood Cemetery, 26, 156, 268; Monongahela House, 10, 15, 16, 17, 39; renaissance in, 29–30; Union Arcade, 96, 149, 151, 155–56; William Penn Hotel, 96, 149, 155–56

Pope, John Russell, xi, 80, 156–57, 158, 215

Pratt, Schafer, and Slowik, 32

Prince, Frederick H., 86

Pullman, George, 91

Raeburn, Sir Henry, 122, 194

Rafaëlli, Jean-François, 57, 59

Regency style, 213

Rembrandt van Rijn, 24, 27, 42, 194

Renoir, Pierre-Auguste, 171, 200

Reynolds, Sir Joshua, 30, 43, 122, 189, 238

Rico y Ortega, Martin, 67

Riesener, Jean-Henri, 33, 152, 180, 203

Rockefeller, John D. Jr., 29, 156, 182, 197

Rockefeller, John D. Sr., 26, 28, 86

Romney, George, 43, 176, 209

Roosenboom, Margaretha, 59, 67

Roosevelt, Archibald B., 262

Roosevelt, Theodore, 47, 63, 277

Rouse, Henry C., 86

Rousseau, Pierre-Etienne-Théodore, 202

Ruysdael, Salomon van, 194

Saly, François-Jacques-Joseph, 205

Scalamandré, 33

Shoumatoff, Elizabeth, 205, 240, 242, 246

Smith, Benjamin and James, 176

Starr, Theodore B., 39

Stephany, Annie Blumenschein, 35, 45

Stephany, Lewis, 30

Stuart, Gilbert, 199, 252

Tacca, Ferdinando, 107

Taft, William Howard, 93, 94, 277

Tiepolo, Giovanni Battista, 201

Titian, 185

Troyon, Constant, 15, 41, 202

Trumbauer, Horace, 158

Turner, J.M.W., 171, 172, 189, 211

Twachtman, Robert, 201

Union Arcade (Pittsburgh), 96, 149, 151, 155–56

Vanderbilt, William H., 28, 88

Vandervort, Benjamin, 16

Van Dyck, Sir Anthony, 176, 194

Van Reisen Burg family, 182

Vaux, Calvert, 219

Velázquez, Diego Rodríguez de Silva y, 194

Vermeer, Johannes, 194

Veronese, Paolo, 194

Victorian style, xii, 18, 23, 27, 30, 36, 80, 87

Vollon, Antoine, 49

Wallace Collection, London, 138–39

Walton, Frederick, 39

Warren, George B., 33

Watts, George Frederic, 65

Webel, Richard K., xii, 228

Westmoreland County (Pennsylvania), 3–11, 278; Abraham Overholt Homestead, 5, 8; Frick family history in, 3–4; Henry Clay Frick birthplace, 3, 5, 8; Henry Clay Frick's business endeavors, 9–11; Henry Overholt Homestead, 4; Overholt Homestead, 6–8; West Overton village, 7, 8, 9, 11

Westmoreland Farm (Westchester County): xiii, 28, 278–81; author's memories of, xi, xiv; purchase of, 278; sale of, 281; as sanctuary, 280

Westmoreland railway car, 91, 156

West Overton, Pennsylvania, 7, 8, 9, 11

Wharton, Edith, 27, 41, 75, 86, 87–88, 89, 139, 143, 220–21, 229, 267

Whistler, James Abbott McNeill, 171, 199, 200

White, Allom & Company, 137, 146, 175, 219, 226; see also Allom, Sir Charles Carrick

Widener, P.A.B., 94–95, 140, 158

William Penn Hotel (Pittsburgh), 96, 149, 155–56

Williams, John, Inc., 267

Willkie, Wendell, 91

Wilson, Woodrow, 277

Woodwell, Joseph R., 49, 85, 90

Woolworth Building (New York), 149

Wren, Christopher, 171

Yale Company, 44

Yandell, C. & Company, 44

Yellin, Samuel, 137, 147, 165, 167, 169

Ziem, Félix, 111

THIS BOOK

WAS DESIGNED AND COMPOSED BY

ALEX CASTRO

IN CENTAUR AND SABON FONTS

AND WAS PRINTED BY

EUROGRAFICA, S.P.A.

VICENZA, ITALY